THE DOMAIN-MATRIX

THEORIES OF REPRESENTATION AND DIFFERENCE
General Editor, Teresa de Lauretis

MENU

HELP

FIND

PRINT

OPEN

PREV

NEXT

iii
PAGE

THE DOMAIN-MATRIX

PERFORMING LESBIAN AT THE END OF PRINT CULTURE

SUE-ELLEN CASE

INDIANA UNIVERSITY PRESS
Bloomington and Indianapolis

iv
PAGE

PREV

NEXT

OPEN

PRINT

FIND

HELP

MENU

The paper used in this publication meets the minimum requirements of American National Standard for Information Sciences—Permanence of Paper for Printed Library Materials, ANSI Z39.48-1984.

Manufactured in the United States of America

Library of Congress Cataloging-in-Publication Data

Case, Sue-Ellen.
    The domain-matrix : performing lesbian at the end of print culture / by Sue-Ellen Case.
        p.   cm. — (Theories of representation and difference)
    Includes bibliographical references and index.
    ISBN 0-253-33226-5 (cl : alk. paper). — ISBN 0-253-21094-1 (pa : alk. paper)
    1. Lesbianism—United States. 2. Lesbians—United States—Computer network resources. 3. Computers—Social aspects—United States. 4. Performance art—United States. 5. Gays in popular culture—United States. 6. Lesbian artists in popular culture—United States. I. Title. II. Series.
HQ75.6.U5C37 1996
306.76'63—dc20   96-8059

    1 2 3 4 5 01 00 99 98 97 96

00031 4999
4.15.97

CONTENTS

CASE STUDIES: PERFORMANCE & THE SCREEN

Bringing Home the Meat:
Materialist Spatial Designs of Nation and Stage   127

Los Angeles: A Topography of Screenic Properties   189

The Bottom   233

ACKNOWLEDGMENTS

As this book has been produced over too many years, it has been helped along by a large number of different people. I will attempt to construct their support chronologically. First, the English Department at the University of California/Riverside dared to hire me upon hearing a paper derived from these techno-interests. Diana Taylor helped me with the sections on Cherríe Moraga and *Duel in the Sun*. Terry Pedersen secured my lodging for two summers in Berkeley. Several people gave me wonderful feedback at Swarthmore, where the Lang professorship provided me with time to write: primarily Alan Kuharski and George Moskos; my assistant, Tellory Williamson; Tom Blackburn, who has already discovered most of these texts; Chin Woon Ping; and Peg Bloom. Nina Auerbach encouraged the more daring experiments with form. Back at Riverside, Townsend Carr suggested the format of italic passages in "The Computer Cometh," and Joe Childers responded to an early version. Students in my graduate seminar on technology illustrated how some of these critical passages come to life in discussion. Philip Brett and George Haggerty gave me the courage to work on the critique of "queer." For direct work on the manuscript, I thank Katrin Sieg, who revised some of the worst grammatical errors and offered suggestions for clarity. Teresa de Lauretis provided a wonderfully critical reading of the whole manuscript in its many stages. Her example of writing lesbian critical theory continues to inspire me. Earl Jackson caught some of my theoretical leaps. Janelle Reinelt gave me courage to publish some sections and critically responded to them. Finally, Susan Foster choreographed our life together so that writing remains possible.

Portions of this book have been previously published:

The section "Commodity Dildoism" appeared as part of the chapter "The Student and the Strap: Authority and Seduction in the Class(room)," in *Professions of Desire*, ed. George E. Haggerty and Bonnie Zimmerman (New York: Modern Language Association, 1995).

Other sections appeared as "Performing Lesbian in the Space of Technology: Part 1" and "Performing Lesbian in the Space of Technology: Part 2" in *Theater Journal*, published by the Johns Hopkins University Press. Reprinted by permission.

THE DOMAIN-MATRIX

DOMAIN-MATRIX

 MENU
 HELP
 FIND
 PRINT
 OPEN
 PREV
 NEXT
 1 PAGE

The immediate problem is how, or where, to begin to write the conjunction "performing" and "lesbian" in this time of slippage and upheaval, when medical technologies are redefining basic definitions of gender assignment, even the deep structures of corporeality itself, in genetic codes; a sexually transmitted pandemic is loose in the world, taking (safe) sexual practices out into more virtual, abstract realms; political categories such as "race" and "sexual preference" are scrutinized at the deepest level as unstable, and even the seismology of such instability doubts its own methods.

The very term "lesbian" is slipping semiotically on the banana peel of mainstream and academic fashion, signifying everything from Banana Republic's "My Chosen Family" of jeans and tanks tops, k.d. lang posing for a shave on the cover of *Vanity Fair*, and ads for strapping on a dildo, to a way to "read" Hollywood movies, such as *Single White Female*, or staking a critical, theoretical claim in the term "queer." In fact, in some queer circles, the term "lesbian" has been evacuated. Understood as a term of the 1970s, connoting "lesbian feminist," "lesbian," in that sense, has been overwritten by the queer-derived "dyke"—more proximate to gay men in identification than the seemingly woman-signifying term "lesbian." Is there a way to retain the notion of "lesbian" in technology, while still marking a material history of lesbian lives—one that might combine the theoretical tradition of lesbian feminist thought and new "queer" inscriptions through sexual practice? Could the two traditions help to bring about a new form of coalition politics?

While "lesbian" comes under scrutiny, the other term in the conjunction "performing lesbian" is troubled by the changing sense of performance. "Live" performance, still burdened with the problematic of accounting for something called the "body," has, in various ways, attempted to construct a staging of the relationship between the body and the new cybersphere. The tradition of performance as something "live" and embodied has, throughout much of the twentieth century, been challenged by the screen. Movies, television, the computer, and new, virtual systems interrogate the "live" body and its tradition by their screenic context. In performance, is the body poised between its appearance within national and kinship systems and its disappearance among multiple screens, as in Jean Genet's play *The Screens*, in which the protagonist finally disappears from among a series of them? Or is it, as in Steve Reich's *The Cave*, the subject position distributed among stage technologies and screens? Will the body be totally subsumed in an interactive, virtual reality, as in the movie *The Lawnmower Man*? Is performing the body's relation to the screen the repetitive hurling of it against the screen, like Elizabeth Streb's dancers, who hurl themselves against walls, miking the music of thudding bodies? Or is the performing body composed of screens, as in Nam June Paik's "Family of Robot, Uncle" and, respectively, "Aunt"? Paik's arrangement of antique TVs in the humanoid shape of a robot, with performing bodies on their screens, ironically quotes systems of the body and of kinship. Both humanoid systems and their simulation, "Robot," signify a nostalgic, antique, representational system—a quaint notion of themselves. For Paik, screened bodies have overtaken industrial, mechanical ones as video sculpture has overtaken TV.

Yet, if the body persists in standing "live" onstage, not screened, is it caught in the gestures of the routing of human agency through technology, as in Laurie Anderson's live performances, in which her voice is transformed in the mike, foregrounding the routing? Is the "live," gendered, experientially specific body in tension with the seeming neutralization of it as it passes through technological channels? How does the body perform *Big Science,* as Anderson entitles it? Is it in consonance with screens—can the two orders play with and against one another? Or must the body be consigned to the empty stage, alone before the live audience, in the tradition of "poor" theater because of the new, discounted value assigned to the flesh, as the continuing practice of one-person shows insists? Is "performing lesbian," then, some conjunction of these elements, such as a wall of video screens projecting images of dildo scenarios, anonymous, but costumed in appropriate retro butch-femme wear—sex-radical, but also reticent in its feminist memories? Or is it live sex acts in the "poor" theaters of the small, migrant bar culture?

Even these suggestions will not carry into contemporary critical theory, for the new sense of "queer performativity" would challenge the formulation "performing lesbian" as retaining, in its terms, the assumptions of identity and visibility politics—what has been considered to be the essentialist trap of idealist philosophical systems. More than any other charge, "essentialism" has focused critical energy against the notions of "lesbian" and "performance" in recent works, claiming the scope of a paradigm shift to correct the ontological fallacies inherent in identity politics, on the one hand, and the enterprise of visibility in the system of representation, on the other. Retaining the conjunction "performing lesbian," then, willfully challenges the essentialist charge.

This book will engage each of these questions in the context of the dawning of cyberspace and the end of print culture. Within this context, the debates around the status of the body and of identity may be perceived as a register of the anxiety produced by the demise of print culture and the rise of virtual systems. Surveying current treatments of the interface between the coming screen-of-screens, cyberspace, the body, performance, and lesbian will

D O M A I N - M A T R I X

  MENU

 HELP

 FIND

PRINT

OPEN

 PREV

 NEXT

3 PAGE

lead the book into several debates which overlap, interweave, and repeat one another. Each of these terms changes its effect, depending upon the context within which it is raised. Cyberspace provides a convergence of concerns—a swift eddy where notions of nation, screening, sexuality, and the body swirl together to conjoin, finally, in a new organization of space that would relocate their functions. Likewise, the guiding terms of critical critiques, such as materialism, feminism, and sexual politics, find necessary new contradictions and consonances among them in this new conjunction.

"Cyberspace," the word coined by William Gibson in 1984 in his novel *Neuromancer*, has become the accepted term for the developing world of information that will combine the online characteristics of the computer with the 3-D simulation of data in space, called Virtual Reality. The new version of the Heavenly City, built in the electronic simulation of space, cyberspace will be the new architecture of information (see Benedikt, 13–18). Its parameters are topological, conflating how we imagine cities with how we have been trained by screens. Here is Gibson's famous description:

> Cyberspace. A consensual hallucination experienced daily by billions.
> . . . A graphic representation of data abstracted from the banks of every
> computer in the human system. Unthinkable complexity. Lines of light
> ranged in the nonspace of the mind, clusters and constellations of data.
> Like city lights, receding. . . . (51)

The complexity of data in space would need some sort of navigating tool—some method of moving quickly through it. While Microsoft is now developing "agents"—software programs that will act like secretaries, designed to navigate the World Wide Web and bring back only the kinds of data the operator "desires"—Gibson originated what has now become the common notion of how we will ultimately interact with such space—with neural implants, or wires directly into the brain:

> People jacked in so they could hustle. Put the trodes on and they were out
> there, all the data in the world stacked up like one big neon city, so you
> could cruise around and have a kind of grip on it, visually anyway, be-
> cause if you didn't, it was too complicated, trying to find your way to a
> particular piece of data you needed. (1988, 13)

Gibson's "jack" that fuses consciousness with urban environment, with techno-screen, foresees the conflation of affects this book would trace. His world is full of commodity fetishism and high capitalist waste—both human and material. The coming collusions between capitalist markets and the new technology call for a renewed vigor in establishing a materialist critique that could account for and intervene in such structures.

D O M A I N - M A T R I X

4
PAGE

PREV

NEXT

OPEN

PRINT

FIND

HELP

MENU

While cyberspace promises to include everything within its screen, the hype of possibilities should not be wholly consumed without an eye to its exclusions. Certainly, it is expensive—especially in terms of world economies. Even though the emphasis in cyberpunk culture is on hacking, building cheap systems out of used parts, stealing time on industrial and military systems, and other like strategies for those who would remain outside the military-industrial net, the majority of time online and software/hardware access to the "information superhighway" remain in the hands of institutions. Cyberspace grew out of military invention and retains violent military images in many of its entertainment offerings. The first computer game was called Space War; the first MUDs (Multiple User Dungeons), where users could meet online, derived from Dungeons and Dragons, and the first virtual environments were built for the Air Force. Moreover, the computer is a kind of mental hot rod, marketed for speed and access. A quick glance at the journals surrounding the growing virtual subculture quickly reveals what boy fantasies, patriarchal privileges, class oppressions, national agendas, and market forces drive its production.

Nevertheless, to stand as some prophet of doom, with raised finger, warning against this future, or to pretend to stand outside its effects, would be mere self-indulgence. The more practical response would be to find a way to be active in its construction. Some critics would construct it as the new "town meeting," where democratic debate will be housed. George P. Landow, in *Hyper/Text/Theory*, concludes his discussion of the coming online and hypertext possibilities with a consideration of their democratization. Taking off from the Frankfurt School's view of technology as Enlightenment domination of both nature and social systems, and the view that it is merely an instrument of social control, Landow uses Jürgen Habermas's theories of communicative action to work away from such condemnation to a theory of the democratization of technology. Landow wants to hope for the familiar goal of "access for all" as a guiding principle for the building of the "net." Communication becomes the cry, supporting "open, free-ranging discourse" (252). How appropriate, or possible, these goals may be will, hopefully, emerge in the working out of the ideas in this book. Likewise, socialist ideals, subcultural strategies, issues of community and nation will be tested in the consideration of the coming technologies. Labor conditions in microchip factories, gendered hiring practices, unemployment caused by the "new world order," and other like considerations must also bear on any analysis of cyberspace.

Beginning to identify the issues surrounding cyberspace begs another immediate question: how to write about these convergences? The book version of computer data is called hypertext: "an information technology consisting of individual blocks of text, or lexias, and the electronic links that join them" (Landow, 1). The links are not visible—the user may proceed as if page by page through the text, or may click on a word or a symbol to "travel" to another part of the text. Thus, the computer navigation of texts can move among ideas in multiple orders, as the user chooses. Hypertext would be the ideal form for this particular work. However, the time has not yet arrived in academic publishing, or in my own software skills, to accommodate that form. Moreover, as I have experienced reading on the screen, it seems most appropriate for "bits" of information. Appropriate to its own time, then, this book will continue the traditions of print culture even as it considers its demise and its transformation into cyberspace. The result of this compromise and contradiction between the engine of this writing and its substance is that the organization of ideas becomes fraught with ambivalence. The multiple relationships among the ideas afforded by computer navigation are reduced to the single, linear mode of print. At first I considered a print emulation of computer possibilities in order to signify this new configuration, but multiple colors of print, icons in the margins, and numerous fonts, while suggesting this form, actually simply render print the poor imitation of the screen, finally serving neither the author nor the reader. Flipping through pages to the next instance of the icon, for example, where the idea intersects with another, then flipping back to the initial icon is cumbersome and often requires yellow stickies and other book prostheses. The speed and simplicity of clicking on an icon to arrive at another instance of the idea in a hypertext is an entirely different order of relay.

My solution is simply to list the various sections of thought so the reader may proceed at will through the parts of the text. The reader may browse the table of contents to select which sections to read first, or in what order. The order of thought, as it appears in the linear structure of the book, represents merely the final decision before going to print. The sections have been variously arranged during the writing process, and aptly so. After all, the geography of the book assumes that the body, performance, and lesbian are produced at various intersections and among differing contexts of nation, screening, print traditions, etc. Thus, I will come back to the same points, but from a different "direction." Calling this "field" of inquiry the Domain-Matrix plays with the gendering and seductive operations within the dominating matrix that congeals around technology.

Sometimes, in the tradition of the dominatrix, I have created a hierarchy of ideas in the traditional outline symbology, to indicate ideas more proximate to one another than to others surrounding them. I have created a sense that some sections might subsume others, as in the signs of Ia, Ib, etc. These are more historical than discursive choices in their signing. They reflect more the ordering traditions of print than any necessary relation of dependency among the ideas. Nevertheless, one could imagine that certain assumptions attempt to overtake others. Such a layout reminds me of Wittgenstein's

DOMAIN-MATRIX

6
PAGE

PREV

NEXT

OPEN

PRINT

FIND

HELP

MENU

Tractatus Logico-Philosophicus. The opening line "The world is all that is the case" is precisely the effect that cyberspace seeks to produce in its technological take-over of material and social relations. Wittgenstein:

> It was my intention at first to bring all this together in a book whose form I pictured differently at different times. . . . After several unsuccessful attempts to weld my results together into such a whole, I realized I never would succeed. . . . My thoughts were soon crippled if I tried to force them on in any single direction against their natural inclination.—And this was, of course, connected with the very nature of the investigation. For this compels us to travel over a field of thought criss-cross in every direction. (In Landow, 87)

After a cursory discussion of surfing the net, the print matrix "begins" with a deconstruction/reconstruction of current critical theories of performance, the body, and lesbian. This deconstruction is something like an amulet to ward off haunting spirits that would impede the directions, the wandering maze, the too-steady matrix this work would weave. I am aiming, in part, for the roll of ceaseless contradiction, learned from Trotsky and Mao, and corrected by feminist and lesbian critical theory. The second part is entitled (pun intended) "Case Studies." "Bringing Home the Meat" deals with specific strategies for the "live" body in "performance" within considerations of nation, community, and global capitalism. "Los Angeles: A Topography of Screenic Properties" traces the rise of the circulation of screens that constitute the habits and practices specific to the dawning cyberspace, through movies, TV, video, and other screens. Each of these chapters concludes with analyses of specific cultural artifacts that illustrate the functions of performance, on the one hand, and screening, on the other. Indiana University Press kindly consented to design the pages of each section in a way suitable to the argument.

Finally, the book assumes a correlation among the constitution of "virtual identities." The virtualizing of identity has occurred in many critical, practical, and technological discourses, but this work focuses on the evacuation of identity in both electronic and poststructuralist discourses and its virtual substitutions in corporate, screened identities and "queer" ones. Taking as its premise that the notion of "queer performativity" appeared in critical discourses as a correction to "essentialist" practices of identity politics and performance at the same time as the rise of virtual reality systems in technological developments and criticism, this work pairs the two virtualizing discourses. The book thus oscillates between the debates and representational strategies around sexual politics and those of technoculture.

Within the oscillation, "lesbian" is a term that deploys the polemic against global capitalist virtualizing tendencies. "Lesbian" intertwines other terms in

D O M A I N - M A T R I X

MENU

HELP

FIND

PRINT

OPEN

PREV

NEXT

7
PAGE

various ways among the sections. Often, as in "Lesbian, Siamesian Space Cadets" or "*Screen/Skin/Utopia*," it serves as a final, utopic, compressed meditation on the topic. It may also be a source for critical strategies, as in the discussion of Gertrude Stein and encryption. It is a body that stands, along with materialism, in contradiction to masculinist, transcendent projects. It is a particular imaginary of space, as it intermingles with homosexual/gay. Along with homosexual/gay, it is a source of authors and works to be cited, from Wittgenstein to Melissa Scott. In the topography of the Domain-Matrix, it is the tendentious dynamic nesting among the sites. Lesbian, here, straddles a discursive examination and a performative discourse. Yet, only in one section ("Commodity Dildoism") does it break into the camp discourse I practiced in other articles to mark its historical, social practices. In its tendentious nesting and sometimes camp articulation, it is haunted by the lesbian vampire I performed in the article "Tracking the Vampire." I refer the reader back to that site for the practice of invisibility that this use of lesbian takes for granted.

CRUISING/SURFING THE MATRIX

The construction of the Domain-Matrix is to encourage the reader to move freely from section to section, or within a section, to a part of another, without any single developmental prescription. This organization hopes to emulate more the web sense of cyber-reading than the traditional composition in print. So that what used to be called fragmentation (still presuming there was a whole to fragment), privileged in earlier decades as they began to pull away from the linear mode, gives way to the sense of a net of notions, intersecting in different ways, depending upon the style of navigation. Yet even the term "navigation" still presupposes a destination, or at least a particular route, privileged as the most efficient. In computer parlance, both terms, "fragmentation" and "navigation," are still employed, retaining traces of their original connotations. "Fragmentation" represents the dispersal of files across noncontiguous sectors of a disk, leading to slower processing and possible damage to the hard drive. Unity, in this case, of location still operates as the most efficient organization. Likewise, navigating the net implies an efficient route through the ever-increasing multitude of sites in order to arrive at the websites most appealing to the user. Yet online practices often encourage the abandonment of such structures, encouraging a sense of hapless accretion and fortuitous accident in the play of the net. This ambivalence about the appropriate practice of methods reveals the way in which new hyper-activity is poised upon the threshold of a possible new managing of knowledge, information, and entertainment and the replication of traditional print concepts within the new engine of space.

D O M A I N - M A T R I X

8
PAGE

PREV

NEXT

OPEN

PRINT

FIND

HELP

MENU

To push the organization of this print text toward its own terminal limit, I want to suggest a strategy for reading that is borrowed from television practice and studies—"surfing." Surfing the channels means zapping through them with the aid of the remote control—the mouse of television **(see "The Flowing Locks of TV" for a discussion of "zapping").** In this practice, the viewer does not conform to the programming of a single channel, but organizes for herself a kind of surfing through the waves of TV reception, watching, briefly, the bits of narratives and images that appeal to her particular, changing impulses of the moment. Interestingly, particularly in terms of the argument in the section on Los Angeles and topography, the term "surfing" is borrowed from that notorious water sport associated with Los Angeles, the land of screens. Without waves, in the arid practice of print, I have organized this print text into short print bytes, or print sites, to encourage the reader to visit each of them in any order that appeals, suggesting a matrix, rather than a line of thought. I retain the term "surfing" because of its popular usage, and because it explicitly suggests white, blond surfer boys on the Los Angeles beaches. I have appended the term "cruising" because of the criticism launched in net debates by people of color and by lesbians and gays against "surfing" as connoting whiteness and straight maleness. Cruising suggests, instead, those low-rider cars discussed in the section on "Chicano Chariots of Fire," as well as the practice of sexual cruising in the lesbian and gay bar scene. "Cruising" thus offers a term for alternative net practices. However, the dominant practices in cyberspace still retain the training in adolescent male popular culture that "surfing" implies. The popular comic book series *The Silver Surfer* raised surfing to a salvationary mode of universal travel long before "surfing" the net imaged virtual relations with the screen. So "surfing" proceeds here as a term for proceeding through this text, as one watches TV and relates to other screenic practices.

Moreover, I hope that the reader might read not only by navigation, surfing, and cruising, but even more by a kind of aimless "drifting," as the Situationists called it. Intervening in the dominant notion of space travel, Guy Debord and his fellow "Internationale situationnistes" devised the project of creating a map of Paris they would call *The Naked City*. The map project took place in the 1950s—the era I am imagining, in the section on murderous heavenly creatures, to be the era of first contact with the virtual. By titling such mapping *The Naked City* after the noir screening of the city produced by the movie of that title and the later television series, the Situationists marked the screen into the city through a notion of what they called "psychogeography." They cut up the map of Paris into sections they linked by red directional arrows. The links represent "spontaneous turns of direction taken by a subject moving through these surroundings in disregard of useful connections" (McDonough, 60). So, rather than the traditional process of mapping, conducted from the "omnipresent view seen from nowhere," the Situationists' psychogeography is constituted through "spatializing actions" which they called "dérives" (drifts or drifting) (64). They posited the dérive as a kind of "blindness" in the modernist scopic economy "drawn by the solicitations of the terrain" rather than detached or controlling (73). Drifting is, then, without the guidance of the instrumental—there is no objective use, or even subjective use, that controls the movement among the sites. The order of access is not a controlling one, but one seduced by the "solicitations of the terrain." Such practices of contradicting the instrumental are central to dealings with technology and science, which would imprint the instrumental onto their management.

In the instance of this book, the section titles call out, in a "bold" manner, to entice the reader to their web-like site, where pleasure may not even endure throughout the section. "Turbo-Lesbo," for example, might accelerate certain readers to consider that section. (By the way, the reader, at this point in the text, might skip to the end of the matrix to note that Nicole Brossard, who appears in the section entitled "*Screen/Skin/Utopia*: The Lesbian Body," named the protagonist of her novel *The Mauve Desert* Claire Dérive.) In other sections, surfing becomes enmired in national, social, and commercial spaces. Yet national and commercial spaces have also helped to recommend such drifting. Walter Benjamin's notion of the flâneur, the urban wanderer, is prompted by shop windows. Print here, then, tries to emulate the spatial relations and their associations that others have made between urban, commercial, and subversive wanderings and texts. George Landow, in his book on hypertext, employs de Certeau's notion of "Walking in the City" to describe the relation between reader and hypertext. The "act of passing by," in which "the virtualized bodies of the walkers . . . are writing their own text, or rather, the interaction between their bodies and space constitutes a highly codified calligraphy," suggested by de Certeau, seems apt to the process of hyper-reading. Using de Certeau, Landow is able to produce a working description of "the networks of these moving, intersecting writings . . . shaped out of fragments of trajectories and alterations of spaces" (in Landow, 137).

Caught in the difference between Benjamin and de Certeau is the role of writing itself. De Certeau presumes inscription as the major trope for social processes. If, as cyberspace portends, we are at the end of print culture, how do we regard the privileged status of such tropes? Putting print aside, away from its dominating position, what other orders emerge as metaphors for the production of meaning? If print composes a certain type of subject, created in consonance with a passing form of capitalism, what new compound of subject, body, sexuality, gender, and class is being constituted in cyberspace? Without the popular trope of "inscription" that has brought writing onto bodies, institutions, and social spaces, what figures manage the emerging spaces

DOMAIN-MATRIX

10 PAGE
 PREV
 NEXT
 OPEN
 PRINT
 FIND
 HELP
 MENU

of information? Surfing these sections, the user will surely hit the shoals of these obdurate problems in many different sections. Borrowing from the novel about the lesbian Trouble and her problems online with her "friends," we might launch carefully into the Domain-Matrix of this book:

> Trouble's on the nets tonight, riding the high data like a cowboy, the plains of light stark around her. The data flows and writhes like grass in the virtual wind. . . . At the starpoint node, she falls suddenly into shadow, its warning cool along her skin.
>
> IC(E) rises to either side, prohibiting the nodes. . . . She can almost taste what lies behind that barrier, files and codes turned to candy-color shapes good enough to eat. . . . She leaves the way she came, sliding oblique along a trail of untouched data. . . . This night's city flows beneath her, data streams like rivers of cars, and she walks the nets down again, merging with the data until it pools and slows and feeds out into the great delta of the BBS. Here are all the temptations of the world, spread out in the broad meanders and bottomless swamps, where slow transfer is common and the sheer volume hides a multitude of sins. The air thickens around her as the brainworm reads the data as sensation. . . . She is never lost, not here, where the brainworm does its best and a lesser netwalker could drown in the sheer overload of sensation—but savoring the taste and scent of rich and unprotected data, the salt ebb and flow of freedom. (Melissa Scott, *Trouble and Her Friends*, 41–42)

Re-charging Essentialism

Immediately upon launching into the matrix, we find the critical shoal that, while seeming to prompt such a performance of reading, actually seeks to hinder it. The depth charge of essentialism would sink such a surfer.

In writing "performing lesbian" in the face of "queer performativity," I want to directly confront the charge of essentialism. This charge has been leveled against both "lesbian" and "performance." The contention of essentialism implies, without directly stating it, the anxiety around the end of print culture. It actually operates in the service of retaining the dominance of print culture by rewriting, or correcting its traditions. In this process, lesbian and performance, identity and visibility have seemingly been evacuated so that writing and reading may continue to exercise the dominance of print culture.

Briefly, the charge is that identity politics rest on the base that one might "be" a lesbian, thereby invoking an ontological claim. According to the poststructuralist critique, such a notion posits the formation of the subject position as prior to other social constructions—possibly even determining them. Moreover, it charges that identity has been imagined as visible, demanding space in the regime of representation as one of its political projects. Identity and visibility are both made to claim the notion of presence in their constitution of the "live" and the body. In order to evacuate the regime of identity and visibility, the charge of essentialism has attended so diligently to the problems inherent in the claim of "being" that it has obscured the broader, structural function of the term.

What is essentialist, or at least metaphysical, the ruinous worm buried in essentialism, is the kind of argument that is ultimately based on a self-generating self-referentiality, which has, in the eurocentric tradition, historically secured its closed status by an appeal to "ontology." In other words, what is structurally essentialist or metaphysical in an argument is the claim that the system rests, finally, on some self-generating principle—that it cuts loose from outside dependencies—operates outside the historical, material conditions of change. Essentialism procures the metaphysical through a notion of Being as

D O M A I N - M A T R I X

12 PAGE
PREV
NEXT
OPEN
PRINT
FIND
HELP
MENU

an essence. An essence, as Teresa de Lauretis notes in "The Essence of the Triangle, or Taking the Risk of Essentialism Seriously: Feminist Theory in Italy, the U.S., and Britain," claims the function of *"the reality underlying phenomena"* or *"that internal constitution, on which all the sensible properties depend"* (4–5). In other words, an essence functions in a philosophical system as the location where "the buck stops," or where "the thing" is, beyond any other referent "in itself." De Lauretis counters the charge of essentialism by distinguishing a "nominal essence" in contrast to a "real" one; the former would, within a feminist project, proffer an "embodied, situated knowledge," as mutable and historically contextualized (12). She slips the rug out from under or from within the "thing," resting its identity claim as contingent upon volition, on the one hand (the feminist project), and material circumstances, on the other. Her aim is to retain the project of identifying in order to challenge "directly the social-symbolic institution of heterosexuality" (32). Within this critical environment, "performing lesbian" would be taking what de Lauretis calls "the essentialist risk" to perform the identity of lesbian against that of heterosexual. Certainly, this is a familiar and welcome strategy.

De Lauretis redefines essence to counter the essentialist charge. Borrowing her adjustment to recontextualize the issue, I want to reverse the charge—to identify a metaphysical base within the poststructuralist argument. For the assumption that that base is corrected by abandoning a certain kind of materialist critique will have debilitating effects on notions of the body and of nation in the course of dangerous conservative agendas. The loss of discourse's ability to pose an outside referent directly unhinges political coalitions around issues of land, wages, processes of social discrimination, etc. De Lauretis, in defense of such prior commitments, reconfirms an open system, in which signs still retain a sense of referents outside their purely textual ones. Heterosexuality in her argument appears as both a social and a symbolic institution. In poststructuralist arguments, the charge of essentialism has been used to erode this sense of a referent outside the linguistic or discursive system. De Lauretis's gesture of reinstating a configuration of feminist politics against the charge of essentialism, through a study of an actual political collective in Italy—a system that accounts for and is accountable to a social movement—traces the critical space in which I would like to counter the poststructuralist charge that would empty out identity and the order of visibility. For, as we will see, such anti-essentialist systems, while they eschew ontology, may rest on other terms which function to set up a self-generating, self-referential, and in that manner metaphysical argument. The poststructural "corrections" operate in the refined atmosphere of "pure" theory and writing, abandoning earlier materialist discourses that signaled to activist, grassroots coalitions while claiming a less essentialist base.

D O M A I N - M A T R I X

 MENU
 HELP
 FIND
 PRINT
 OPEN
 PREV
 NEXT

13 PAGE

IA. QUEER PERFORMATIVITY

Debates over the meaning of performativity have been linked to the adoption of the term "queer" in some critical quarters. As Eve Kosofsky Sedgwick describes it in "Queer Performativity," Judith Butler's proposal of gender-bending performativity in *Gender Trouble* has been a central tool for the "recruitment" of graduate students into gay studies (1). The journal *glq (a journal of lesbian and gay studies)* even dedicated its inaugural issue to a dialogue between Sedgwick and Butler on queer performativity. If queer corrects the tradition of lesbian identity politics, performativity corrects the attendant regimes of the "live" and performance. Looking to Sedgwick's and Butler's articles as concise summaries of the positions, the necessary bond between "queer" and "performativity" may be seen to focus several critical anxieties that the departure from the troubled territories of "lesbian" and "performance" seeks to allay.

Performativity describes a critical strategy seemingly more deconstructive in its account of "performance" as sign. It strips the mask from masquerade that would still retain an actor/subject behind the show. In contrast, queer performativity identifies its operation as iterations of power contested at the sites of gender identification and legal, medical discourses concerning sexual practices. Performativity, as Sedgwick sees it, "carries the authority of two quite different discourses, that of theater on the one hand, of speech-act theory and deconstruction on the other. . . . Spanning the distance between the *extroversion* of the actor, the *introversion* of the signifier" (2). Sedgwick attributes the exclusive relation between performativity and the performance of gender to the Butler compound—particularly drag performances. Sedgwick would extend performativity to "coming out, for work around AIDS and for the self-labeled, transversely but urgently representational placarded body of *demonstration*." In other words, the "live" body is performative when "self-placarded [in] demonstration."

Certainly, the hard-won "visibility" of ACT UP! demonstrations has spurred critics such as Sedgwick to account for such activism in writing theories dependent on some notion of the subculture. Sedgwick's sense of "self-placarded" admits agency and the visible, while semiotizing it. To those familiar with the standard practices of agitprop theater, or the Brechtian notion of "distanciation," ACT UP!'s strategies and Sedgwick's representation of them do not seem to diverge from numerous historical models. The Brechtian tradition of political theater has long regarded any modes of suturing as empathetic structures that retain mystified class relations, thus rendering every performing body a placarded demonstration of social gesture—either complicit with dominant practices or, in Brechtian epic practices, a challenge

D O M A I N - M A T R I X

14
PAGE

 PREV

 NEXT

 OPEN

 PRINT

 FIND

 HELP

 MENU

to the status quo. However, what Sedgwick identifies as the queer-specific mode of performativity is one catalyzed by "shame," distinguishing it from those propelled into representation by other mechanisms of oppression, such as class relations in the Brechtian model. Unlike the material relations of class, the catalytic relation of "shame" to "performativity" establishes a bridge between internal dynamics and the order of the visible. This crossing of the internal/external divide may provide the key contribution of "queer" to "performativity" that has made the compound so inviting to theorists in recent years. Diana Fuss, in her introduction to the influential anthology *inside/out,* marks this relation as the signature of new critical practices. We will see in a later discussion just how this works along the borders of the visible and writing. Yet Sedgwick only passingly admits demonstrations into her discussion. Instead, she ultimately settles upon Henry James's prefaces in the New York edition of his work as the prime site of performativity.

Before addressing the consequences of that settlement, I want to turn briefly to Butler's use of "queer performativity" to explore just how reading and writing have been made to overtake traditional notions of performance. In "Critically Queer," Butler emphasizes that "there is no power, construed as a subject, that acts, but only a reiterated acting that is power in its persistence and instability" (1993, 17). Butler's mission is to evacuate traditional notions of the subject/agency from within the system of performativity. She emphasizes that "performativity, then, is to be read not as self-expression or self-presentation, but as the unanticipated resignifiability of highly invested terms" (28). Butler continues, working from J. L. Austin, to locate such performativity within studies of speech acts, asserting that "performative acts are forms of authoritative speech." Reframing the operations of "queer" within those of "performativity," Butler finds that "the term 'queer' emerges as an interpellation that raises the question of the status of force and opposition, of stayability and variability, *within* performativity" (18). The term "queer," operating within these parameters, provides the solution to earlier conundra that Butler identified in her influential article "Imitation and Gender Subordination," in which she problematizes the rubric "lesbian theory."

> To install myself within the terms of an identity category would be to turn against the sexuality that the category purports to describe; and this might be true for any identity category which seeks to control the very eroticism that it claims to describe and authorize, much less "liberate." . . . For it is always finally unclear what is meant by invoking the lesbian-signifier, since its signification is always to some degree out of one's control, but also because its specificity can only be demarcated by exclusions that return to disrupt its claim to coherence. (1991, 14–15)

For Butler, "lesbian" as an identity is overdetermined by heterosexuality. It is actually produced by homophobia, articulates the, by definition, unarticulable

in its claim to sexuality, is both "out of control" for those reasons and oppressive in drawing exclusionary borders of specificity. "Queer" evacuates
the fulsome problematic of "lesbian" to operate as an unmarked interpellation,
thus avoiding that exclusionary specificity.

"Queer" occurs within "performativity," which Butler in the earlier article
defines as evacuating "performance" by denying "a prior and volitional subject"; in fact, as she would have it, "performative" "constitutes as an effect
the very subject it appears to express" (24). Unlike Sedgwick's, Butler's sense
of performativity sets out to contradict traditional agitprop or Brechtian theatrical strategies that encourage actors and spectators alike to imagine themselves as an agent of change. Butler gives over that agency to a "reiterated
acting that is power in its persistence and instability . . . a nexus of power and
discourse that repeats or mimes the discursive gestures of power" (17). She
insists that the subject is merely a product of such iterations:

> Where there is an "I" who utters or speaks . . . there is first a discourse
> which precedes and enables that "I." . . . Indeed, I can only say "I" to the
> extent that I have first been addressed, and that address has mobilized my
> place in speech; paradoxically, the discursive condition of social recogni-
> tion *precedes and conditions* the formation of the subject. (18)

Generally, this treatment of subject formation is familiar to readers of
poststructuralist or even Gramscian theory. The signature of Butler's strategy
here resides in its own emphasis on "precedes and conditions."

Moving an argument through the notion of "preceding" is reminiscent of
an earlier philosophical move that would also confront idealism, the mother
of essentialism, but that also, finally, reinscribes a metaphysical presumption
at its base: Aristotle's notion of the prime mover in his *Metaphysics*. Marking
his base as "substance" in contrast to Plato's Ideas, Aristotle finds himself
within the currently familiar dilemma of the contradictions between compound, or heterogeneous, "substances" and the unity of "identity." Against
the essentialist stasis of identity, Aristotle also arrives at the function of acting
(read performativity) as mutable and motile: "Nothing, then, is gained even
if we suppose eternal substances, as the believers in the forms do, unless there
is to be in them some principle which can cause change—for if it is not to *act*
there will be no movement" (1071a 14–18). But the cause of action, or change,
suggests prior agency—a problem that both Aristotle and Butler would solve.
Butler poses discourse as that which precedes and "mobilizes" the formation
of such agency in the subject position. Then how do discourse and power
avoid the same correction as the subject—to be preceded by something that
determines their agency? Butler posits "reiterated acting that is power" as
the generator of the system. Aristotle strikes a structurally consonant tone,
as his chain of "precedings" resolves in the self-referential notion of "thought

thinking on itself" (1072b 19–22; 1074b 34–36). Since thought is both the subject and the object of its operations, argues Aristotle, it iterates itself and thus becomes the "prime mover." "Reiterated acting" describes a similarly self-referential function that "precedes and determines" agency, without begging a further precedent. Now, Aristotle literalizes the theological implications in such a strategy, calling the prime mover "god," while still insisting on substance against Idea. Butler, in overwriting human agency with self-iterating acting as "power," embeds the theological, self-referential "preceder" in what she emphasizes is an anti-essentialist move. In order to deconstruct the location of the subject as preceding the social, Butler reverses the equation, necessarily retaining what is metaphysical in both postulations: a self-iterating function that "precedes."

In Butler's argument, iteration itself, mediating the relation of power to acting, finally functions as re-iteration. Whereas Aristotle found, in thought thinking on itself, a self-generating collapse of subject/object positions, Butler fires up the motor of iteration by repetition. When all referents fail to signal anything outside the system, repetition becomes its dynamic, as is obvious in several of Butler's key concepts: "the psyche calls to be rethought as a compulsive repetition" (28), "repetition is the way in which power works to construct the illusion of a seamless heterosexual identity," "the very exercise of repetition is redeployed for a very different performative purpose" (1991, 24). Repetition, then, the dynamic of self-generating self-referentiality, is the action, the activism, proposed by the argument.

Yet lurking in the project to make writing active, to make theorizing a significant actor in spite of all repetitive iterations, or theoretical stomps, is the writer. Ironically, but fittingly, the evacuation of identity, the old political compound, by self-referentiality becomes literal, concluding the argument at the site of the self—the author. Finally, "queer performativity" is located in Butler's decision to accept (mis)readings of her own writing:

> It is one of the ambivalent implications of the decentering of the subject to have one's writing be the site of a necessary and inevitable expropriation. . . . yielding of ownership over what one writes [and] not owning of one's words. . . . the melancholic reiteration of a language one never chose. (29)

In spite of moves to the contrary, Butler has reinstated the subject (of writing) as herself. "Melancholic reiteration" motivates her critical production; as she reported in an interview, "I've just finished writing another manuscript in which I spend page after page trying to refute the reduction of gender performance to something like style" (1992, 31). When the author, by virtue of her own theories, forgoes her role as representative of either a movement, an activist group, or even, through identity politics, the conditions of lesbian or

D O M A I N - M A T R I X

MENU

HELP

FIND

PRINT

OPEN

PREV

NEXT

17 PAGE

some form of social oppression, self-referentiality can become either formalist philosophical arguments, or prey to media adulation, as the troubling (to Butler) appearance of the fanzine *Judy!* illustrates. Writing, as Derrida set out to illustrate, cannot, in spite of alluring, queer performative gyrations, wriggle free of the metaphysical—even if it scapegoats lesbian and feminist writings as sites of identity and presence.

And this brings us to the way in which a notion of performativity, as in both Butler and Sedgwick, while referencing activist demonstrations, is finally most alluring as an effect of writing and reading. In fact, one might argue, the project of performativity is to recuperate writing at the end of print culture. In Sedgwick, queer performativity is best enacted by the prefaces of Henry James, and in Butler it resides in accommodating misreadings of her own writing. The critical discourses of speech-act theory and deconstruction ultimately bring the notion of performativity back to their own mode of production: print. It is confounding to observe how a lesbian/gay movement about sexual, bodily practices and the lethal effects of a virus, which has issued an agitprop activist tradition from its loins, as well as a Pulitzer Prize–winning Broadway play (*Angels in America*), would have as its critical operation a notion of performativity that circles back to written texts, abandoning historical traditions of performance for the print modes of literary and philosophical scrutiny. Queer, then, moves identity to readership, and "performativity" imbues writing with performance.

IB. BURYING THE LIVE BODY

What happens when critics of "live performance" attempt to accommodate this new sense of performativity and its privileging of print culture? Positioned at the intersection of the realm of the visible with the "live," within a tradition that foregrounds the body and resists recording technologies, such as the camera or print, performance seems unable to partake in the strategies of performativity. In addressing performativity, the critics of "live performance" detail a clear axis of dependencies along the notions of "performativity," "queer," and the realm of the visible in relation to that of writing. They must discover a way in which to rid the "live" of the contamination of "presence" and install writing at the scene of visible action.

Not all performance critics have been seduced by queer performativity. Janelle Reinelt, in "Staging the Invisible: The Crisis of Visibility in Theatrical Representation," identifies one danger inherent in these operations of performativity. Reinelt challenges Butler's arguments for their extraction of visibility and identity politics from theatrical production. Moreover, she concludes that Butler's only notion of political action, to perturb the system, is a

DOMAIN-MATRIX

18 PAGE
 PREV
 NEXT
 OPEN
 PRINT
 FIND
 HELP
 MENU

dangerous one. She argues that the notion of subversion, by abdicating any clear program for change, offers what seems to be a subversion of the dominant order, but in fact leaves hegemonic codes of visibility in place. Reinelt deems the subversive strategy "theological," operating on the "blind faith" that once the dominant system is perturbed, the hold of the hegemonic will somehow give way, and the lot of oppressed people in the system will be improved. Reinelt quotes one example of Butler's leap of faith: "Subversiveness is not something that can be gauged or calculated. In fact, what I mean by subversion are those effects that are incalculable" (Reinelt, 5).

In order to illustrate her point to the contrary, Reinelt describes how a cross-gender, cross-racial casting of the character of Betty in Caryl Churchill's *Cloud Nine* served to feminize markers of race in challenging those of gender. Reinelt describes the audience's laughter when the colonial, white Clive kisses the African American male actor playing Betty, as celebrating the feminization of the African American man in white, colonial practices. In this case, perturbing gender roles by cross-gender casting does not destabilize the gender and racial markers; instead, it reinscribes the negative way in which markers of gender and race are used against one another in dominant practices. In spite of perturbations of the system, the traditional codes reassert themselves. Likewise, Reinelt argues, Butler's analysis of the film *Paris Is Burning*, which focuses on Venus Xtravaganza as a subject who "repeats and mimes legitimating norms by which it itself has been degraded," actually illustrates the lethal power of these "norms" by selecting the "performer" in the film who is murdered by someone for whom "she apparently didn't 'pass'" (Reinelt, 7).

In contrast to Reinelt's skepticism about politics without programs or outside referents, Lynda Hart's recent work seeks to reconcile the notions of performativity with the visible realm of "live" performance. The terms "queer" and "performativity" offer a direct challenge to Hart, who previously has written within a tradition of critical accounts of "performing lesbian." While she does not evacuate the term "lesbian," she does attempt to move it from its traditional context of visibility politics to function more like the term "queer" in regard to performativity. Yet the retention of "lesbian" causes an oscillation between the two systems that Hart cannot quite resolve. Her solution lies in adding Lacan to the formulation.

Hart begins her article "Identity and Seduction: Lesbians in the Mainstream" by addressing the traditional question: How does a lesbian look or act like one? In a consideration of a butch/femme performance by Peggy Shaw and Lois Weaver, the performing duo that has catalyzed most theorization in the field, Hart aligns the term "lesbian" with the politics of visibility, as tainted by essentialism. Yet, rather than situate "queer" as the correction to this traditional sense of "lesbian visibility," Hart posits psychoanalytic theory:

> According to such responses, Weaver and Shaw were unsuccessful in presenting themselves *as* lesbians. But what is this "something-to-be-seen" that is presumed to be so crucial to the political project? Why do we always assume that visibility always and everywhere has a positive sociopolitical value? Visibility politics, the dominant agenda of gay and lesbian activism, clashes with psychoanalytical constructions of sexual subjectivities. The former's assertion of identity politics is unraveled by the latter's destabilizing identifications. (124)

The lingering problem for Hart, which had been abandoned by the textual return effected by Butler and Sedgwick, is in the realm of what is seen—the "meat" of the matter. Hart is still looking at live performance. However, she finds that such visibility "risk[s] reinstating a metaphysics of substance in order to maintain a political perspective that can be referred to as lesbian" (128).

"Substance," once the base of a materialist critique in contradiction to an essentialist one, now associated with visibility and identity, risks essentialism by turgidly resisting the psychoanalytic strategy of positing "sexual subjectivities." Hart would not "see" the contaminated meat of the material, nor its double, identity, yet she will continue to look—to remain a spectator. If she will not risk the sight of lesbian *identity*, what could she see? Following in the Butlerian mode, Hart actually manages to see the binary—the slash— the pole that runs through Shaw and Weaver's butch/femme role playing. Butch/femme is no longer a way to make "lesbian" visible, with its marking of experience and history; rather, for Hart, butch/femme performance provides a "challenge [to] the construction of the heterosexual/homosexual binary, adulterating the first term and foregrounding the *production* of the second term" (128). Putting it another way, lesbian visibility gives way to the visibility of the production of the binary. All that the spectator sees is the structure of the binary.

Hart's argument actually seems to offer a new version of structuralism rather than poststructuralism, coming full circle to the essentialism once leveled at its tradition. Consider Claude Lévi-Strauss's work on the face and body painting of the Caduveo in *Tristes Tropiques*, for example. Opening with the assertion that "the customs of a community, taken as a whole . . . are reducible to systems," Lévi-Strauss perceives in the body paintings "a dualism that is projected onto successive planes" (178, 191). The dualism, he argues, becomes dynamic in the intersection of themes, which destabilize the hierarchy of the dualism. Lévi-Strauss claims to see both the representation of the tribe's social practices, as in their endogamous/exogamous marriage practices, and their utopic solutions in these paintings (196). Structuralism allows this particular brand of spectatorship, as in Hart's example, to perceive, in both cases, the binary pole that organizes the sociological status of the performers.

D O M A I N - M A T R I X

20
PAGE

PREV

NEXT

OPEN

PRINT

FIND

HELP

MENU

In mobilizing this structuralist method, Hart still does not turn away from the designation "lesbian," which is generally associated with other claims of visibility. Valiantly, while arguing with visibility politics, Hart resists the term "queer." However, as Hart's critique oscillates between the two strategies of lesbian visibility and queer performativity, it slips through several positions, as she proposes "lesbian desire," the ability of spectators to "see lesbians," and "lesbian subjectivity." Hart finally arrives at the solution in retaining both the visible, the live, and its evacuation in the notion of a "hallucination" of lesbian within the "specular economy." What Hart has accomplished by the revision is this: Subjective processes have been empowered to absorb the realm of the visible. Hart resolves the initial dilemma between visible/identities and internal, discursive functions by empowering the latter to swallow up the former. Once firmly on the ground of subjectivities, through the notion of hallucination, Hart can actually "see" Shaw and Weaver produce the binary.

Finally free of the axis of visible/identity/body/live through her unique blending of Lacan with Butler, Hart can *write* about a lesbian performance. Without recourse to a written text for the move—that is, without reading a playscript, but remaining tuned to live performance—hallucination allows Hart to textualize what it seems to "mean" outside of linguistic systems. She can employ the master narratives of writing out the internal available within psychoanalytic discourse. Hart can then make the return to writing that Sedgwick and Butler effected in their notions of performativity, while seemingly retaining a focus on live performance.

Hart has overcome the way in which performance has traditionally perturbed the interpretive power of print. After all, critics of theater, dance, and music are familiar with the long, precarious tradition of *writing* arts' criticism. Yet, within current critical debates, the contestation between these two orders seems to have overrun the borders of the traditional dispute. The obsession with the performative aspect of writing from within many critical quarters marks a reconfiguration of strategies through which print may once again claim the production of meaning for the realm of the visual and the active. Establishing writing as performative both admits its limit and reestablishes its dominance. In terms of performance, it becomes the victory of the spectator over the performance—the old idiom "beauty is in the eye of the beholder" becomes constitutive and all-embracing in this new formula. Performance is made to yield this precise point.

Whereas such debates over writing's role in regard to performance may reside in the subtext of the above critics, Peggy Phelan, in the chapter of her book *Unmarked* entitled "The Ontology of Performance," directly addresses this struggle. After setting out the familiar charges: "Performance implicates the real through the presence of living bodies" and "live performance plunges into visibility" (148), Phelan situates these critical problems with performance at the site of writing. First, she notes that "to attempt to write about the undocumentable event of performance is to invoke the rules of the written document and thereby alter the event itself" (148). She then reverses the direction of the critique, however, to lead her argument back to writing as performative:

> The challenge raised by the ontological claims of performance for writing is to re-mark again the performative possibilities of writing itself. The act of writing toward disappearance, rather than the act of writing toward preservation, must remember that the after-effect of disappearance is the experience of subjectivity itself. (148)

The use of performance, then, is to challenge writing to become performative. The contradiction between performance as mutable and nonreproductive, and writing as stable and reproductive, motivates writing to somehow perform "mimicry" and "to discover a way for repeated words to become performative utterances" (149). Not surprisingly, J. L. Austin does not follow far behind.

These new strategies of writing follow on the heels of deconstruction, a strategy linked to the role of writing. They seek a way to extend writing to those whom it had previously dispossessed. While Phelan never writes "lesbian" or "queer," she does situate the performance of writing in terms of gender, deploying the category of "women" and finally "mother" as the dispossessed, as body. How can writing finally accommodate them? Once again, performance enters the scene as that which insists upon the body and clarifies the problem:

> For performance art itself however, the referent is always the agonizingly relevant body of the performer. . . . In performance, the body is metonymic of self, of character, of voice, of "presence." But in the plenitude of its apparent visibility and availability, the performer actually disappears and represents something else—dance, movement, sound, character, "art.". . . Performance uses the performer's body to pose a question about the inability to secure the relation between subjectivity and the body per se; performance uses the body to frame the lack of Being promised by and through the body—that which cannot appear without a supplement. (150–151)

The supplement is the gaze, which is constituted through castration and the invisible genitals of the mother. As Phelan puts it, seeing is the fear of blindness: castration. Through a Lacanian oxymoronic formulation, sight, the body, and performance become the site for loss, lack, and disappearance (152). As the body attains subjectivity through the promise of disappearance, the anx-

D O M A I N - M A T R I X

22
PAGE

PREV

NEXT

OPEN

PRINT

FIND

HELP

MENU

ious eye writes performativity—securing for writing that same promise of disappearance, freeing it from its fetters as a recording device.

Likewise, the critical/political role that Phelan assigns to performance is that of "radical negativity" (165). As she sees the blindfolded Angelika Festa hang from the pole of the binary, effectively resisting being "absorbed by history" and the effects of representation, Phelan's writing "mimics" that contingency and negativity, promising a fulsome discursive marking of the "unmarked." Both writing and the body actively access their incapacities, mediated by "articulate eyes" (158) whose enunciations are, as Butler would propose, "subverted." Phelan celebrates the end stations of the engines of writing and seeing, offering up, as political and performative, blindness and the unmarked, what Reinelt has pointed out in Butler as "blind faith" in the effects of subversion as a radical potential. Phelan thus distinctly addresses the issues emanating from the contestation between performance and writing. Yet she shifts contestation to homology, "mimicry," insisting that writing is both unlike and like performance when caught in the Symbolic web of Lacanian principles. By dis-abling both, she retains both in terms of one another.

Accordingly, "queer performativity" and its concomitant charge of essentialism serve to bring together several different issues and to reflect several different anxieties: self-referentiality has overcome an argument that would set determining referents outside its own symbolic system, identity and visibility politics have been replaced with unmarked interpellations into such symbolic systems, and the body and the order of the visible have been subsumed by writing and the order of print. "Queer performativity," in withdrawing from these arguments, not only has evacuated the sites for certain debates but has successfully isolated the various elements from one another.

Accompanying these absorptive strategies is the alteration in the critical study of performance from a perspective based on the practice to one based on its reception. Hart, Phelan, and others actually write out the position of the spectator. For those versed in the history of critical writing on performance in this century, the shift is a crucial one. The early exemplars of performance criticism were written by practitioners, with an eye toward production: Antonin Artaud's *The Theater and Its Double*, Peter Brook's *The Empty Space*, Grotowski's *The Poor Theater*, Herbert Blau's *The Impossible Theater*, and of course, the critical works of Bertolt Brecht and Heiner Müller. Each practitioner imagined the ground of the theater in terms of how it embodied the agonistic positions, appearances, and gestures of their communities or of their historical, social moments. Artaud went in search of collective enactments to Balinese and Tarahumara Indian ritual practices in order to discover the masks of the agon between the perceptible and the imperceptible: the theater and its meta-double. Blau produced the first U.S. staging of *Waiting for Godot* in San Quentin—to be acted by an invested community.

Brecht invented the *gestus*—developed stage positions, crosses, and proximities as maps of social relations. The crucial difference here is between the assignation of power into agonistic roles (the deliberations of its partitions through characters and spatial relations) and the absorption of it into the arena of the spectator—the singular envelope to which it is addressed.

As the agonistic collective fades away, in its performance traditions and in critical reception, the rise of the individual may be seen as part of the victory of advanced capitalism and its market strategy. Private property is celebrated in a new way. Rather than individual ownership in the traditional sense, of something outside oneself, the self has been amplified across the terrain of what was once an "outside" to finally encompass all property within its subjectivity. In the rise of the individual as the theater, and the conflation of audience member with performer, the private individual has become the arena of the public. For example, the desire for the neo-individualist stage is manifested in the prominence of the work of Anna Deveare Smith, who subsumes cross-ethnic debates in her one-woman shows. Individual performance representing different ethnic communities in crisis seems to be far more acceptable to contemporary audiences.

There is a model of performance lurking behind these several critiques of it—one that actually "embodies" those who write about theater. While they seek to confute performance and its assumptions, they themselves continue to perform in a way that replicates what they would contradict by reading academic papers.

IC. PERFORMING READING

Much of the preceding debate has centered upon how certain uses of the poststructuralist critique and "queer performativity" operate in the service of reading and writing to imbue them with the seductive, pleasurable qualities of performance and, consequently, to relegate bodily performances to a prior, essentialized mode of production. Performing reading, then, within these critical treatises takes on several complex maneuvers. At the heart of academia, at the center of intellectual performance, dwells an age-old tradition of reading that continues to constitute authority within the institution and to provide the most prominent practice of collectivity within academic circles— reading a paper. Reading a paper is academic performance.

The performance of reading an academic paper emulates the theatrical setup. A performer stands in front of a group of listeners who are constituted as an audience. They listen quietly, respond appropriately (such as laughing at some critical witticism), and applaud at the conclusion. In fact, oral interpretation, the practice of reading well in front of an audience, was once part of the traditional curriculum in theater studies. Unlike theater, however, which distinguishes in kind between performer and audience, reading a paper brings together a group of academics who are paper readers themselves, in other venues or at other times. The performer and audience come together through this sole scholarly practice. To make the point succinctly: The oral performance of print forms the sociality of the academic community. Since the major performance of reading and writing research is done in isolation, this reading of it is *the* social instance. No wonder these "readers" perceive live performance through a textual lens. Their perspective has led to the creation of a theatrical canon focused on performance from text, with Shakespeare at its center, and cabaret or other traditions of improvised theater relegated to the wings.

"Reading" the paper foregrounds the condition of having written the paper elsewhere, and at an earlier time. As an import rather than an improvisation, the paper foregrounds the stability of print and thus of knowing. Improvisation is perceived as a kind of "fallen," unprepared performance that borders on "opinion" rather than research. The performance of reading, in this way, often undercuts the aim of a paper to encourage the sense of postmodern slippage, or deconstructive strategies. The style of reading also testifies to this solemn, stable style of delivery of postmodern instability. The voice is assumed to be one's "own," as original to the owner of the intellectual property. At my first academic conference, I heard a paper about Hrotsvit von Gandersheim, in which the reader created a voice for the quotations from Hrotsvit, a voice for the several chroniclers of her life, and a voice for her own emendations. Appropriate as the technique might have been to the work of the first woman playwright, the "strong voice" of Gandersheim, it seemed to produce a skeptical response to her paper. A "serious" scholar could not read as "playfully" as her delivery of sources as characters seemed to be received. Instead, the academic reads a paper in the style of news anchors, who perform "reading" the news on television in order to emphasize its solemn accuracy and stability amidst frolicking sitcoms and teary soaps. Unlike the news, however, the academic paper will be published in some form, may be cited—and, most important, may be copyrighted. Print is the very ground of intellectual property, and the reading of it as the performance of the social nature of ideas rests on their presentation as private property.

The prominence of this sense of performing reading saturates not only the formulation of "queer performativity," but also the structures of other basic poststructuralist notions, such as masquerade. Joan Riviere's founding article on masquerade, after all, was based on the instance of a woman reading an academic paper. There, gender as masquerade was revealed through the citation of such a performance. Whereas Riviere's work is generally received in its address to gender issues, it may be that its enduring paradigm is, in fact, its setting at the site of reading a paper. The homology may be thus framed: Gender is to masquerade what print is to reading. Masquerade, like reading, is derived from a base order of gender (print), but inverts it through performance. Derived from "reading, " the structure of the notion of masquerade emulates the relations inherent in the mode of performance as reading a paper. Other theorists of masquerade were also thinking of the notion specifically in terms of print culture, such as Bakhtin, who considered the novel. The structure of a stable base, be it gender, or class, or print, subverted by a performance of it, drives the concept of masquerade as well as the performance of reading a paper.

Performance, then, when derived from a "community" of academics, whose social practice resides in performing reading, and whose structures of performance saturate poststructuralist notions around performance itself, is posited as an after-effect of print. The construction after-effect is acted out in all sorts of theories, from those of dominant culture and resulting subcultures, to social constructionism itself. Queer theory, with its emphasis on "performativity," replicates the relationship that performance has held to print. The nature of the medium of print, so embedded in the production of knowledge, has bled out into the critical structuring of cultural production and its social implications. The law, the legislated, the written, in book culture, in print culture, precedes and determines performance. The difficulty in proposing any conjunction such as "performing lesbian" runs aground of arguments over such "precedings" (as in Butler). "Performing" cannot seem to inhabit any originary space—that is precisely, those critics would offer, its merit. It is posed as an after-effect, albeit a subversive one—of a stable condition.

Opting out of the tribal customs of academia, of the dominance of performing print, through reading, in order to constitute performance, what if we turn to the cultures of improvisation in order to re-imagine it—even wordless improvisation, such as mime or dance? Must improvisations inevitably be "read," as current critics maintain? Are they really "texts" that operate as other, primarily written ones? What about the experiments of twentieth-century performance: Artaud, for whom language failed, seeking Balinese dance to invoke the ground of meaning through performance; Grotowski's school of gesture first and sound as root emanations of corporeal, anatomic poses; Cunningham's dance that sought to leave narrative and symbolic structures behind in a choreography of unadorned, simple "bodily" movement. Improvisation first, as a mandate, acts differently. During improvisation, elements of different orders of things are necessarily contingent upon one another; whereas print stands alone, as cheese does at the end of "The Farmer in the Dell." Improvisation elicits an exploration of space by something moving in it. Intention is situated within conditions outside its purview. As Cynthia Novack has decribed the project of contact improvisation, "it was one of a number of enterprises during the late

'60s and early '70s in dance, theater, therapy, and athletics which were trying to realize a redefinition of self within a responsive, intelligent body" (3). Novack stresses the maintenance of a state of ambiguity between "allowing things to happen" and the process of collectively "reaching a definitive decision" as the process of such improvisation (216-217).

These avant-garde performance traditions took on print as an adversary as far back as the early decades of this century, deploying improvisation as its destabilizer. Take Dada, for example, with its exploration of random sound, random altered arrangements of letters, type, and its emphasis on one-time-only performances. Recalling Artaud's and the French Surrealists' early relation to communism recalls the direct relationship these innovations held with social and material conditions. The fascination that works such as Nietzsche's pre-symbolic Dionysian celebrations in his *Birth of Tragedy* held for these innovators offered a philosophical argument with print posed as the symbolic, or in Nietzsche's case, the Apollonian. They sought to posit performance as prior to print, rather than as an after-effect of it. The debate raged on around the role of print. The Lacanian obsession with words, the Symbolic and its power, may have been a last-ditch effort to resuscitate its power, the power of the talking cure, the writing of it, as Freud began it, and the resulting pathologizing of bodily knowledge (hysteria). Within the context of these experiments, academics who continue to collect around the valorization of print culture seem almost superstitious in their cult performances.

While some academics continue to perform the mysteries of print, online pleasures register its passing. One of the leading computer games, Myst, literally begins with the falling of the book through space. To begin the game, the operator clicks on the book, which opens to a page that houses a screen. The screen reads animated pictures through the empty shell of the book, as it leads the player out into its graphic environment. The images of books are haunting, nostalgic references in the game, constituting a kind of fallen, half-destroyed origin from which the play of the computer is generated. In their place, landscapes—connected worlds—envelop the player, who wanders through pictorial fields of information. Movies, screens of an earlier order, also narrate the coming of the screen-of-screens in relation to the demise of print. For example, the movie *In the Mouth of Madness* portrays the end of the book as a nightmare—its pages open to a cyberhell. In the movie, the book, like the Bible a victory of the printing press, claims a positive status for its mode of production, promising a better world through reading. As the book fades, the dark forces overcome it. Either way, whether as entry into cyberlandscapes or into hell, the demise of the book is set at the opening of the screen.

At this point in history, reading an academic paper, even one written on a computer, enacts this same kind of melodrama between print and screen. The lamp of knowledge is lit against the darkness through the reading of writing.

D O M A I N - M A T R I X

MENU

HELP

FIND

PRINT

OPEN

PREV

NEXT

27
PAGE

The community collects around that light, maintaining its glow by insisting that the social production of knowledge is best performed by reading aloud. Freud read papers to learned societies; Joan Riviere was inspired by the sight of a woman reading one. Even those who propose postmodern theories of slippage maintain the stabilizing of print's dominion by reading their works aloud.

Improvisation stands in contradiction to this practice. It sets up an "intelligent body," as Novack puts it, through which response rather than intention is prioritized. It is a body among bodies—in space. The space also retains its own mandates, actively shaping the possible through its exploration. More like ecology, more like coalition, improvisation provides a mode of performance where performative textuality would pronounce through print.

ID. THE END OF PRINT CULTURE

The contest between two orders, previously perceived as alphabetic and visual but technologically represented by print and the screen, has run throughout the twentieth century. Print and the screen have organized their own cultures—their own virtual communities. The two technologies produce their own structures of value. In fact, one could trace cultural production in the twentieth century through a history of their relationships through Dada and Futurism, Benjamin and Brecht, feminist critical theory and film. *The Name of the Rose*, by the semiotician Umberto Eco, could be read as the narrativization of this current print/image struggle, masquerading in the robes of medieval monks. Whereas these two orders have traditionally run their separate courses, challenging one another by difference, the coming dominance of the computer as the new engine of writing has finally assigned print to the screen. The victory of the screen, accompanying the victory of global capitalism and the new virtual construction of social and economic practices, yields a variety of consequences. The dominant position of postindustrial nations will become even more exaggerated—particularly the prominence of the top cyberproducers, the United States and Japan.

Print and the screen contest the role of the image. Print's page encourages a linear, orderly, generally black and white visual arena. If images are introduced into the arena of print, they are relegated to the role of illustration, as if they somehow duplicate or extend the meanings produced in the print. They are additive in a certain sense, intrusive in another, embellishing in yet another. The screen, however, is constructed for the image. It inverts the relationship, situating print as mere proof of ownership of the images, as running credits introduce or follow a movie, or locating print upon an image in the narrative. From the perspective of the screen, where techno-color enhances the image through saturation, and magnification celebrates its domain as vast

DOMAIN-MATRIX

28 PAGE

 PREV

 NEXT

 OPEN

 PRINT

 FIND

 HELP

 MENU

and worthy of survey, the manners of print culture, which forgo such pleasure, are foregrounded:

> Print represents a decision of severe abstraction and subtraction. All nonlinear signals are filtered out; color is banned for serious texts; typographical constants are rigorously enforced; sound is proscribed; even the tactility of visual elaboration is outlawed. Print is an act of perceptual self-denial. . . . Not the least implication of electronic text for rhetoric is how the implicit self-denials of the print contract are being renegotiated. (Lanham, 74)

Print's puritanical practices clearly run afoul of the wriggling, color-filled, spectacular attributes of the screen. Learning's dedication to print's values has produced a panic among writers about its durability and its assimilation into the screen—that cartoon-laden, movie-queen engine of recorded performance. The panic concerning the role of writing has fueled deconstruction, French feminist theory, and the Lacanian writing cure. It seems the academy, in crisis, has organized two strategies to retain writing amid screens: writing about writing, in order to maintain its ground through self-referentiality, or writing in emulation of the screen's potential for hypertextuality.

Deconstructing writing's role is a melancholy manner of writing about writing in order to maintain a central role for print. Discovering a role for print as a site either of contamination or of salvation (in relation to the oral) at least keeps it centered in the practice of academic production. Yet some deconstructive writing sought to enhance print's culture by encouraging experiments which would illustrate spatial coincidences in writing, reading, and the academic performances of both. Jacques Derrida in many of his works, such as *Glas*, or "The Double Session," in *Dissemination*, plays with the black/white register of print, its spatial organization and performance: "These [on the recto page] quotations on the blackboard are to be pointed at in silence. So that, while reading a text already written in black and white, I can count on a certain across-the-board index standing all the while behind me, white on black" (177). Derrida falls back on another academic performance—standing between the blackboard and the listeners, in order to animate print. Sometimes called teaching, this kind of "live" performance seeks to compel an audience for learning that makes the classroom into an intermediary for print. Presumably, silently pointing at print draws one's attention to it. One can sense how desperate the situation has become when, looking out at students who will probably watch TV on a weeknight and go to the movies on the weekend, one silently points to print, in its black and white register, to enhance its tradition.

The interplay between new technologies and the "alphabetic culture" (as Gregory Ulmer terms it) of philosophical traditions has brought other innovations to print that, in some way, emulate the other technologies rising up around its borders. Such authors as Avital Ronell have written explicit instructions into their books in order to encourage the enhancement of print. Ronell, writing on the philosophical contiguities of the telephone, the precursor of online virtualities, arranged her print in varying columnar, diagonal, spatial relations, further complicated by various styles of print, print sizes, line spacings, etc. As the "textual operators" instruct in the opening page of *The Telephone Book*:

> Your mission, should you choose to accept it, is to learn to read with your ears. In addition to listening for the telephone, you are being asked to tune your ear . . . to the inflated reserves of random indeterminateness . . . stay open to the static and interference that will occupy these lines. . . . At first you may find the way the book runs to be disturbing, but we have had to break up its logic typographically. . . . To crack open the closural sovereignty of the Book, we have feigned silence and disconnection. . . . *The Telephone Book* releases the effect of an electronic-libidinal flow using typography to mark the initiation of utterances.

Here it seems that writing is actually borrowing from the technological advances of other media to remain alluring. Yet, as in much of Ronell's work, the space of technology seems to vivify the critical powers of writing. Her critical models are from the print past, and rarely from works which actually confront the technologies themselves. Outside Lacan's minor association with television, Ronell imagines a relationship among her print philosophical models and virtual technologies.

Feminist critical theory has produced its own tradition of the deconstruction, or reconstruction, of writing and print, aimed at gender practices. Cixous's gender project in "Laugh of the Medusa" was to encourage women to write: not only to wrest the means of production from patriarchal hands, but also, and crucial here, the notion that "by writing her self, the woman will return to the body" (250). Cixous's relation between "woman" and her "body" seems to be inscribed in a writing which organizes a specific kind of inscriptive space: "A feminine textual body is recognized by the fact that it is always endless, without ending; there's no closure, it doesn't stop, and it's this that very often makes the feminine text difficult to read" ("Castration or Decapitation," 53). The body here, read as historical and metaphoric, suggests a certain kind of textual space (that of no closure), which is a reading space, a writing space, and a social space, all at once. This "body" is gendered by its formal, spatial definition, and its parameters are drawn by writing. In other words, the impact of the social, material conditions of women's bodies is brought to bear on writing as if it were its first and final cause. Writing in an "open" space heals the separation of the woman from her body. Its role is

D O M A I N - M A T R I X

30 PAGE

 PREV

 NEXT

 OPEN

 PRINT

 FIND

 HELP

 MENU

heroic, then, and all-encompassing. Anxieties around gender oppressions finally come to rest on the failures of patriarchal print.

Luce Irigaray continues to critique not only the linear effect of writing, but also the organization of pages, and the play of vertical and horizontal as inscriptions of gendered, hetero-social constructs. In "The Power of Discourse," she calls for the disruption of the "recto-verso structure that shores up common sense," asserting that

> we need to proceed in such a way that linear reading is no longer possible: that is, the retroactive impact of the end of each word, utterance, or sentence upon its beginning must be taken into consideration in order to undo the power of its teleological effect. . . . That would hold good also for the opposition between structures of horizontality and verticality that are at work in language. (80)

While Gertrude Stein eschews the print highway as heterosexual grammatical practice **(see section IVe, "Turbo-Lesbo")**, Irigaray takes the analysis out into teleology—the "nature" of spatial design. Print culture spatializes patriarchal mechanisms. Irigaray perceives the contest between spatial orders as gendered. Print, as the progression of integers, with its obdurate, concrete character will ultimately lead her to consider "fluid mechanics"—a physics of gender. Perhaps among these authors, Irigaray is the most prescient in perceiving writing, print, as a spatial, material order of things requiring a fundamental physical reorganization.

As Irigaray brings a spatial politics to print, those who are theorizing the organization of future information screens are also aware of the way in which certain spatial locations signify value. For example, Michael Benedikt in his book on *Cyberspace* notes that "Spaces have their own 'value-laden lefts/ rights, ups/downs, ins/outs, objects/voids—top of screen as icon/menu territory with Macintosh trashcan at bottom right —vestiges of horizons, of pages, of body with eyes to anus' are retained on organization of information onscreen" (130–131). Notably, Benedikt envisions these matrices as without the inscription of gender or sexual orientation. Reading Benedikt after Irigaray, one can deduce that as the screen emulates the traditional order of spatial values, its very organization will imprint dominant practices. These future visions need to be addressed by feminist, lesbian strategies, in order to intervene in the construction of the coming social space.

Irigaray deploys strategies beyond Müller's and Stein's guerrilla occupation of spatial fields **(see section IVc, "Blanking Out")** in order to design a utopian space, which would imprint a gender unlike that of the hot rod computer boys. Irigaray's spatial morphology nests in what she calls a "feminine syntax," which "would involve nearness, proximity, but in such an extreme form that it would preclude any distinction of identity, any establishment of ownership, thus any

D O M A I N - M A T R I X

MENU

HELP

FIND

PRINT

OPEN

PREV

NEXT

31
PAGE

form of appropriation" ("Questions," 134). Rather than the space of difference and boundary, Irigaray seeks a way to design space as shared at the root of its construction, locating the functions of capitalism in its very organization. For, while emphasizing gender operations, Irigaray nevertheless compounds the space of private property with the space of gender. "Feminine," in her sense, means a space of proximity which confounds spatial "properties." In "This Sex Which Is Not One" she recommends a "nearness so pronounced that it makes all discrimination of identity, and thus all forms of property, impossible" (31). Ultimately, Irigaray pushes proximity into cohabitation: "you/I are neither open nor closed. We never separate simply: *a single word* cannot be pronounced, produced, uttered by our mouths" (Roof, 145). Employing the trope of orality, Irigaray keeps the sharing of space as corporeal and sensual. Ultimately, the integrity of a defined space yields the base formation. Integers, the occupied territories of spatial imagination, stand in opposition to the notion of women together in a shared space. Consequently, Irigaray turns to "fluids" for a concept of space which reorganizes the sense of boundary and integrity.

Irigaray, through gender, finally implies a kind of sexual practice in writing. The "you/I" she addresses are women, and thus the cohabitation is a lesbian one. Her utopic sense of space, then, is one of lesbian cohabitation **(see section IIe, "Lesbian, Siamesian Space Cadets")**. Unfortunately, she does not pursue the explicitly lesbian connotation of her position. In contrast, D.A. Miller's *Bringing Out Roland Barthes* develops a specifically gay method of reading and writing, through a combination of semiotics and the way that signs might spatialize a text. The force in Miller's argument is that one can read gay writing only when one is acquainted with the subculture. His book begins in the Saint Germain Drugstore—a cruising site for Barthes, where, at first, Miller couldn't read the subcultural signs. Later, his growing acquaintance with gay pickup practices taught him to read the question *"avez-vous l'heure?"* as a *"leurre"*—a lure, encrypted in a figure of speech (4). As Miller proceeds to learn to read the subculture, he discovers that Barthes's map of Tokyo in the *Empire of Signs* actually charts a "gay Tokyo" (4–5). Both cruising and navigation are like reading and writing, in Miller's analysis—they rely on correctly reading the signs of gay subculture.

Miller then goes to the alphabetic plane of reading to illustrate, once more, gay writing at its base. To make his point, Miller concocts something like an intermedia strategy. Miller attends to Barthes's treatment of the letter "M" in Erté's alphabet, quoting Barthes:

> This inhuman letter (since it is no longer anthropomorphic) consists of fierce flames; it is a burning door devoured by wicks: the letter of love and death (at least in our Latin languages), flames alone amid so many letter women (as we say Flower-Maidens), like mortal absence of that body that Erté has made into the loveliest object imaginable: a script. (Miller, 19)

DOMAIN-MATRIX

32
PAGE

 PREV

 NEXT

 OPEN

 PRINT

 FIND

 HELP

 MENU

Miller reads this elevation of the letters as "a smoke screen" for the association of that letter with a particular name that the "imprudence of divulging it consigns, like many another love letter, to the fire." Now comes the performance of the spatializing strategy, which "embeds" images amid print to create a text that moves across signs into subcultural meaning. Miller writes, "On which conjecture, the writer fond of," then the reader turns the page to discover a two-page photo spread. On the recto is Erté's flaming "M," and on the verso, the almost nude buttocks of a leather man before a billboard, stretching one hand onto the mouth of the Marlboro man, as if to seal his lips, and his other hand stretched to the edge of the "M" in Marlboro. Again, turning the page, the sentence picks up:

> eliding himself into R.B., and his friends into A.C., E.B., D.F., will have been secretly banding, say with Shakespeare, as he is repeatedly supposed to have needed to conceal the identity of W.H.; say with Wilde, a character in whose *Dorian Gray*, when he likes people immensely, never tells their names to anyone; say with the entire long line of sodomites, inverts, homosexuals, and gay men to whom "safer sex" has ever had to mean, for themselves or their partners in crime, securing an incognito. (22)

Written across signs, the alphabet's graphic quality is read as gay. The "M," "flaming" in several senses, becomes a cigarette in the photo, a penetrating oral/anal device, sheathed in safe-sex initials. As Miller suggests, gay writing is a form of encryption. One might argue that Miller could not control the page breaks in the printing. Yet the precision of the break could not have been better. The image replaces the print, revealing its connotations in the middle of the meaning.

If Irigaray imagines a politics of the organization of print, Miller offers a strategy across a combination of print and image. The encrypted wit in his text relies on reading the suggestions embedded in the play between print and visual image. However, breaking (into) the code relies upon a third position—that of familiarity, through experience, with the "live" practices of the gay subculture. Unlike Derrida's use of live performance to enhance reading and writing, Miller subjects print to "live" performance. He could not successfully "read" Barthes until he had cruised the drugstore. Moreover, cruising provides the key to the code that arranges meaning across print and image. Gay sexual practices, then, are necessary for the combined reception of the alphabetic and the imagistic. Alone, they cannot be successfully "read."

Miller's example introduces a crucial issue in the transversal of virtual identities. He proffers a model of relations among "live" body, text, and image that is antithetical to the one proposed by queer performativity. Miller reverses the direction of dependencies among the elements, from queer performativity's move away from body to text, back to body from text. The

D O M A I N – M A T R I X

MENU

HELP

FIND

PRINT

OPEN

PREV

NEXT

33
PAGE

historical and specific development of these conditions is worked out here in the sections "Sexual Stages" and "Slipping into Subculture." It suffices to note that a transverse position between the two cultures, the alphabetic and the imagistic, is performed through a gay "live" performance.

While the above authors were led from the nature of their critique to the material production of print, radical alterations in the technology of writing itself, caused by the widespread adoption of the computer, have encouraged authors and publishers to experiment in print forms closer to the functions of data and print management which these new engines of inscription perform. The multi-colored, icon-ridden print of *Mondo 2000: A User's Guide to the New Edge* simulates the interactive screen. Terms are outlined by colored brackets, leading the eye to an outside column of print where the term may be defined. Images are nested in the text to lead the reader to the section at the end of the book where sources are listed for items to purchase. The illusion is that these brackets and icons are operating as if in hypertext, where clicking on them would lead to another space in which linked information about them may be found. Another new practice is to co-produce a print text with a hypertext, as in Jay David Bolter's *Writing Space*, or George P. Landow's *Hypertext*. One may read the text in its hard-copy version or in its hypertext version. These are productions at a pivotal point in the emergence of the hypertext and the demise of print's single domain—the reader may move from one to the other as she needs, or wishes, without making a complete transition into the hyper-realm.

The play between the order of the sequential and multiple, branching arrangements of information is now being staged on the computer screen. The printed page, by the nature of its technology, enforces the sequential development of ideas, whereas the computer screen offers multiple arrangements of data, allowing the reader to form the development of materials in a multitude of ways. Icon mandalas at the beginnings of hypertext novels, as in Stuart Moulthrop's *Victory Garden,* offer a topography of episodes, which the reader may link in several different patterns. One may read the text in a sequential order, or click among terms in the different episodes which provide a variety of possible arrangements. In Bolter's *Writing Space,* the reader is offered the illusion that some terms are "deeper" than others, leading in to the hub of the text. Bolter uses the shape of the software links to perform a spatial pun on "subtext."

Reading this electronic novel resembles more wandering in a maze than adhering to the sequence of pages. Gender and sexual practices, as Irigaray has noted, have long been inscribed in the sequential architecture of meaning. The linear prescription was aligned with gender difference and the institution of heterosexual marriage as early as the myth of Ariadne and the Minotaur. Ariadne's thread translated the maze into the line, leading both to the con-

D O M A I N - M A T R I X

34
PAGE

PREV

NEXT

OPEN

PRINT

FIND

HELP

MENU

quest of the Minotaur and to her own marriage. What was the Minotaur, part animal, part human, but a kind of sex-radiating cyborg? The labyrinth, or maze, a mapping enabled by and more appropriate to computer writing than the emulation of pages, thus brings us back to that early Minoan threat of Other, civilized by the linear technologies of meaning.

The end of print's secure hold on the production of meaning releases the possibility of a new politics of spatial organization. Transvisual print or transscriptural images may organize in a space that hails a different kind of social organization. Recalling once again Eco's novel *The Name of the Rose*, we can see how the medieval production of scripture brought on the debates over architectural space in the design of the cathedrals and monasteries that housed it, along with proscriptions against performance. Similarly, the new engine of meaning invokes a reconsideration of space. Gender and other power differences are inscribed in the architecture of print and image. The body, as gendered or engaged in sexual practices, is assigned either a productive or a nonproductive role in the process. All of these considerations may lead to a notion of a politics of space.

Toward a Politics of Space

The critical anxiety set off by the fall of the wall, which capped the erosion of the grounds of the Marxist, or postMarxist, materialist critique, dispatched several strategies into exile. While eurocommunism, particularly in France, continued to be ratified in intellectual circles, Althusser, Baudrillard, and Foucault could argue for continuing adjustments of the notion of the subject as within the materialist critique and its social, activist movement. When the framework of such a dialectic fell away, when the terms of the debate were no longer ratified because of the seeming failure of such a critique in the historical moment of the late 1980s and early 1990s, strategies concerning the subject sought to distinguish their critical, political operations from the failures of socialist, Marxist practice. An ambivalence, an anxiety blocked the bridge between theoretical, critical systems and activism—a bridge which had been mandated in Marxist/materialist systems. Without that bridge, the deployment of critical strategies onto outside referents collapsed into self-referentiality. In his "Cultural Studies and Its Theoretical Legacies," Stuart Hall poignantly traces of the collapse of such a bridge out of the system and continues to insist upon it:

> What decentered and dislocated the settled path of the Centre for Contemporary Cultural Studies certainly, and British cultural studies to some extent in general, is what is sometimes called "the linguistic turn": the discovery of discursivity, or textuality. . . . Unless and until one respects the necessary displacement of culture, and yet is always irritated by its failure to reconcile itself with other questions that matter, with other questions that cannot and can never be fully covered by critical textuality in its elaborations, cultural studies as a project, an intervention, remains incomplete. (283–284)

Similarly, feminist critical theory began to withdraw from its 1970s necessary link to grassroots, activist agendas, which, if not ideologically materialist, were engaged in social change. Lesbian theory, on its way to queer theory,

D O M A I N - M A T R I X

36
PAGE

 PREV

 NEXT

OPEN

PRINT

FIND

HELP

MENU

sought to distinguish itself from 1970s lesbian feminist agendas, with their identity and visibility politics. The charge of essentialism blocked the major throughway from theory to what had been constituted as practice, turning theoretical arguments to strategies of signification, such as overdetermination or excess. The positing of economic conditions such as class oppression became impossible to accommodate, as they called for that referent outside the system. Capitalism could not, effectively, be introduced as a concept. In *Materialist Feminism and the Politics of Discourse*, Rosemary Hennessy traces this withdrawal through the effects of Foucault, Laclau, and Mouffe, and the charge of essentialism. Yet, she notes that the very project creates strategies in consonance with global capitalism, installing "a decentered, fragmented, porous subject [that] is better equipped for the heightened alienation of late capitalism's refined divisions of labor, more readily disciplined by a pandemic corporate state, and more available to a broad nexus of ideological controls" (9). Evidence of just how this use of the postmodern subject is installed in the electronic structures of the media, as well as in the critique of them, may be found in the section called "Transition: The Subject Position" in "Los Angeles: A Topography of Screenic Properties." However, the aim of this section is not to look forward, but to recover the materialist concerns embedded in the Marxist tradition which were truncated by the anxiety produced by the fall of socialist countries and the charge of essentialism. One legacy of the 1980s critique was to imagine the subject as single—as individual in contradiction to the collective.

Looking back to the 1970s, one is reminded that the notion and the practice of the collective produced one of the signature structures of lesbian feminism, as of the Marxist tradition. Both traditions posited a challenge to capitalist structures through notions of collective ownership and its social practice. Lesbian feminism presumed that capitalism was a patriarchal form of economic practice, deployed against women. Therefore, lesbian feminist events and businesses were organized collectively in order to avoid replicating patriarchal structures in commerce among women. The majority of the collectives had closed down by the late 1980s. If the East bloc fell to a successful take-over by global capitalism, lesbian food collectives, bookstore collectives, living collectives, and theater collectives fell to traditional capitalist practices. The subject was multiple—not in its singular oscillation among multiple positions, but in its very composition across different individuals. The identity "lesbian feminist" was one that groups sought to produce. As socialism waned, postmodern individualism gained ground. Sexual practice was thus extracted from its association with other social and economic practices.

By the 1990s, "postmodern lesbian" or queer articles trace the way in which capitalist projects have appropriated such abandoned territories for their own uses. For example, Sasha Torres's sense of the "prime time lesbian," and Danae Clark's "Commodity Lesbianism" describe how the media and market make use of the "sign" lesbians to sell their products. While I would contend that this commodification of what were once collective practices and market uses of the term "lesbian" is the result of the queer retreat, some of the postmodern protectors would, as Robyn Wiegman has done, fault identity politics for it, arguing that "it is along the modernist axis of self-assertion and visibility that both a lesbian consumer market and a marketed commodity repeatedly named *lesbian* has been achieved" (10). Yet, in the face of such high capitalist aggressivity, these authors can offer only celebrations of commodification or, as noted in the section "Queer Performativity," isolated strategies of subversion. In particular, "subversive shopping" has been formulated as an apt action within the commodified realm. It is difficult to perceive, finally, what is subversive in buying the version of the sign "lesbian" that ad campaigns have developed. (For a fuller description of the structures of commodification of "lesbian," see "Slipping into Subculture" and "'Subversive' Shopping" in "Bringing Home the Meat.")

Thus, the critique of the commodified lesbian, severed from any program for change—in isolation—actually promotes commodification. The evacuation of the outside referent has effectively coupled the body and the materialist critique only to give them over to, as Reinelt has pointed out, the hegemonic practices that endure in the codes. The new "queer dyke" thus appears as commodity fetishist—the dildoed dyke who makes of herself an ad as politics. What remains is mapping the exact route of the retreat through deconstructive critiques. Meanwhile, the collusion with global capitalist uses of such strategies, as noted by Hennessy above, or of national agendas, still remains untested. As the critique withdraws from notions of communities or subcultures into the sign "lesbian" slipping among market strategies, it often becomes what it seeks to critique.

From the beginning arguments around "performativity" and "queer" on through the matrix, we can begin to perceive a critical axis forming along the abandonment of the term "lesbian" for "queer," in its class operations, and in its imperialist uses, along with the evacuation of the body, as a subject-suspect. Within the poststructuralist critique of those two terms, textualization and inscription are deployed to cleanse "lesbian" and "body" of their material(ist) accretions. "Queer performativity" thus runs the "race into theory" away from the site of material interventions. Sagri Dhairyam, in "Racing the Lesbian, Dodging White Critics," states the case succinctly:

> The rubric of queer theory, which couples sexuality and theory and collapses lesbian and gay sexualities, tends to effect a slippage of body into mind: the monstrously feminized body's sensual evocations of smell, fluid, and hidden vaginal spaces with which the name resonates are cleansed, desexualized into a "queerness" where the body yields to intellect, and a spectrum of sexualities again denies the lesbian center stage. (30)

D O M A I N - M A T R I X

38
PAGE

PREV

NEXT

OPEN

PRINT

FIND

HELP

MENU

The challenge of the "live" body needs to be cleaned up by the abstracting efficiency of theory. But how do all of these theories happen to conjoin with the rise of global capitalism, the new techno-era, and the coming supremacy of the computer screen?

One obvious relationship between the poststructuralist critique and the move into cyberspace is in the move away from the "live" and the material into a clean, textual world. Online sex, after all, is the "live" writing of sexual desire across the chat-space of the screen. The exchange of sexual practice for textual practice in the poststructuralist critique could train one to enjoy sex online. The rush of transcendence, like that of a drug, is produced by the evacuation of the sordid material world into the white screen space of America Online, gleaming the way that the "alabaster cities gleam, undimmed by human tears" of an earlier imagined America. The poststructuralist, queer critique, then, growing up along with the construction of cyberspace, trained the critical mind to understand and imagine that "coming" textual body and its textual, screened social space. Rather than a subversion of the in-corporation of the new economic cyberproject, these critiques actually trained a generation of intellectuals to inhabit the new cyberspace. Sexual politics provided the successful transition into the cyber. By turning away from the 1970s blend of socialist, gender, and lesbian politics, extracting the sexual and realigning it with textual politics, the transition into the cyber could be made. Strangely, print paved the way to the screen.

In the light of such a discovery, what kind of a materialist critique could remain useful within the emerging cyberland? What intervention into the pure space of commodity fetishism might still be made? Harking back to another project of the 1970s, certain postMarxists in France began to argue that a political critique of space would better serve contemporary politics than the prior model based on time, or history. Their concerns were of a new, geographical structuring of capitalism, produced by economic production zones assigned to so-called developing nations, and the role that urban planning began to play in zoning class and market relationships into cities. Clearly, however, considerations of the construction of a new cyberspace could also benefit from a politics of space. Leaving the subject behind for a moment with the issues of "presence" and "absence" that attend its construction, a critical examination of space could relocate the terms of the social. Moreover, developing a politics of space might directly inform interventions into the screenic interface with the cyber that the late twentieth century is constructing **(see "Los Angeles: A Topography of Screenic Properties"** for the historical development of screenic and urban spaces).

Erecting a politics of space rather than one of history does not imply that history would become unnecessary in critical thought, but it does explicate how its dominance in the critique has hindered the exploration of space as a critical category. Space as a category crucial to political critique began to languish in the late nineteenth century. The success of the historical model of "time" as the primary critical apparatus for reviewing social relations relegated spatial considerations to the realm of the arts, architecture, and geography. Even though the early experiments of the Dadaists and some Cubists implicate the design of spatial relations with political concerns, these graphic experiments have carried little weight in subsequent discursive analyses of political situations. With the rise of urban planning, however, critical notions of space began to intersect with social paradigms. A broad postMarxist correction to the traditional hold that history had in the social critique constitutes the new field of the "politics of space."

By examining the trajectory of spatial considerations back through this century, one can return to two turn-of-the-century French cultural experiments with philosophical and formal explorations of time and space which might have led to a reformulation of the politics of space. Henri Bergson and Marcel Proust explored the subjective interplay between time and space. Their philosophical and aesthetic discoveries of the relationship of subjectivity to space might have led to a deeper understanding of how the construction of social spaces implants both ideological and pscyhological structures in, for example, the city, or the screen. Unfortunately, their work took the opposite turn, away from social space altogether and into the hermetic isolation of the solipsistic individual.

In one sense, it might seem that Bergson, in proposing the notion of duration, *la durée,* over segmented space, was heading in the same direction as Irigaray, who proposed "fluid mechanics" over divided space, or in the direction of this critique, in which I will attempt to somehow posit a shared space beyond segmentation. Bergson's aim to overcome the idealistic inner space of integers seems sympathetic to the politics of space this work would suggest. Bergson abandoned space as a category because it serves as a "principle of differentiation other than that of qualitative differentiation" (95). Yet space continued to reside in the realm of the external, not the subjective. One could manage to read Bergson's notion of duration, a form of time, as a co-producer, perhaps of a different sense of space. The barrier in Bergson, which led away from any construction of a politics of space, as the century wore on, was the antisocial projection of the subjective realm that he would privilege. In order to overcome segmented space, he offers only the tool of "deep introspection, which leads us to grasp our inner states as living things, constantly *becoming*, as states not amenable to measure" (231). Along with Bergson, Proust's intricate structuring of time and space through subjectivity, navigating by memory through such representations of space as impressionist canvases, Romanesque architecture, and *fin de siècle* drawing rooms, brings him finally to the subject in isolation, alone in introspection. Thus, at the start of the century, the philosophical

D O M A I N - M A T R I X

40
PAGE
  PREV
 NEXT
 OPEN
PRINT
 FIND
 HELP
 MENU

and aesthetic reconstruction of space was based upon a retreat into an antisocial subjectivity. Rather than transforming the notion and practice of social space, these works charted a withdrawal from it.

In contrast, at the turn of the century, the materialist critique took an opposite position in regard to the categories of time and space. In his chapter "Space and Time" in *Materialism and Empirio-Criticism* (1908), Lenin evidenced a negative response to the new philosophies of Mach and Poincaré, who would account for subjective elements in constructing time and space. To begin, Lenin emphasized the independent, objective nature of time and space, branding subjectivists such as Mach as "idealist." Ultimately, however, Lenin rejected space altogether as a critical category because of its association with subjectivity. He perceived the new theorems of subjective space as merely "one manifestation of a general disease of doubting material reality that was infecting modern society" (Kern, 135). While Lenin did retain space as an objective, empirical category, space ultimately devolved into a static concept within the developing Marxist critique. At most, space represented traditional geography—national divisions of land. It was time that took on the dynamic potential for change. History would become *the* critical category for analysis and change.

As we can now see, Bergson/Proust and the Marxist critique constructed a divide that ran between subjectivity and instrumental rationality, between the isolated individual and the social, and between time and space. Subjectivity, the isolated individual, and time were to be set up in opposition to instrumental rationality, the social, and space. This divide continued to run through these categories throughout the century, as Marxist theory tried to accommodate the subjective and theories of subjectivity strove to accommodate the social. What would bring space back into consideration as a possible critical category, would be the combination of structuralism and Marxism.

Edward Soja in *Postmodern Geographies* traces the uses of history and space through the alterations made to the Marxist critique during the twentieth century, proposing that the French postMarxists, already acqauinted with structuralism, were the best positioned to produce the combination of the two (53). In his later writings, Michel Foucault described the traditional attitudes against space and the burgeoning recognition of its social role:

> Space was treated as the dead, the fixed, the undialectical, the immobile. Time, on the contrary, was richness, fecundity, life, dialectic. (Soja, 4) If one started to talk in terms of space that meant one was hostile to time. . . . that one "denied history," that one was a "technocrat." They didn't understand that to trace forms of implantation, delimitation and demarcation of objects . . . the organization of domains meant the throwing into relief of processes—historical ones, needless to say, of power. (Foucault in Soja, 21)

Foucault turned away from the devaluation of space as a possible critical category. In his article "Of Other Spaces," he advocates that "the anxiety of our era has to do fundamentally with space, no doubt a great deal more than time. Time probably appears to us only as one of the various distributive operations that are possible for the elements that are spread out in space" (Foucault in Soja, 18–19).

In 1974 (the same year Irigaray published her "'Mechanics of Fluids"), Henri Lefebvre published his book *The Production of Space,* which became the first major document in the new critique. Lefebvre reverses Lenin's charge to label the notion of independent, empty space as idealist. Bringing the Marxist critique into the construction of space, Lefebvre insists that space is only a social construction. By exchanging the notion that space "always already" exists as an objective category, for the sense that space is socially produced, Lefebvre made a place for the role of labor in space: "physical space has no 'reality' without the energy that is deployed within it. . . . Energy cannot . . . be compared to a content filling an empty container" (13). Although Lefebvre goes on to develop an "isomorphism" between notions of "outer space" and "inner, mental space" (14) which could lead to the way space is imagined that directly forms notions of epistemology, or the borders of spectacle, both Foucault and Lefebvre were working with urban planners, which led their considerations into a relation between space and social labor reminiscent of traditional Marxist formulations.

Space, then, in the early postMarxist critique is finally urban space. Consider Jameson's treatment of Los Angeles in his book *Postmodernism, or The Cultural Logic of Late Capitalism,* Soja's last section, "It All Comes Together in Los Angeles," and Mike Davis's *City of Quartz.* Interestingly, in all these works, the urban site for arguing these politics is provided by the city of Los Angeles **(see the section "Los Angeles: A Topography of Screenic Properties").** In this study, the city is incorporated within cyberspace—an online social organization that acts like a city. Although an exploration of how Los Angeles works together with the screen to set up the cyber, urban planning is not the final goal of his study. Rather, city and nation will compose a certain residue of social space, operating with the perceptions and practices of cyberspace, or online interactions.

The postMarxist tradition makes a donation to the politics of cyberspace, but by retaining many of the traditional Marxist categories of critique, such as labor, it continues, as classical Marxism did, to take little account of gender, ethnicity, sexual practice, and an emotional or subjective inner life **(see "Transition: The Subject Position"** for an example of these omissions). Certainly, the ownership of cyberspace and the conditions of its production are crucial to any understanding of how it works. In the section "Los Angeles: A Topography of Screenic Properties" I develop a sense of the growing corpo-

D O M A I N - M A T R I X

42
PAGE

PREV

NEXT

OPEN

PRINT

FIND

HELP

MENU

rate circulation of value. Likewise, the discounted labor of women in the production of microchips and other elements of the hardware reflects the ongoing patriarchal ownership of the production and the profits. The assignment of labor to production zones in developing countries allows for its distribution in first-world countries. Yet, as I will argue in section IVf, "The Hot Rod Bodies of Cybersex," and elsewhere, the fact that the production of much of the software is accomplished by adolescent white men integrates their own sexism, sexual performance anxieties, and violent aggressions into the games and other functions. These relations may also be revealed through the postMarxist treatment of space.

Fredric Jameson's study of the relations of postmodernism and capitalism illustrates the contraction of spatial concepts into familiar Marxist categories, concluding with a confession that the conception of "space" functions for him as a masquerade. Jameson reviews his theoretical venture with a description of three kinds of space which align themselves with three historical periods of capitalist production. The first is the space of "classical or market capitalism in terms of a logic of the grid . . . geometrical and Cartesian homogeneity, a space of infinite equivalence and extension." He points to Foucault's book on prisons, but cautions that his own notion of this space is grounded in "the labor process rather than that shadowy and mythical entity called 'power'"(410). Jameson's treatment of the grid is helpful in associating a structuring of space with a form of economic development. While the grid is related to a form of capitalism in one sense, the strict, classical Marxist agreement with periodicity and more traditional forms of history encourage Jameson to relegate that production to a bygone era, rather than imagining a space which might be constructed by continuing, dissimilar forms of production. Because of his ultimate allegiance to historical development, Jameson does not perceive the grid as an ongoing construct, co-producing a more complex contemporary social space. Moreover, by banishing Foucault into the shadows of "emblematic representation," as Jameson calls it, he neglects to consider how representation co-produces social space. Imagination thus plays no role in the construction of space. In contrast, in the section "Screenic Discourse as Grid," I attempt to draw the relationship of freeways and malls to movie and other screens, in order to reveal a "familiar" Southern California space where representation and geography merge.

Jameson proceeds to describe the space of "figuration" produced by monopoly capital, or "what Lenin called 'the stage of imperialism.'" Here, Jameson does introduce a notion of "lived experience" to note the difference between it and the structural model (410). Situating "art" in the space of lived experience, Jameson concludes that the distance between experience and its social space "poses tremendous and crippling problems for a work of art." For Jameson, this distance produces modernisms:

> I have argued that it is as an attempt to square this circle and to invent new and elaborate formal strategies for overcoming this dilemma that modernism or, perhaps better, the various modernisms as such emerge: in forms that inscribe a new sense of the absent colonial system on the very syntax of poetic language itself. (411)

Space in this "phase" is both a "closed world" housing "each consciousness" and the "impossible" social space for the "passage of ships in the night," or, geometrically expressed, a "centrifugal movement of lines and planes" which never intersect (412). The operations of Jameson's space of figuration are similar to those described in section IVc, "Blanking Out." Yet, once again, Jameson contains them within a historical period—a developmental sequence. In the notion of the Domain-Matrix, they remain in circulation, alongside the grid and as disrupted by counterhegemonic spatial strategies.

For Jameson, the current space of multinational networks abandons spatial models of city or nation-state, to configure "the suppression of distance (in the sense of Benjamin's aura) and the relentless saturation of any remaining voids or empty places" where "the postmodern body" is racked by the "perceptual barrage of immediacy" (412–413). Surely Jameson is referring here to the space of the first world, where the products produced (but not consumed) in the economic zones of the third world return to deluge the markets. Nevertheless, for Jameson, in this space of production, the only representation of space is one which embodies the failure of political agency—the space of spectacle that Guy Debord or Jean Baudrillard has configured (412–413). By relegating these structures of space to historical periods, Jameson neglects to perceive how the grid and the figural space interact. Yet, even more to the point of the argument in this book, space continues, in the tradition of Lenin, to house the instrumental. "Art" or "spectacle" is the result of economic structures, spaces where subjectivity fails. No wonder, then, that critiques of gender and sexual practice, working within subjective, imaginary spatializing, are absent from both Jameson and Soja's "postmodern geography."

After rehearsing his proposal for a new "cognitive mapping," which would spatialize social relations, Jameson admits that something like "a new postmodern version" of the "base and superstructure formula" emerges (416). Finally, he confesses that "cognitive mapping" is indeed "in reality nothing but a code word for 'class consciousness'" (418). PostMarxist postmodern geographies, then, retain the classical Marxist privileging of time or history, which guides a developmental study of space that continues to disallow a productive role for subjective, ludic, or aesthetic experience. In saturated space the media are not so much actually co-productive of space as the "*interpretant*" or "*analogon*" of other active structural forces. Space is simple—constructed by a single mode of capitalist production, while subjective processes are situated in space only as receptors and never as co-producers. The postMarxist construction of space thus retains the divide set up by Bergson, Proust, and Lenin.

DOMAIN-MATRIX

44
PAGE

 PREV

 NEXT

 OPEN

 PRINT

 FIND

 HELP

 MENU

Now, cyberspace, the new "house" of social and economic relations, is in itself already a representation of space. For this reason, the urban planners' critique must be melded to some method for analyzing representational space. To this end, I have set up the city of Los Angeles as screen or as screening in order to assume that instrumental and subjective, aesthetic space are one. In "It All Comes Together in Los Angeles," Soja moves in this direction, noting that any notion of a downtown, or central area, is merely a node—"a strategic vantage point" or "an urban panopticon" (235–236). L.A., he contends, is actually a "semiotic blanket." However, in a traditional Marxist move, he adds that "underneath this semiotic blanket there remains an economic order, an instrumental nodal structure" (246).

Soja's introduction of the semiotic into the understanding of space may provide a productive direction for the critique when it is perceived as an integral structure in the space, rather than as a blanket covering the "real" instrumental spatial structure. I think a particular use of semiotics might serve to amplify the relationship Lefebvre wanted to draw between "inner" and "outer" space, or between discursive and material space. It may offer a key to opening up a space that melds the two orders together. After all, the etymological root for "semiotics" resides in the Greek word *semion*, which means a sign, mark, or point in space where things meet. It is precisely the way that space organizes a meeting, a coming together, that is at issue in its social structuring. How both "real" social spacing and cyber-social spacing organize the meeting provides the inroad to their operations. To paraphrase Wittgenstein, in cyberspace, the semiotic blanket is all there is.

IIA. SEMIO-SPACE

Semiotics clicks into space through the same device the screen uses—the icon. While the icon moves the computer operator through linked objects and textual sites, in semiotics it links discourse to its outside referent. The role of the icon has occasioned multiple and lengthy debates within semiotic circles. I hope to be able to skirt their contentions to focus in very tightly on a single discussion that situates the icon within spatial terms. I want to see how space is organized, both in Euclidean boasts of just how material space is defined, and in provisional claims within discussions of discursive space.

Umberto Eco, in rereading Peirce, treats the central function of the icon, resemblance, as a spatial relationship. The relationship sometimes termed resemblance, argues Eco, is actually a structural one, within "the perceptual structure, a *perceptum*" that is shared with both the "actual object" and the representation of it. Eco is coming, as Goethe did in his *Elective Affinitives*, to some notion of correspondence. Icons are "*surrogate stimuli* that, within the framework of a given representational convention, contribute to the significcation; they are sheer material configurations that simulate perceptive conditions or components of iconic signs" (194). Unlike Goethe, Eco configures this correspondence, perception, as conventional, emphasizing the role that social conventions play in structuring such correspondences. In that sense, there is no "objective world," per se, but only "the criterion for similitude" that is based on "precise rules that select some parameters as pertinent and disregard others as irrelevant" (196). Eco is struggling to hold onto the link between discourse and an outer referent, while maintaining the ideological construction of that link. Thus, on his way to a configuration of discourse as spatial, Eco emphasizes the link whose loss this work earlier mourned in the formation of queer performativities that would recede from outer referents into the rarefied, privileged atmosphere of pure discourse. Eco retains the notion of a perceptual bridge between two orders of things, while (unlike Jameson) also retaining the force of representation.

As Eco proceeds in his treatment of the icon, he moves increasingly into graphs. Finally, he sets up an "isomorphic topology," in which correspondences are spatially represented (199). Within this topography of representation, Eco constitutes the icon as a point in space. He emphasizes that "geometrical similitude and topological isomorphism are a sort of *transformation* by which a point in the effective space of the expression is made to correspond to a point in the virtual space of the content model" (reiterating the fact that the correspondence is culturally learned) (199–200). Eco arrives at a kind of Euclidean semiotics, which hinges on the point as the organizer of the correspondence between two realms configured as spatial: the "effective space of the expression" and the "virtual space of the content." "Iconism," then, may be understood as "a visual relationship between similar spatial properties" (198). It is an isomorphic point which organizes correspondence.

The icon provides a figure for the relationship among kinds of space. We recognize it as just such a convention within the computer menu of functions. Also, it might be perceived as the way to connect orders of space, from an external, expressive one to an internal, virtual one. How can Eco's spatiosemiotics combine with the postMarxist critique of space as political? I pose this question only in terms of the organization of the coming cyberspace. Before it can be answered, however, some of the consonant considerations within the architecture of cyberspace must be added to the equation.

IIB. CYBERSPACE

In terms of the computer screen, considerations of labor look to the future dominance of virtual systems as storing and organizing data, what was formerly called on the one hand "money," and on the other "communications." The manner in which that space is designed will both reflect and determine hierarchies of labor and ownership. Economic crises in the 1990s suggest a period of transition into cyberspace as workspace. Unemployment, caused by the disappearance of traditional industrial functions, is running at high rates in several first-world countries. Social services such as travel agencies and real estate are increasingly working online, making their functions available to users. In the future, many of these types of "middlemen" will be replaced by the online functions. These kinds of jobs are already disappearing. Grocery stores have installed lasers that relay prices directly to the cash register, which in itself is disappearing before the appearance of credit card slots at the counter. Soon the cashier and the bank clerk will have no function. The emphasis on retraining in social welfare systems generally means learning software or hardware skills. Movies such as *The Net* build their intrigues upon how many functions are already online, from fingerprints, drivers' licenses and passports, money, medical records, prescriptions, house listings, phone numbers, to personal correspondence. These consequences of cyberspace in the spheres of wages, state control, privileged access, first-world power, and social organization are already upon us with both the promise of a better life for some and the threat of ruination for others.

The politics of space are formed, partially, by these kinds of considerations. Yet the kinds of politics this section is working toward are those involved in the construction of the space itself—its structures and assumptions. How is workspace represented? How is it defined? How is it re-created online? How is it simulated? Michael Benedikt, in his essay "Cyberspace: Some Proposals," outlines the present state of the art (at least present in 1992, a long time ago in cyber-developments). Benedikt begins with a correspondence, not unlike the one Eco described:

> In cyberspace, information-intensive institutions and businesses have a form, identity, and working reality—in a word, and quite literally, an *architecture*—that is counterpart and different to the form, identity, and working reality they have in the physical world. . . . So too with individuals. Egos and multiple egos, roles, functions, have a new existence in cyberspace. (123)

Much has already been written about the slippage in the correspondence between the "physical," the "real" world and its representation in cyberspace. The body figures into this slippage, as does identity, desire, etc. Later (a concept imposed here by print's linearity) this slippage will provide an exploration of how identity is constructed online. For now, the architecture itself is of interest, in order to understand how these correspondences will be constructed. The project of creating an architecture or city online

TOWARD A POLITICS OF SPACE

 MENU
 HELP
 FIND
 PRINT
 OPEN
 PREV
 NEXT
 47 PAGE

brings together the postMarxist geographies of urban planning with the vicissitudes of representation.

Benedikt first asks, "What is space?" (125). Given the mandate to construct a workplace, he reasons that a phenomenological approach to space is the most useful for those who would design it. What operations does it permit or deny? Any sense of natural or universal aspects would be beside the point in this workspace/playspace, which is designed to house functions. Phenomenologically, he asserts, through Piaget, that the initial sense of space is through movement. Movement introduces contingent terms such as "location," "continuity," "freedom," and "change" (127). The functions that follow are finding places, retaining the identity of the objects as they move, and the sensation of travel. (In section Va, "The Body Acts," a similar return to phenomenology, by Judith Butler and Elizabeth Grosz, resituates discussions of the body through movement and location.) Benedikt concludes: "This set of phenomena, with its logical bounds and experienced character, we call *space*" (127). These are, then, terms defined operationally and phenomenologically in Benedikt's study. Without "necessary grounds," or essences, these "immediate conditions, consequences, properties and manifestations" are regarded, finally, by Benedikt as "signs" (128).

Benedikt collapses the two distinct systems of phenomenology and semiotics into one. In designing the architecture of cyberspace, he requires the spatial sense of movement and location for the performance of different functions along with their signifying properties. "Working" in cyberspace is both functioning and signifying. Like Eco, Benedikt assigns the perceptual recognition of these functions, the sense that they emulate bodily experiences "in the world," to social conventions.

In Benedikt's project, the engine of cyberspace is the computer screen. The screen organizes the perceptual qualities of space through an emulation of the conventions of print:

> "Why is the . . . Apple system menu—happy and edenic—positioned . . . at the top left? Why have almost all GUI designers agreed that the top of the screen is icon/menu territory?" These are vestiges of the organization of *pages,* which . . . have given different value to top and bottom, center and margin . . . of things in general and then to fields of inscribed textual and graphic information. (131)

As print culture, in the strictest sense of its meaning (as the production and reception of the body of print), declines, its conventions move onto the screen to organize the signification of its space. For precisely this reason, it is important to remember the attack on these conventions proffered by Luce Irigaray **(see section Id, "The End of Print Culture").** Yet, in spite of the control of spatial organization that phenomenological and semiotic systems exercise,

D O M A I N - M A T R I X

48
PAGE

PREV

NEXT

OPEN

PRINT

FIND

HELP

MENU

Benedikt moves on to address the essential figure of the spatial divide: the point. As Eco centers his notion of the isomorphic quality of discourse on the iconic "point," so Benedikt deems the point as the basic figure in the organization of space. Enter Euclid.

The aspect of the point in Euclid that first suggests itself to Benedikt is the fact that it has no character: no size, no "intrinsic, inherent properties" (134). The point is pure position. As an icon—a point of correspondence—this is its difference to a point "in the world" which is always a "something" with "a color, a shape, a frequency of vibration, a weight, size, momentum," and so on (135). In "data space" it is always an "address-point (or, simply an address) that functions to identify accurately its position" (135). Accepting this notion of a point, or address, as the basis of the construction brings with it the principle of exclusion, mandating that you cannot have two things in the same place at the same time. Ah, we now recognize the point as the basic element in the construction of difference. In fact, within this system, not only must points be different from one another, but space is revealed as the second term in the point/space binary. This means, even to the architects of a completely simulated social space, that address or identity is constituted by difference. We might well ask of space, then, the questions we have asked of other such systems: What does it produce when based upon the principle of difference? What kinds of interactions are legislated by its very architecture? Will difference as its base re-create the hierarchy of differences already in place? Will the so-called "freedom" in cyberspace be regulated by its very structure?

Both Eco and Benedikt have led us to a consideration of the point—specifically the point of correspondence revealed as a structuring of space. Yet cyberspace need not conform to the construction by the point, and all that it brings with it. Instead, cyberspace has great potential for building on what Marcos Novak calls its "liquid architecture." It need not replicate gravity, or two-dimensionality, but may produce a "continuum of edifices. . . . a building's *performance* akin to . . . dance and theater" (251). This is its promise. In this sense, one might return to the great modernist experiences in painting—the abstract or abstract expressionist movements—in order to imagine space in another way. What if it were to imagine space as Arshile Gorky or Joan Miró has done? The design of cyberspace might abandon realism and even geometric principles in exchange for a playful, eccentric sense of space that is mandated by imagination and invention rather than by replication. The sober, calculating principles of phenomenology or the exclusionary principles of the point might be left behind in their scientistic constraints of the body. Instead, the painterly revolution in the twentieth century might inform the construction of this new space, encouraging new social relations that might exit the regime of realism.

Novak's notion of "liquid architecture" returns to performance as a strategy that would disrupt the Euclidean regime. He suggests a "building's *performance . . .* akin to dance and theater." The point as *the* figure of structural difference gives way to the liquid (similar to Irigaray's move of fluid mechanics) through performance. These several notions appear again and again throughout the matrix to converge in varying manners. Here it would seem that considerations of the actual design of cyberspace rely upon the status of the critical terms that this work has deemed at issue in the transition from print to cyberculture. Systems that treat the body in space provide the critical hinges that swing between identity and social practices, on the one hand, and online cyber-relations, on the other. Novak wants to imagine buildings akin to theater and dance. The missing term in his equation is the body. Buildings would act or dance as the body has done. While the actual body is absent from cyberspace, its most radical activity, performance, is caught in the design.

Reversing the direction of the critique, we might ask how the body relates to the point. We might configure the cybersystems in relation to the body's domain.

IIC. GETTING THE POINT

In the instrumental sense, the body is hooked into cyberspace either by "driving" a mouse (with the nostalgic reference to the car), by wearing a glove and helmet to enter Virtual Reality (VR), by "jacking in" (a cyberpunk fantasy of actually jacking the brain into the system, appearing in novels such as William Gibson's *Neuromancer* and Melissa Scott's *Trouble and Her Friends*), or by some psychological/mental correspondence established between the body in physical space and its location in cyberspace. In many instances the body is imagined as "meat," the cyberpunk sense of it as the too, too solid flesh that will not melt into the cyberdew. The body, in that sense, is something to be evacuated as the mind enters the "free play" of cyberspace. Even as "meat" it still registers the effects of cyberspace as physical, whether it be as virtuality sickness, the dizziness and nausea caused by the lag time between a physical movement and the concomitant movement in the simulation, or as the aches and stiffness in the body occasioned by the repetitive, constrained, cramped motion in interface with the system, but most definitely, as Allucquere Rosanne Stone notes in "Will the Real Body Please Stand Up?," in death:

> The discourse of visionary virtual world builders is rife with images of imaginal bodies, freed from the constraints that flesh imposes. Cyberspace developers foresee a time when they will be able to forget about the body.

D O M A I N - M A T R I X

50
PAGE

 PREV

 NEXT

 OPEN

 PRINT

 FIND

 HELP

 MENU

> But it is important to remember that virtual community originates in, and must return to, the physical. No refigured virtual body, no matter how beautiful, will slow the death of a cyberpunk with AIDS. (113)

In this way, the body is the point of contact, of correspondence between the virtual and the "real" worlds. The history of philosophy registers this concern in a variety of ways. For instance, Descartes already imagined such a point, a meeting place for body and mind, in the pineal gland. Imagining a point, a hook for those two entities of different orders, is at the base of such concerns.

The dawning of cyberspace spreads the attraction and anxiety around such a point across the horizon of cultural production. Hooking into the meat has become a fashion in some lesbian, gay, and queer circles. Piercing the tongue, the lip, the nose, the eyebrow, the nipple, the penis, and the clitoris marks '90s fashions. Piercing signifies, in bodywear, the social plenitude that Eco and Benedikt isomorphically assign to the point as icon. The performance artist Bob Flanagan acts out this hooking of the body into social space by publicly piercing his penis or other particularly sensitive parts of his body. As he drives nails into his penis, he performs an apt image of the patriarchal effects of Euclidean space on the body. As he hangs from metal rods driven into his body, Flanagan images the way in which the point constructs position and identity in space. The point, then, performs its Euclidean distribution of space across the body and through the body into surrounding space. One might say that Flanagan performs the point in the flesh.

As the subject position shrinks from the collective to the individual, the points that hook it into the cyber multiply. Multiple hooks into the nose, the nipples, and the genitals point to the growing assimilation of the body into the corporate cyberspace. Multiple entries, pointing into the body as Euclidean spatial difference spatializes the global, pierce the individual, extending the cyber into the flesh. The point of "queer" constituted at the site of piercing performs the new cyberglobal citizen. Allucquere Rosanne Stone argues that this kind of contingent relationship between citizenry and body is, in fact, the traditional setup. She terms the manner in which the body links the two spaces of the virtual and the "real" world as "warranting." The body is configured as something like the apprehensible citizen, a proper inhabitant of the space, warranted by social and ideological conventions that associate it with a specific location—in this instance, a body. For Stone, the "'social disciplines of pain and pleasure' create a specific and bounded site for the citizen, requiring that it be assigned a body. The tie between the two orders of space is through the convention of assigning citizenship (location) to something bounded and apprehensible—the body (the point)" (1995, 41). The point creates what Stone perceives as "relentlessly monistic articulations of physical and virtual space that law and science favor" (42). In other words, the sense of integers, or unified wholes, as the basic elements of space, enforces the structures of law and science. For Stone, the body is just such an integer, displaying a unitary organization, operating as a location, in constructing citizenship—the right to occupy space—in its traditional social role. The body, in its traditional use, operates as a point in the system that mandates a single, whole subject. Performing the hook, the piercing merely literalizes the function.

Stone would set some other notion of citizen or subject against this tradition in order to interrupt the gridding effect of the Euclidean, or to encourage an "unruly multiplicity." She would stave off the law of exclusion (42–43). So, rather than the single, integral body of the citizen, she poses some effect like that of "multiple personalities" warranting through the assignation of multiple subject positions, rather than through a single physical body. Stone works out in detail the effect the syndrome of "multiple personalities" has on legal structures as well as institutions of psychological "health." Virtual subject positions, then, promise what the body cannot. In section Ve, "Performing the Cut," I want to offer a different possibility from the argument that Stone offers here. There I want to consider Stone's work on the transsexual, written under the name of Sandy Stone, along with the example of her own two authorial personae to provide an understanding of the relation between the changing body and virtual technologies. In other words, I want to identify a changing body, rather than a multiple personality, in contradiction to the single integer or point of difference.

IID. VOUDOU

Thus far, debates among systems of space and the body have presumed eurocentric models. Science and technology, in the spaces and points they would emulate and discover, incarnate Enlightenment notions of rationality, empiricism, the city, and the citizen. The cyberpunk imagination, however, written from the perspective of hackers, miscreants, cyborgs, queers, and others outside the legitimate net, finds a use for a model of space taken from the so-called third world: voudou. One character in Gibson's *Count Zero* describes it this way:

> Vodou . . . isn't concerned with notions of salvation and transcendence. What it's about is getting things done. You follow me? In our system, there are many gods, spirits. . . . Come on, man, you know how this works, it's street religion. . . . Vodou's like the street. Think of Danbala, who some people call the snake, as a program. Say as an icebreaker. (91)

Gibson's character perceives voudou as the language of doing, of functions, not of abstract concepts. Voudou is used by the outsiders who hack into this net that would transcend their miscreant spaces to represent a belief system that thinks by doing. Like the street, voudou is a system which takes found

DOMAIN-MATRIX

52
PAGE

 PREV
 NEXT
 OPEN
 PRINT
 FIND
 HELP
 MENU

objects, the trash or litter that the transcendent system leaves behind, and redeploys them in a useful, hopeful manner. Voudou vessels, for example, on the altars, are empty bottles reworked with sequins and ribbons to aid in invoking the loas, or spirits, who work on various problems the petitioner submits. Online, Gibson's character takes old computer parts or software functions to grab some online time—the unit of value.

The cyberpunk use of voudou could be perceived as part of what Mark Dery, in "Black to the Future," terms "Afrofuturism"—a broad category that includes films such as John Sayles's *The Brother from Another Planet* and Lizzie Borden's *Born in Flames,* Sun Ra's Omniverse Arkestra, black drawn comics such as *Static* and *Icon,* and certain forms of graffiti art. "Afrofuturism," argues Derey, interconnects multiple practices derived from the African diaspora, such as voudou, to virtual technologies:

> It's worth pointing out, in the context of what I've chosen to call "Afrofuturism," that the mojos and goofer dust of Delta blues, together with the lucky charms, fetishes, effigies, and other devices employed in syncretic belief systems, such as voodoo, hoodoo, santeria, mambo, and macamba, function very much like joysticks, Datagloves, Waldos, and Spaceballs used to control virtual realities. (766)

In other words, voudou functions like virtual systems to access other kinds of space. "Afrofuturism" resituates technology within systems that had already discovered a complex signification of space before eurocentric scientistic rationality began to construct it. Scott Bukatman, in *Terminal Identity*, addresses how Gibson's use of voudou undermines the presumptions of rationalist technology:

> The interface of voodoo superstition with cybernetic certainty has a literally subversive effect upon the rational, geometric perfection of cyberspace. The modernist "mythology" of rationality, the mechanisms of instrumental reason, are undermined. . . . The data is reappropriated in the name of an appropriated religion as the *loas* of disembodied intelligences circulate through the instrumental spaces of information. (214)

Voudou's origins also signify a different social order from the eurocentric, dominating discourse of science, which is linked to class privilege and gendered male. Voudou originates on the still-troubled island of Haiti, specifically linked to the history of slave revolts. And, whereas Gibson comes to voudou through the depiction of an imaginary, punked-out, basically male, urban context, "conjuring" and "hoodoo" have a long tradition in this century of empowering, in performance and in writing, women of the African diaspora. Marjorie Pryse, in her introduction to the book *Conjuring,* extrapolates how Zora Neale Hurston "would write out . . . hoodoo as a source of power." Pryse illustrates how Janie, the protagonist in *Their Eyes Were Watching God,* brings the power of the representational system to those who are able to see her, but especially to Pheoby, her "kissin friend" for twenty years, who gets the power of such "conjuring" by being able to "feel and do through Janie" (12–13). Pryse follows the tradition of the "ancient power" through black women writers, up to Alice Walker (15). Employing voudou as a model of the navigation of "other" spaces, as useful in imagining cyberspace, then, brings a tradition with a history of revolts against oppression, the empowerment of women in the history of representation, and a communally-based participation to the design of space.

Perhaps because of its practice among peoples caught up in the African diaspora, voudou imagines a navigation of space that deterritorializes rather than colonizes the space it imagines. Nevertheless, as Bukatman suggests above, employing voudou for purposes of imagining a deterritorializing of electronic space is an appropriation of it for first-world high-tech purposes. Recolonizing the imagination of these peoples may certainly provide an instance of how a high capitalist theorist reaches out into Caribbean labor to extend the net. But if, at this point in history, another "new world" has already been processed past its initial "Columbus effect," and cyberspace is in place with nationalist, internationalist, and Big Science goals, then some strategies of spatializing, which may be set against the eurocentric sciences, will be necessary to provide a "place" for the unempowered in the data management of the future. Voudou would once again operate on the side of the oppressed. Perhaps it could provide a hacking into the system that is marked with African diasporic history. After all, technology has not invited the participation of African Americans in its production. Samuel Delany points out that "when one talks about 'black youth culture as a technological culture,' one has to specify that it's a technological culture that's almost entirely on the receiving end of a river of 'stuff,' in which the young consumers have nowhere near what we might call equitable input" (in Dery, 749). Delany continues to note that there is "a naive assumption that the redistribution of commodities is somehow congruent with the redistribution of wealth—which it is not"(749). Strategies for manipulating the net, for taking over the functions of software and the production of online value, associated with those peoples excluded from its ownership and employment, seems a worthy project.

However, rather than perceiving the project as moving from within Enlightenment science out into voudou, one might note that, actually, voudou was navigating virtual space for a long time, and Western science is running to catch up. Sandra Richards suggested this direction to me in a conversation about voudou and virtual reality. When she heard about the connection, she laughed, saying, "Wouldn't you know that the old trickster Shange was already there." Rationality and geometry are being used to construct the engine of the other space that voudou has traditionally already perceived.

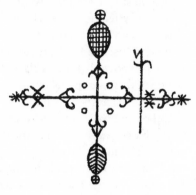

Fig.1 Voudou vever for Legba, loa of the crossroads.
Teiji Ito, from Maya Deren, *Divine Horsemen*.
Courtesy of McPherson & Company, Publishers, Kingston, N. Y.

Crucial to the study of performance and the body is the way voudou links the production of virtual space to the body. The vever (fig. 1) is a figure drawn to chart the particular course through space that the need of the moment would employ to invoke the appropriate spirit. The vevers are drawn with various materials, most importantly, again, with materials produced as "leftovers" from other functions. For example, the black markings within the white lines of a vever may be made with coffee grounds. The vever signifies the figure of space to access the particular loa, or window of space that opens up into the web. There is a multitude of loas and vevers, opening to intersections, sites, and paths in the voudou "net." No part controls another, but each stabilizes momentarily into a pattern of possibilities designed specifically for a given communal rite. The vevers could thus be read as contingent spatial negotiations far more sophisticated than the current software "templates," which organize a functional, unyielding space, or the Euclidean-based point that organizes space through difference.

The particular vever illustrated here is for Legba—the god of the crossroads. Legba is both male and female, the womb and the phallus, as well as the means, the avenue, the axis, the intersection where the two orders of space, the two worlds, meet (Deren 96–97). Legba is the "sacred gateway," who opens the way to the loas (Deren 98). The vever for Legba, the gifts left at crossroads, the chants for Legba constitute the password, the signing on, the access to the net. Note how the vever, unlike the point, produces by bringing so-called opposites together. A figure for both womb and phallus, an intersection rather than a differentiation, the vever is a more welcoming form of spatial organization.

At the same time that these vevers figure the choreography of space, they do so in terms of the moving, dancing body. They are figures for the communal dance to work with, producing "possession" by the loa—a term that signifies the way the body opens as a window into the virtual space. The practice of "dancing space" plants flesh at the root of spatial relations. Rather than "meat," the term that cyberpunk culture employs for the body, intimating its "dumb," rather useless status, which cyberspace purports to transcend, voudou creates such space through the body, which, rather than a computer, or software program, or virtual-reality body mask, dances a window into the web. In this way, voudou provides what Michael Taussig, in his book *Mimesis and Alterity,* describes as "a knowledge adhering to the skin of things" (44). Taussig notes that science sets a eurocentric tradition against "this tactile knowing of embodied knowledge. . . . Thus . . . the whiteness of lab coats, the laboratory, the scientifically prepared and processed sociological questionnaire" (31–32). Voudou reinstates the active body as the producer of the virtual space—the link in the communal web of spaces.

Contrast this fleshly emphasis on the body's relationship to the virtual with the concept of the cyborg, which relates, more often, to relations with the mechanistic **(see section IVg, "Driving My Mouse")**. Voudou centers production within flesh rather than metal. Dancing flesh still may signify something other than instrumental uses of the body within the global capitalist structuring of technospace; whereas the cyborg, the robot, imagines the body as already appropriated by the system. As Patricia Rose notes, in answering "what Afrika Bambaataa and hip-hoppers like him saw in Kraftwerk's use of the robot was an understanding of themselves as *already having been robots* . . . labor for capitalism that had very little value" (in Dery, 771). Rather than moving toward the machine, voudou configures technology within fleshly productions of space that do not necessarily originate in the instrumental uses of the human body. Voudou is the "liquid architecture" of flesh, drenched in dazed dancing, intersecting material and virtual systems.

Along with anthropologists such as Taussig, performance theorists turned from the European stage to find a fleshly co-production of space and meaning—a "theater of alchemy" as Antonin Artaud described it. Artaud's influential concept of the "double" in performance was worked out through his perception of Balinese dancing and the rites of the Tarahumara Indians in Mexico:

> Not a movement of the muscles, not the rolling of an eye but seem to belong to a kind of reflective mathematics which controls everything. . . . Setting aside the prodigious mathematics of spectacle, what seems most surprising and astonishing to us is this aspect of *matter as revelation* [sic], suddenly dispersed in sign to teach us the metaphysical identity of concrete and abstract. . . . developed to the nth power. (59)

D O M A I N - M A T R I X

56
PAGE

 PREV

 NEXT

 OPEN

 PRINT

 FIND

 HELP

 MENU

Artaud terms such performance a form of "primary Physics" (60). Voudou, then, creates a sympathetic mapping through the vever, a fleshly production of science, through performance, a nonhierarchical organization of space and a model for imagining space that does not come with all of the eurocentric, scientist privileges already installed. Imagining cyberspace through such a model may be more critical than novelistic, more empowering than cyberpunk.

IIE. LESBIAN, SIAMESIAN SPACE CADETS

The voudou vever is one talisman to be held in the techno-imaginary to ward off the piercing Euclidean point. Another is the talismanic sense of lesbian as a compound rather than simple space. The adjective "siamesian" refers to siamese twins, who image two bodies in one space. Accordingly, "lesbian" as defying the commands of exclusion embedded in Euclidean space, as performing Benedikt's "superidentical," and as an icon, offers a pleasurable coupling within a space as an organizing principle for the construction of space **(see section IIb, "Cyberspace")**. This means that lesbian would be the sign of the possibility of inhabiting a space together—of a space not constructed upon the principle of difference. Posing lesbian as this structuring of space is to set up a challenge to the point (pounding into the penis of Bob Flanagan, or hooked into the queer clitoris) of difference **(see section IIc, "Getting the Point")**.

Lesbian, as in the 1970s lesbian feminist practice, necessarily implies a collective, multiple position. After Irigaray, lesbian performs a gender-specific proximity in space which challenges property, dis-organizing the hierarchies inscribed in print culture. Figural rather than geometric, lesbian (in spite of Jameson) produces a social space rather than consumes the products of a commodified one. Aligned, through identification, with social movements against oppression, outside of bourgeois "private" space by collective constitution, producing through physical pleasure, defying the principle of exclusion by sameness, lesbian, as space, is a site where many of the liberatory imaginings of space scattered through the Domain-Matrix cohere.

If constructions of cyberspace were to originate from such a site, how would its operations be altered? How would exclusion be set up on a base model of coupling? It will take the entire book to imagine this position—in fact, it is the anti-point of this work. I place it here, in the space of the Domain-Matrix, only to reveal one of its locations—its address within the grid of the argument. Polemically, I close the section on a politics of space with lesbian as the final frontier that cyber-trekkies may imagine in the consideration of space.

First Contact:
Murderous *Heavenly Creatures*

The 1950s may be considered the era of first contact with the new, virtual technologies. The Soviets launched their first satellite, *Sputnik*, which sent the United States into a frenzied state of catching up. The schools were given federal monies to upgrade and emphasize the sciences, new scholarships were founded, and intense new partnering relationships between the military and education multiplied throughout the high schools, colleges, and universities. *Sputnik* was the first in an era of satellites. They now control communications technology. The "heavens" are alive with commercial satellites launched by both federal and private industries. The 1950s was also the founding era of television. The virtual screen entered domestic spaces with surprising success. **(See "The Flowing Locks of TV.")** The new virtual expansion invigorated advertising. Its placement in domestic spaces created new markets aimed at women and teenagers. Resultant commodity fetishism produced the new phenomenon of the teenage fan. At the same time, anticommunism and homophobia intensified their policing practices, inventing new judicial and cultural forms of the witch-hunt. One myth that fueled the fear and hatred of queers was the story of murderous, intellectual, homosexual teenagers. This is a myth of first contact, within the project of organizing the virtual by screening out the lesbian from the state.

IIIA. MATRICIDE ENGENDERS NATION

In the Greek classical theater, and in the myths, matricide set up the origins of trial law. The trial of Orestes for the murder of his mother was represented as the originary trial that replaced the bloody vengeance of the Furies. Athena, that woman born of man, presided over the selection of judges, and celebrated Orestes' acquittal from matricide by relegating the Furies to a cave and declaring Athens the new seat of reason and justice. With the help of Apollo,

D O M A I N - M A T R I X

58
PAGE

 PREV

 NEXT

 OPEN

 PRINT

 FIND

 HELP

 MENU

Athena argued that she was not born of woman, and that was proof sufficient that the father, not the mother, is the blood relative; therefore, Orestes' crime was not really a blood crime (*Eumenides*, second stasimon). In the stage version of the story, *The Eumenides* ends with a triumphal procession into the bloody, violent patriarchal future.

If the origins of democracy proceed from the murder of a mother by her son, women are prescribed the role of fit accomplice. In the play *Electra,* the murder of Clytemnestra is encouraged and aided by a chorus of women citizens, along with Electra herself. During the actual murder, the audience sees Electra onstage, discussing its necessity with the chorus of women, while hearing the offstage screams of Clytemnestra. These screams can be heard down the halls of patriarchal forms. At the conclusion of *Electra*—the *ekkuklyma*—that stage as agent speeds out to the audience, from the unseen action deemed "within," to offer up the tableau of the triumphant Orestes and the bloody corpse of his mother. The stage lays bare what Freud later configured as the oedipal-imitating Electra complex—that women may enter the bloody realm of the Symbolic as accomplices in the absolved murder of the mother.

If Apollo and Athena are the heavenly creatures involved in this originary crime, what of the heavenly creatures in the current film by that title—the two teenage girls who committed lesbian matricide? The film *Heavenly Creatures*, based on an actual matricide committed by Pauline Parker and Juliet Hulme in New Zealand in 1953, represents the vengeful borders of the patriarchal symbolic order secured by the originary matricide. If the myth and the tragic trilogy represent the origins of the law, the state, order, and the entrance into the social symbolic that drove the maddened cloud of Furies into a cave, *lesbian matricide represents the crime at the end of print culture.* Thus, matricide shores up the boundaries of the eurocentric tradition of reading and writing catalyzed into representation by the son's murder of his mother and concluded by lesbian matricide. How is it that these lesbian murderous heavenly creatures are cast as the agents of panic at the beginning of the end of print's dominion? How do they represent the conditions of first contact?

The film *Heavenly Creatures,* produced in the 1990s, provides an example of how the present era, moving beyond the initial virtual contact into cyberspace, revises the myth of first contact. *Heavenly Creatures* depicts the events in the lives of Pauline Parker and Juliet Hulme that led to the murder of Pauline's mother. The directors and writers of the film, Fran Walsh and Peter Jackson, thoroughly researched the case in order to build a sympathetic portrayal of their characters from diaries, interviews, and court records, in contrast to the negative stereotypes of the young women that circulated through the press, the testimony of court experts, and general apocryphal sources. Pauline Parker kept extensive diaries that recorded the details of her relations with Juliet, as well as the premeditations of the matricide and the announcement of the dawning of the day of the murder with the words: "this is the day of the happy event." Writing, print culture, was central to their relationship and to the events that would determine their future.

Pauline and Juliet met in school, where they were top students in their classes. Pauline was a working-class girl, in school on fellowships. Juliet was recently arrived from England—a child of the moneyed professional class who had enjoyed the benefits of private education. The girls bonded through their intellectual superiority and their general enthusiasm for and dedication to cultural production. They performed a mutual fandom of Hollywood movie stars and Mario Lanza, which they interwove with their creation of a fictional world based on a *faux* royalty that sexualized and ironized their colonial heritage. As the two girls retreated further and further into their mutual fictional creations, their parents became concerned about the intensity and exclusivity of their relationship and its distance from the "real" world. Following the breakup of her parents and her father's involuntary exit from his post at the university, Juliet was to be sent to live in South Africa. The girls panicked at the threat of separation. Pauline's mother would not allow her to accompany Juliet. The threat the separation posed to their cultural production, as well as to their emotional and sexual relations, led them to devise the murder of Pauline's mother.

Both the film, made in 1994, and the crime, committed in 1953, set this lesbian matricide at the site of print and its demise. The 1950s, even in New Zealand, may be marked as the period of the rise and the suppression of a new sense of the virtual that would challenge print's dominion. The extension of commercial radio and television into the home created what Lynn Spigel has termed "the theatricalization and specularization of the domestic space—the home as a theater" (12). Ever ensconced in the domestic, women were particularly involved in this new virtuality. They became the new audience as well as the new addressee of the virtual and of its ad campaigns. The new hunger for the virtual, created by serials on radio and TV and the promise of opening "a window to the world" within the domestic confine, created a new social persona called a "fan." The 1950s gave rise to this term—particularly denoting teenage girls. Pauline Parker and Juliet Hulme represent these new fans of the dawning virtual age, who constituted their relationship through the circulation of fan materials and, eventually, the creation of their own, original "other" world.

Critics who set the beginning of the current sense of "fans" in the early 1950s argue that the concept functioned as a conceptualization of identity in relation to the new power of mass culture. Joli Jenson in "Fandom as Pathology: The Consequences of Characterization" asserts that the term "fan" "mobilizes related assumptions about modern individuals" from the "alienated, atomized, 'mass man'" to the "irrational victim of mass persuasion." In

DOMAIN-MATRIX

60 PAGE

PREV

NEXT

OPEN

PRINT

FIND

HELP

MENU

other words, Jenson perceives the concept of the "fan" as "a psychologized version of the mass society critique" that focuses the fears and seductions of the individual's relation to mass culture (16). She continues to develop the image of the deranged fan as situated "on the dangerous territories of fanaticism—the line always proximate and crossable." Jenson makes the point that such notions of the "fan" are marked with class assumptions. Fans of high culture are called aficionados, or collectors, or even professors (19). She compares the Barry Manilow fan to a Joyce scholar, in order to emphasize the class assumptions that treat the regard of such behavior in different manners. Jenson concludes that "by conceiving of fans as a lunatic fringe which cracks under the pressure of modernity . . . we tell ourselves a reassuring story—yes, modernity is dangerous, and some people become victims of it by succumbing to media influence or mob psychology, but *we do not*" (24). The concern with fans in the fifties, then, created a moral landscape upon which relations to the virtual may be organized. "Fans" organized the border between proper and improper involvement with the virtual, contextualizing the growth and lure of the media within fifties moral concerns.

As usual, the sense of those who are identified as most seduceable, who were "prone" to the virtual, were women and, in the 1950s, adolescents (157–158). The virtual and its ads became a way of domesticating sexual impulses for teens and housewives. At the time (as well as now), teens were pushed into celibacy and then toward marriage and the role of housewife. A study of girl fans conjectures that: "part of the appeal of the male star . . . was that you would *never* marry him; the romance would never end in the tedium of marriage. . . . The star could be loved noninstrumentally, for his own sake, and with complete abandon" (Ehrenreich, Hess, and Jacobs, 96–97). For Pauline Parker and Juliet Hulme in their lesbian relationship, this fandom offered a zone outside the expectations of compulsory heterosexuality—a possible realm for circulating images of desire between them. Thus, the new fandom of the virtual created a signifying and, in their case, relational space for constituting lesbian desire. Their lesbian relations, then, were inextricably caught up in the virtual realm of fandom.

This realm also offered them the possibility for cultural production. John Fiske, in "The Cultural Economy of Fandom," identifies it as an opportunity for "semiotic productivity" (37). Fiske argues that fans are not merely receptive, but are making social meanings, and even finding a self-empowering way to create textual productivity (39). Their participatory sense in the circulation of fan images is a way of refusing to distance the cultural object (40). Parker and Hulme, two talented, intelligent young girls living in the hypermasculinized social space of New Zealand in the 1950s, found in fandom a space in which to configure lesbian desire outside heterosexuality and to empower their own facility for cultural production. Yet, while fandom does offer a mode of cultural production, it should not be taken as enabling in the broader cultural field. For, although teenage girls were the addressee of the marketing of virtual relations, they were not encouraged to imagine that they might produce the actual images themselves. Women, after all, were still confined in the domestic space. (Surely, the origins of which Athena's expulsion of the Furies into a cave represented—they were to remain secluded and confined, away from the trials of patriarchal justice.) Moreover, women were disallowed the controls of technology. Lynn Spigel offers several images of women in front of the new television in the home—operated by the man. This contradiction was expressed through the relationship of Parker and Hulme, who enthusiatically took up virtual relations and their production and suffered under the censoring of their production. They could produce them *only* vis-à-vis one another, which enforced the exclusivity and withdrawn nature of their relationship. The violence of their containment, eventually leading to their imprisonment, prodded their anxieties around such production and their intense, singular need for one another. Within this context, the mother, as the intimate representative of normalized social relations, and as the agent who would separate them, became the symbol of their repression that offered the opportunity for violent revolution. If Lacan proffers that castration, what he calls "the pound of flesh," must be offered up for entrance into patriarchal cultural production, these girls made the sacrifice of the mother's body. At the threshold of virtual relations, some body, or all bodies, must be sacrificed in order to enter the meatless, transcendent realm. The masculine sacrifice of the mother in order to secure the line to the father enacted the entrance into print. The mother, in that case, needed to be sacrificed only once, and the father continually, within print's symbolic realm. The lesbian murder of the mother in the 1950s secured the necessarily exclusive, withdrawn, but possible virtual creation of the relationship.

But why the revived interest in the Parker/Hulme relationship in the 1990s? Why film its revision? If the 1950s performed the new allure of the virtual, it was also obsessed with policing it—particularly the specific combination of homosexual attraction, intellectual brilliance, the disclosure of class privilege and oppression, and violence. In fact, the 1950s project of violent repression, of crime and punishment, invigorated the form of the trial, as Athena and Apollo had done, but this time specifically through the air waves and the video signals. The trials of the 1950s, however, did not offer the celebration of acquittal. They were designed to encourage outrage on the part of the public chorus, now constituted by the media. They organized virtual judges across the nation, in their own homes, to decide the guilt or innocence of the accused. The media organized the spectacle of punishment for the collusion of the representation of class as an agent in the social field, with intelligence, the presumption to produce culture and homosexuality—a configuration now back to haunt us in the 1990s. It is this connection of the 1990s with the 1950s, along these axes, that points to the panic around the passing of print culture and the dawning of the virtual. The connection, not surprisingly, is being formed through film production—the queen of the screens.

IIIB. *ROPE*-ING IN THE VIRTUAL

The film *Heavenly Creatures*, the Parker/Hulme case, is joined in its retrospective handling of this 1950s cultural compound by the film *Swoon*, which offers a revised treatment of the Leopold and Loeb case. Although the Leopold and Loeb murder actually took place in 1924, Alfred Hitchcock's treatment of it in the film *Rope*, produced in 1948, provided a prologue into the fifties, while Meyer Levin's book on the case, *Compulsion*, published in 1957, followed by the play, and finally the movie, in 1959, closed the decade. Once again, in 1993–94, two films were produced that revised the representation of these cases. The similarities in the cases are obvious. Leopold and Loeb were two brilliant, wealthy boys, eighteen and nineteen years old, who enjoyed a homosexual relationship. They determined to commit the perfect murder, choosing a young boy as victim, and smashing his skull with a chisel in fashionable Hyde Park. The trial, like the Parker/Hulme trial, hinged on theories of mental competence, the damning evidence of homosexual attraction, also related in diaries, along with the premeditation of murder. Both couples, Leopold and Loeb and Parker and Hulme, were tried for homosexuality, intellectual ability, the lure into virtual worlds, writing, and murder.

While the two cases are similar, they also compose different structures of circulating the virtual and homosexuality. D. A. Miller points out that the homosexuality of the two men is never indicated in Hitchcock's *Rope* through bodily contact, constructing "a homosexuality of no importance" (122). As covert, implied, but unsaid, the murder committed, but undisclosed to others as part of narrative action, creates the pairing of the two "mysteries." Both homosexuality and murder work to both disclose and conceal. In *Rope*, both the corpse and the homosexuality are unseen—only implied—begging for the disclosure of evidence and the closure of a trial. Miller attributes the implied/disclosed status of the "crimes" to Hitchcock, but also to a broader social practice. The class privilege of the boys also aided in constructing the circulation of "unsaid." Miller: "murder is a crime for the masses, a privilege for the elite" (127). The shared upper-class status of the two boys created a shelter for their secrets, which, even when publicly tried, were sympathetically articulated by the best of defense lawyers, Clarence Darrow. Parker and Hulme also secreted their mutual life from the public, circulating popular images through their restricted, private fantasy world, but their class differences allowed a wedge of disclosure to splay open what they would hide. The families shared no privileged exclusivity, encouraging the upper-class parents to reveal the "crimes" of both homosexuality and murder as Parker's—as the always "open book" of working-class lives.

The 1950s would publicly manage the virtual by assigning to it the power of revelation—it could pry into the secrets of the domestic, where it now was lodged, and publicly reveal hidden "crimes," bringing them to the forum of justice. Revealing covert sexual practices and domestic murder ratified the virtual's breaking into the home. If the notion of the fan policed proper contact with the virtual, its own security system of rooting illicit fan practices out of polluted relationships illustrated how the virtual installed virtue into its practices. In the Cold War era, posing the virtual as a virtuous revelatory device allayed anxieties about its own powers of secrecy. However, this was the public face, the organization the virtual was to have in mass communications. The actual deployment of its most sophisticated means was in the service of national secrets. Nevertheless, secret state security organized their virtual system's virtue along the same lines. If the virtual empowered secret state activities by the FBI, it also spied on the state secrets of the "Russians," legitimating its practices. Hitchcock's *Rope* spies on the "open secret," both retaining and disclosing it as the state organized the role of the virtual and its claims to virtue.

IIIC. *SWOON*-ING INTO CYBERSPACE

The current film *Swoon* redresses the omission of explicit homosexuality in *Rope*, taking long, beautifully composed shots of the boys' sexual and romantic association and relegating the trial to frozen, distant, documentary cuts of condemnation. Filming homosexual contact is the focus of the film. Likewise, *Heavenly Creatures* overtly portrays the sexual liaison between the girls. The "open secret" is a mode of the past. Revelation as a political tool lost its efficacy after Watergate. In these films of the 1990s, the authorities, such as the psychologist in *Heavenly Creatures*, who suggest that homosexuality is a "problem" are portrayed as distant, foolish characters. In the film, there is almost the sense that the girls beat their relationship into the manifest as they strike the mother. If intellectual, teen, homosexual relations channeled the virtuous control of the virtual by telegraphing violence and punishment through the electronic imaginary of the 1950s, they have become the privileged site for explorations of the virtual in the 1990s.

Lesbian, gay, queer, and transgender studies are the site where interiority and exteriority meet in critical theory. Their academic élan springs from the way in which their subcultural sexual practices challenge the codes of interi-

DOMAIN-MATRIX

64
PAGE

 PREV

 NEXT

OPEN

PRINT

FIND

HELP

MENU

ority and exteriority. Desire's relation to the social is cycled through the articulation of lesbian and gay constructions. In other words, lesbian and gay politics, when theorized, raise the issue of the relation of the virtual to the flesh—the relation of desire to social relations. Their current fashionable status in the academy and in the media performs this moment of the second virtual coming, as it were, as the 1990s ushers in Virtual Reality itself. As the book is challenged by the hypertext, writing by the transmission of digitized images, print culture, in its hermetic, colorless, linear form is intersected by the morphing, multi-spaced environments of new technologies, money is abstracted through virtual banking procedures, and fleshly social relations transmit through MUDS, MOOS, bulletin boards, and email courtships, the representation of lesbian and gay relations, their political work, is offering up some of the critical strategies necessary to comprehend this new form of exchange.

Let's go to the movies again to watch how the screen queen displays this transformation in terms of a narrative structure—cinematic realism. *Heavenly Creatures* cuts its realistic narrative with morphing scenes of the girls' entry into their virtual, other world:

> Pauline: . . . but we're all going to heaven.
>
> Juliet: I'm not. I'm going to the fourth world. It's sort of like heaven only better because there aren't any Christians. It's an absolute paradise of music, art and pure enjoyment. James [Mason] will be there, and Mario [Lanza]—only they'll be saints.
>
> Pauline: Saint Mario.

The other dimension is a virtual one, inhabited by the arts along with the objects of fandom—the signs the new electronic communication circulated around the world.

The fourth world actually opened up for the girls while they were on vacation in Port Levy. The film shoots the scene as a park, shot in saturated colors, replete with unicorn. Pauline described it this way in her diary:

> Today Juliet and I found the 4th world. . . . We saw a gateway through the clouds. . . . We have an extra part of our brain which can appreciate the 4th world. Only about 10 people have it. When we die we will go to the 4th world, but meanwhile on two days of every year we may use the ray and look into that beautiful world. (In Glamuzina and Laurie, 62)

As virtual contact, this passage displays their almost arrogant sense of being "chosen" to observe this window to the other world, locked as it was within the context of fandom. While Hollywood must be our guide to the film, from the perspective of the U.S., two feminist authors in New Zealand offer another explanation of this virtual sphere—one they borrowed from the Maori cosmology. Apparently, the Port Levy area is one of special spiritual significance to the Maori. Morover, there is a possible window to the other world which opens about twice a year, when certain planets are fortuitously aligned. If one can make contact with the Karakaia, one can open up into another order of space and time. The privilege of passing through the gates, however, requires a blood sacrifice (Glamuzina and Laurie, 147). This is a complex theory, which I cannot unpack from the brief explanation of it. Certainly, several specifics of the Parker/Hulme case seem to match its form of the virtual. The point is merely to raise a local knowledge of these events—an indigenous reading—in contrast with the way I have positioned these events in the book. Nevertheless, in terms of the film and the fandom, we can presume the virtual as the media have begun to organize it.

The director of the film, Peter Erickson, turned to this subject after a prior film, *Dead Alive,* which mixed animation and the breaking through of mimetic "natural" forms by transformative morphing in the horror genre. In *Heavenly Creatures* he uses the lesbian relationship, set in the narrative of matricide, to produce the window into the other world—the intense breaking through of their relationship in a homophobic culture. However, the haunting relationship between that breakthrough and the breaking into the mother's skull gives pause to the sympathetic viewer. What does Saint Mario promise these girls? Erickson brings together the two genres that render the breakthrough—horror and fantasy—the two most successful genres of the early 1990s. Traversing a lesbian, matricidal relationship in this bonding, Erickson situates the taboos of matricide and lesbian sex at the center of the spectrum—this is where inside and outside, "real" and virtual meet.

If the 1950s virtualized the trial, the 1990s produce trials as the virtual. The O. J. Simpson phenomenon, substituting miscegenation for homosexuality, tries sex and murder—the crucial difference for this context, however, is that the trial is a part of watching television, rather than the other way around. The courtroom, bedecked with flowers sent by those who hope to see their arrangement on TV, is a TV series, similar to those others it is nested among. The moral landscape the 1950s organized for the virtual has been transformed into a virtual landscape upon which morality is situated. The panic now is around the dissolution of that order and the coming of virtual reality.

IIID. THE PRISON OF PRINT'S RETURN

The film about the Parker/Hulme case has also created a new interplay between one of the girls and her current social relations—an interplay which performs the new role to which reading and writing are assigned within the virtual. Because of the success of the film, reporters began to investigate what happened to the girls. Juliet Hulme was discovered to be presently writing

Fig. 2 Open letter to Anne Perry as ad
for movie *Heavenly Creatures*.

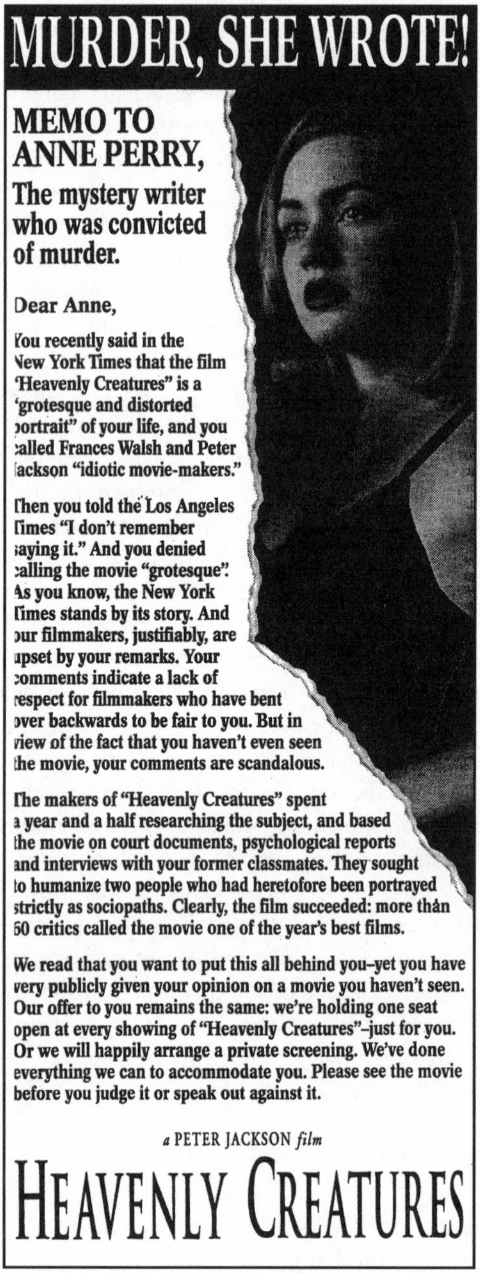

mysteries under the name of Anne Perry. Her mysteries, interestingly, are set in Victorian England. Perry has since been interviewed on NPR and in the *New York Times* and the *Los Angeles Times*. She speaks about her work, her memories of the crime, and the influence it and her imprisonment have had upon her life, and, of course, the film. She has no memory of a lesbian relationship, insisting that they were "innocent girls." In her interview with Terry Gross on *Fresh Air,* Perry admits that the writing of the mystery ultimately traces a return to the guilty self—the author is the criminal. She acknowledges that mystery writing is an obssessive return to the scene of the crime.

Writing, then, for Perry is a form of punishment. The breakthrough, morphing fan world she co-created with Parker has been reduced to the repetitious discovery of criminal acts set in a period of high social moralizing. Constraints of class, gender, and a complex code of social manners oppress her characters as they make their way toward the discovery of the criminal. Writing, for Perry, emulates the order of the virtual that the 1950s deployed against her. She is captive in a print prison of surveillance and discovery, disallowed those morphing fantasy visits to other worlds. Writing and reading, then, after the pleasures of the morphing virtual, are punishments for the crime that allowed it.

Yet Hulme's punishing script has now intersected with the movie of her lesbian, virtual explorations to construct her persona as what the ad in the *L.A. Times* so wittily hailed as *Murder, she wrote!* (Friday, March 10, 1995, F10) (fig. 2). The scripting of the criminal now circulates back through commercialism, to once again make Juliet Hulme the addressee of the market—only this time it is as cultural producer. Her scripted constraint is set against the representation of her revolution. While her actual photo has graced the papers, along with pictures of her twelve-room home in Scotland, the ad for the film, captioned *Murder, she wrote!* is formatted as a letter to Hulme/Perry in regard to her negative comments on the film. The ad is composed to seem as if the letter had been ripped to reveal the sexy actress who portrays Perry in the film standing in a black slip, looking out of the frame. The film breaks through into Perry's life, into her scripting of murder in print as the film breaks through its own ad to haunt the letter. As Hulme denies the lesbian content of her relations with Parker, emphasizes her conversion to Mormonism, and dedicates her novels to her old aunts, she is preparing for a twenty-three-city promotional tour, advertising her novels as a kind of sequel to her actions—a kind of sequel to the film. If print is the punishment, its circulation in the new virtual is its absolution. If nothing else, on the threshold of the biggest conglomerates in history, forming to combine entertainment with computer technology, matricide sells.

D O M A I N - M A T R I X

PREV

NEXT

OPEN

PRINT

FIND

HELP

MENU

68
PAGE

The Computer Cometh

For more than a decade, many academic theorists have been composing their work on the computer, yet the experience of the screen seems to remain unattended in their theorizing. They write as if at a typewriter, or with a pencil, retaining the structures that those engines of text inscribe. Considering the computer as a different material condition of writing reorganizes fundamental concepts about the organization of intellectual and physical functions. This section deals with the new tricks certain pet theories must learn. It does so in the context of sitting at the computer, imagining the import of familiar functions on its screen.

IVA. A REVISION OF THE GAZE

Feminist film criticism produced a notion of the Gaze that became one of the dominant strategies in revealing the status of women in representation. This notion combined the simple observation of how women are constituted as objects of the "male" Gaze with the complex underwriting of the psychoanalytic principles of castration and the oedipal in its constitution. Briefly, the Gaze locked representation within the patriarchal, or more specifically the phallic, regime, constituting men as Gazers and women as the Gazed upon, which likewise characterized men as voyeurs and women as exhibitionists:

> In a world ordered by sexual imbalance, pleasure in looking has been split between active/male and passive/female. The determining male gaze projects its fantasy onto the female figure which is styled accordingly. . . . Woman displayed as sexual object is the *leitmotif* of erotic spectacle. . . . The presence of woman is an indispensable element of spectacle in normal narrative film, yet her visual presence tends to work against the storyline, to freeze the flow of action in moments of erotic contemplation. (Mulvey 1989, 19)

Here, Laura Mulvey, in the pioneering essay "Visual Pleasure and Narrative Cinema," illustrated how the realm of the visual overcomes even narrative flow through an erotic economy that secures an imbalance of power through gender. The active male Gazes his fantasy onto the objectified woman. Yet woman as object of the Gaze "connotes something that the look continually circles around but disavows: her lack of a penis, implying castration." So she is perfected in her look, scanned by the camera for her phallic-like visual potency, both "posing" the castration anxiety and circumventing it (25). The concept of the Gaze thus mobilized gender assignment, erotic practices, and psychoanalytic structures all in one swell look.

In the heady early days of feminist critical practice, those of us engaged in theater/performance studies presumed that we could borrow this strategy for the study of "live" performance. Since the initial experiments in feminist theater collaborated with the art-based, imagistic practice of performance art, we wanted strategies that would account for constructions of gender in the economy of the visible. In spite of the specificity of its title, "Visual Pleasure and Narrative Cinema," feminist critics assumed that Laura Mulvey's notion of the Gaze as gendering had wider applications than cinema studies. We managed critically to perform its acuity, when considering how "woman" was constructed within different scenarios on the stage, employing a notion of spectacle to unite the two different technologies of representation—the stage and film. The power relations of the Gaze in narrative cinema seemed homologous to operations of spectatorship in the theater. Yet the obvious but astonishing fact that this construction of the Gaze helped to inscribe a role for the technology of the camera and the screen in the critical understanding of gender politics somehow eluded our attention. We neglected to comprehend fully how the power relations in the visual were necessarily conjoined with a mechanical apparatus for seeing. Certainly, we noted the prominence of film criticism in the construction of the feminist critique, but what we neglected to perceive was that situating the techno-apparatus of perception, the camera, as constitutive of the Gaze militated against any accounts of the "live," and by extension the "body," outside of the apparatus. When we raised, again, in such circles the notion of the "live" sweating, laboring, productive body, deconstructive strategies and accusations of "presence" were deployed to establish that it was no different from the body within technoland—screened by the industry.

Only problems with the rigid format of sexual difference, of gender as a determining category, sought to adjust the construction of the Gaze. Obviously, not all Gazers of cinema are men, so the initial problem became how to understand the position of women as spectators. Mulvey's "Afterthoughts" and Mary Ann Doane's "Film and the Masquerade: Theorising the Female Spectator" reconfigured the Gaze to accommodate women as spectators

D O M A I N - M A T R I X

70
PAGE

 PREV

 NEXT

 OPEN

 PRINT

 FIND

 HELP

 MENU

through a sense of visual transvestism (Mulvey 1981; Doane 1982). Women's Gaze, they maintained, was enabled by drag—only as transvestites could women enter the phallic, erotic economy of looking. This simple, gendered bifurcation of the Gaze, based on sexual difference, the two basic categories of men and women, became further problematized in gay, lesbian, and queer discourses. Not all men are Gazing erotically at women; some women are Gazing erotically at women, some women who are Gazed upon by women look like men, and some men Gazed upon by men look like men. Although the accommodation of visual transvestism might both retain the divide of sexual difference and heterosexist theories of desire in the Gaze, and account for these permutations, studies of the complexity of identificatory gender processes in lesbian/gay spectatorship and cinema finally render the effect that perhaps the Gaze doth protest too much. In fact, my article "Tracking the Vampire" works out, in some critical detail, how the feminist psychoanalytic formation of the Gaze maintains homophobic practices in regard to the lesbian discursive position.

Meanwhile, the central role that technology plays in the process continued to remain relatively unremarked. While gender theories came under scrutiny, technology's position in the process did not. Now, this does not mean that feminist film critics did not account for the apparatus at all. They certainly encouraged women to take over the camera and thereby alter the Gaze. They dealt with the gendering effects of the lighting, framing, etc. Still, the critique moved away from the consideration of the technology *qua* technologies, or as situated among other technologies, to a primarily psychoanalytic study of the internal dynamics of the spectator. Teresa de Lauretis outlines the movement of the critique in "The Technology of Gender":

> The understanding of cinema as a social technology, as a "cinematic apparatus" was developed in film theory contemporaneously with Foucault's work, but independently of it; rather, as the word *apparatus* suggests, it was directly influenced by the works of Althusser and Lacan. There is little doubt, at any rate, that cinema—the cinematic apparatus—is a technology of gender. . . . not only how the representation of gender is constructed by the given technology, but also how it becomes absorbed subjectively by each individual whom that technology addresses. . . . the crucial notion is the concept of spectatorship. . . . the ways in which his/her identification is solicited and structured. (13)

The study of identification, rather than the study of the industry, the industrial production, motivated the critique forward. The focus shifted from the mode of production to the mode of reception. As we have seen in section Ib, "Burying the Live Body," this shift also occurred in the study of the theater, radically altering the terms of the analysis.

If early feminist criticism centered on film, the majority of current lesbian, gay, and queer work continues to assume film, photography, video, advertisements, and photographic images in the 'zines as the ground of the critique. Consider the centrality of debates on the work of Mapplethorpe, AIDS and safe-sex videos, prime-time television, Hollywood movies, k. d. lang's or Madonna's music videos, the underground cinema of *Paris Is Burning* or *She Must Be Seeing Things*, the pages of *Vanity Fair* and *Ten Percent*, to offer only a few examples. The technology of camera and screen secures the discourse of desire, just as the discourses around desire and gender secure the centrality of screen technology. The techno-screen provides the ground of such cultural theory, and the theory provides the critical ground for the screen. All the world, in feminist and queer theory, it would seem, is no longer a stage but a screen. Yet the prominence that these types of cultural artifacts take over others, say, "live" performance, is presumed rather than argued. The assumption of certain technologies as the key targets of any "alternative" or "subcultural" critique, or desire, constructs the sense that they are always already the producers of "spectators'" identifications without questioning how the mode of production, within the development of technology, has suited these exclusive rights.

Before proceeding to the complementary exclusivities in the practices of technocriticism, I want to note another significant structuring in the Gaze that will be challenged by the coming ascendancy, in the late twentieth century, of the computer screen. The Gaze, as concept and as camera, operates by focus. This point seems obvious enough upon initial consideration. Theater studies have already dealt critically with, for example, the role of perspective in painted flats, the organization of sight lines in respect to the king's Gaze, and, in Joseph Roach's study, the micrographic foundation of imperialist spectacle. Focus has become a controlling trope for acting and directing, but even more for the relation of so-called concentration to learning and thus to the organization of thought itself. The camera is an instrument of focus. Much of the feminist critique concerns how it focuses on the woman, constructing her as the object of that focused Gaze. The computer screen, however, is not, by nature, composed by focus. This screen has no camera—no eye. While the user-friendly aim of software replicates the function of the camera, other functions instate another form of organization.

The increasing anxiety around the loss of focus in the new technological age marks the dawning of a new mode of organization that is unlike that of the Gaze and the camera. Institutions founded on focus, such as schools, are troubled by the increasing loss of it, calling for a resistance to computer games, and screens of distraction, such as MTV programming. Postmodern studies, following Dick Hebdige's sense of subcultural style, have recast Lévi-Strauss's

D O M A I N - M A T R I X

72 PAGE

 PREV

 NEXT

 OPEN

 PRINT

 FIND

 HELP

 MENU

notion of *bricolage* (ironically, in his study as a measure of the "savage mind") to signify this new alteration in focus. If focus has had its day, then how will those entities that it organized be represented? If the Gaze constitutes gender, what happens to gender after the era of focus has passed? Let these questions linger behind the ensuing description of the criticism that would account for this new technology.

The development of critical studies around technology proceeded neither from this focus on the camera and the screen, nor from the critical models proffered by psychoanalytic, gender, or sexual studies. Instead, the theorizing of technology as technology regards computers, cyberspace, and other virtual systems. Its critical models derive from chaos theory, semiotics, postMarxist studies of value, and theories from men whose work by and large ignores issues of gender and sexuality, such as Martin Heidegger, Walter Benjamin, Paul Virilio, Gregory Ulmer, Mark Poster, and Deleuze and Guattari. Significantly, techno journals are entitled neither *differences* nor *Genders,* but *Wired* and *Mondo 2000.* Only a small portion of cultural theories of technology considers gender, such as that by Katherine Hayles, Donna Haraway, and Vivian Sobchack, and none, to my knowledge, attends to lesbian and gay issues.

Now, these broad assertions beg the question of what is meant by the term "technology." Certainly, discourses on gender and sexuality that relate to the technology of camera and screen have developed critical studies of the apparatus and from the apparatus. While they proceed from specific apparati out into a variety of institutions and discourses, they do not tend to link their theories to technology as it is understood in studies of virtual technologies. Of course, even the term "virtual technologies" could refer to anything from a pencil to a computer. However, there is a field growing up around the study of computers, hypertext, virtual environments, and screens that employs the term "technology" to refer to these particular machines and the social/political/economic structures that accompany them. This conglomeration is sometimes called "information technologies," "media," or, as Constance Penley and Andrew Ross term it in their introduction to *Technoculture,* "cultural technologies" (x). Penley and Ross outline the concerns they used to compile their influential anthology, which help readers understand what the concerns of such a study address:

> We selected contributors whose critical knowledge might provide a realistic assessment of the politics . . . that are currently at stake in those cultural practices touched by advanced technology. . . . Like all technologies, they are ultimately developed in the interests of industrial and corporate profits. . . . In many cases, the inbuilt principles of these technologies are precisely aimed at deskilling, information gathering, surveillance, and the social management of large populations. (xii)

It seems, then, that the break between the study of gender and sexuality that is currently addressed through spectatorial identification and the study of technology, addressed through economic and national structures, continues the divide between Marxist studies and psychoanalytic ones. The division between the two critiques, arguably combined by some critics, continues to offer the familiar differences of methodology. Why is it that studies of technology separate out from those other, internal concerns?

Part of the failure to consider technology's role within gender critiques was precisely its association with the *instrumental*. Use has little value in studies of desire. Another part of the failure rests in the post-Heideggerian sense that "technology" is the term for the construction of all comprehension and knowledge. The instrumental is more than the mechanistic and a part of everything. As Verena Andermatt Conley concisely stated it in her preface to the important anthology *Rethinking Technologies*:

> Heidegger's vocabulary is still appropriate, with a *techné* or means that flattens a three-dimensional world into a two-dimensional diagram or map, institutes a separation between subject and object, and inaugurates the quest of the rational, self-possessed subject that soon expands and colonizes. . . . it is one with the "Western project." (x)

While this Heideggerian sense of an almost cosmological status for technology has been useful in understanding the broader epistemological effect of the instrumental, it has also served to obscure the specific role that instruments do play in this new technological culture. For example, one postulate Heidegger holds is that "the essence of modern technology shows itself in what we call Enframing" (xii). Heidegger, in the tradition of German Romanticism, sets this process against the lost golden age of Greek *poiesis*, which he characterizes as a bringing-forth that set one on the path of revelation. In contrast, he posits a technological Enframing that objectifies the world. Rather than using this postulate to proceed to general philosophical principles, one might ask which machines are involved in the process, who is building them, where, and to what end? While this is a Marxist "framing" of the questions, as we will see, practices of gender relations and those surrounding sexual practice are implied in their construction and marketing.

Turning from the move out from machines to philosophical principles back to the "instruments" themselves, assuming that the bygone Gaze no longer focuses gender through its subject/object filter, but that it is becoming a mere citation on the computer screen, and reviewing the mode of production in ways that reveal gender and sexual politics, what strategies might reveal and disrupt the political economy of the new screenic power?

DOMAIN-MATRIX

74
PAGE

 PREV

 NEXT

 OPEN

 PRINT

 FIND

 HELP

 MENU

IVB. OUT OF FOCUS

Above and beyond the obvious centrality of film and photography in late-twentieth-century cultures, the computer screen has ascended as the sublation of screening. Currently, the largest monopolies in history are forming to secure this screen as *the* mode of production in communications, banking, investment, social relations, and entertainment. The new computer multimedia capability to embed (mobile) visual images and sound in a space with print, in the very instrument of "writing," revolutionizes cultural production. In the future, or the late present, moving images, the voice, music, plastic representations of the body, in other words the elements of what has been considered "performing," will be nested at the new combinative base with "writing." Perhaps this new mode of performance/script might be perceived as a late capitalist version of "closet drama." However, "closet," in this case, would not denote the internal, imagined staging of a written text, as it did in the past, but rather a kind of screened performance in the hands of an *auteur*, who could bring all the elements of performance together on the screen for "private" viewing. Whether it be quick-time film segments of Richard Burton playing *Hamlet,* cut in with the text itself, or a more radical mosaic of elements, borrowing images from underground comix, laid alongside digital representations from museum holdings, cut with sound bites of dialogue, music, digital simulations of bird calls, water lapping on the shore, writing graffiti-like scrawls of cultural assertions, followed by paragraphs from Plato, these "performance/scriptings" may now be sent out along the World Wide Web to others who may cut, again, the elements into new combinations, add their own ideas, and send out amended versions, creating, finally, a social circulation of the elements of writing, image, and sound across a myriad of screens, in which authorship and artifact are constituted across and only through net travel.

The particular mix I am suggesting here is not my fantasy of montage, but actually is drawn from a number of hypercard stacks. Something in the cyberpunk imaginary seems to call for mixed citations of natural sound, recognizable bites from popular culture, comix, and "high" theory. For example, *Beyond Cyberpunk: A Do-It-Yourself Guide to the Future* combines industrial sound, comix, and quotations from Deleuze and Guattari. *The User's Guide* of *Mondo 2000,* in a lengthy bibliography designed to introduce the elements of this new sensibility, lists underground digital recordings such as *Sex Packets* alongside Derrida's *Of Grammatology*; Madonna's videos next to Baudrillard's *Simulations.* Cyberpunk gleefully cuts from theory, art, sound, image, and text. Distinctions of genre, or of the relation of theory to performance, or of writing to image are transformed from the discursive to the traversive. Assumptions about the difficulty of texts, or their respective accessibility, are non-operable. Likewise, requirements of preparation, background research—in short, the accessories of focus—no longer provide the key to cultural production. Hakim Bey, a columnist for *Mondo 2000,* has published a new manifesto on the anarchistic potential of the net. Ironically (to some), he enlists Artaud, Foucault, and Baudrillard in his argument for an antischool "voluntary illiteracy," which he perceives as the basis of the revolutionary "counter net" (Bey, 128–133). The perspective effect of education, rendering, through focus, a sense of background, no longer plays a functional role in the transverse, accretional, distracted process of computer screening. What many of the psychoanalytic or even postmodern theorists characterize as melancholic or apocalyptic in this new mode of cultural production is perceived as ecstatic, even anarchistically radical, by the cyberpunks.

Yet this ecstatic, transcendent, assimilating screening of cultural production, while both private and collective, in a completely new sense is also, finally, corporate. And, although traditional elements such as print and graphics do participate in constructing the new environment, the source is a machine— a technology in the literal sense of the word. In his article "Old Rituals for New Space," David Tomas describes the intersection of the new uses of the screen with its instrumental organization:

> In recent years, there has emerged a new form of electronic space that holds revolutionary promise as *the* fin de siecle metasocial postindustrial work space. Variously described as "a space that wasn't space," a "nonplace," and a space in which "there are no shadows". . . cyberspace is a postindustrial work environment . . . that provides a total and sensorial *access* to a parallel world of potential work spaces. . . . *Such sites are the essence of a postindustrial society*—pure information *duplicated in metasocial form*: a global information economy articulated as a metropolis of bright data constructs, whose plasticity is governed by a Euclidean model based on the given problematic of visualizing data, a problematic subordinated, in Gibsonian cyberspace, to the dictates of a transnational computer-based economy. (35; italics his)

Now, if the computer screen is soon to become *the* screen to the world as well as for our own so-called private production, its space will be *the* contested arena of the symbolic organization of cultural and economic power. How, then, can we intervene in that "screening"? What will constitute political resistance?

Katherine Hayles has written about the screen as a site of the "flickering signifier." In her article "Virtual Bodies and Flickering Signifiers," she works in the distance between the kinesthetic sensation of keystroke pressure and the electronic images that are distantly, complexly produced by it. This relationship brings her to an awareness of the play between pattern and random-

D O M A I N - M A T R I X

 76 PAGE

 PREV

 NEXT

 OPEN

 PRINT

 FIND

 HELP

 MENU

ness that working through machine language to software function produces (71). Because the "image-text," as she calls it, of the computer is not resistant, but fragile and changing, she is led to the following association:

> It may seem strange to connect postmodern bodies with print rather than electronic media, but bodies and books share a crucially important characteristic not present in electronic media. . . . Books carry information on their bodies. . . . The book . . . incorporates its encodings in a durable material substrate. . . . Print and proteins in this sense have more in common with each other than any magnetic or electronic encodings, which can be erased and rewritten simply by changing the magnetic polarities. (73)

I think Hayles has raised a key position here about the screen. I have developed the politics around this relationship between books and bodies in the section "Bringing Home the Meat." Books as property and the complex relationship among books, private property, nation, and the "live" body are worked out in some detail there. It is hoped that they will resonate with this position here. But Hayles uses this association to arrive at another point about the politics of the computer screen that I think begins to suggest a direction for the development of a political critique.

Hayles regards the influence of technology and the direction of some of its reception to create a "contemporary pressure toward dematerialization," which affects both human and textual "bodies" on the level of both the "material substrate" and the "codes of representation" (73). On the level of code, she arrives at the phenomenon of the "flickering signifier": "In informatics the signifier can no longer be understood as a single marker, for example an ink mark on the page. Rather it exists as a flexible chain of markers bound together by the arbitrary relationships specified by the relevant codes" (77). Hayles moves from this relationship to issues of ownership, insisting that the world of the "single marker" encouraged the sense of private ownership, whereas access, the key to informational systems, reconfigures the orders of public/private (84). To counter the move toward the dematerialization inherent in this mode of production, Hayles wants to think how the two orders, the material and the virtual, may be reconfigured, not as bipolar opposites, which is leading to the evacuation of the former for the latter, but as interwoven in some necessary way.

In the example below, read in relation to the section "Bringing Home the Meat," I want to imagine how one of the software functions, the screen blanker, might be received as a corporate effect. Establishing the screen blanker as a signal of ownership, how could one imagine resisting its insistence on corporate production and its "flickering" call to the virtual? The following sections set up various responses to experiences at the computer as critical models for imagining resistance.

THE COMPUTER COMETH

 MENU
 HELP
 FIND
 PRINT
 OPEN
 PREV
 NEXT
 77 PAGE

IVC. BLANKING OUT

While writing these sentences, I stopped to consider how I would construct my following section. When my gaze returned to the computer screen, I discovered that the screen blanker had activated, and my written text had been replaced by multicolored, flying windows which seemed to be coming at me from a great distance. They began as mere dots, then grew into full-fledged windows which trailed off, on one side, into a digital fragmentation of themselves. Because they seemed to travel toward me, I "read" the black background as space. When I began to type once again, they disappeared, and my print text once more commanded the screen.

So, effectively, any writing of "performing" or "lesbian" gives way to those windows, those icons of a software program "saving my screen." The scrim of print culture is shot through with the dark screen of icons, representing Microsoft's success in the wildly expanding market of information systems. Corporate ownership of the tools of writing marks its territory in the very space of writing. The function of "saving" the writing screen flashes a corporate billboard, overwriting the script—the high capitalist version of putting the text "under erasure." The "window to the world" effect that the computer produces is claimed by the corporate logo. The claim to the new space has already been filed by Bill Gates. How, then, to recover the screen of my writing from these effects of corporate territorialization? If the computer screen has swallowed performance, perhaps some performance strategies can at least intervene in its digestion.

Obviously, Microsoft Windows is not the only screen blanker in use. One can buy any number of programs that seem to instill one's own taste within the screen, but the critical point remains the same. The consumer buys a screen saver that flashes an image created by someone else, whose signature resides somewhere in the process of viewing the screen. If not in the blanker, one might remember other ways the corporations insist upon their logos. Apple requires the user to click on the Apple logo, for example, in order to access a variety of functions. The aim is to become aware of the familiarity these logos encourage as the user makes daily use of them and how they intrude, in subtle but insistent ways, into her spaces of work and play.

Heiner Müller, the leading playwright of an erstwhile national space that was both constituted and deconstituted in his lifetime, that of East Germany, describes one way in which performance/texts may claim space, while not necessarily colonizing it. He begins by citing Gertrude Stein on Elizabethan literature:

> In a text about Elizabethan literature, Gertrude Stein locates power in
> the rapid change of meaning in language: "everything moves so much."

> Change of meaning is the barometer measuring the pressure of experi-
> ence in the dawn of capitalism, which begins to discover the world as
> market. The tempo of change of meaning constitutes the primacy of meta-
> phor, which in turn serves as a blinder against the bombardment of im-
> ages. (Müller 1990, 125–126)

By turning to dramatic practices adopted along with capitalism, Müller seeks
to identify just how capitalist processes are inscribed in performance scripts.
He discovers that the bombardment of images and the tempo of rapid change
enact processes of commodification and market practices. Yet they also produce their own limits. Against their alluring flicker, "blind" metaphor stands
as a transient but stable space within which something other than shifting
market economies may be inscribed. For Müller, the blindness of metaphor is
produced in language by its retreat from explanation, and within concerns of
social activism by the pristine distance it keeps from any specific directives.
Hence, "blind" metaphor may "take" and hold inscriptive space against the
market's "bombardment of images" without inscribing any precise logo of
meaning or ownership in either its discursive or its social space.

Müller then composes performance scripts which emulate high capitalist
advertising modes by bombarding the performance space with accelerating,
accumulating images, which nevertheless founder at the occupied territories
of blind metaphors. For example, in *Hamletmachine*, "characters" such as
Hamlet and Ophelia display no history or psychological makeup. They suggest the production of an internal, private, capitalist space of self, but do not
actually produce it. Instead, Hamlet and Ophelia organize sites onstage where
images produced by the specific effects of nationalism, capitalism, gender
subordination, and defeated desire bombard the empty but occupied site of
Hamlet/Ophelia. Ophelia, in particular, as woman within patriarchal capitalism, organizes a site of the dispossessed. She is assigned a particular space
within production, but dispossessed of value within the system. Ironically
citing her drowning, Müller sets Ophelia amid the garbage, the waste of capitalist colonialization: *"The deep sea. Ophelia in a wheelchair. Fish, debris,
dead bodies mad limbs drift by"* (Müller 1984, 58). She lingers there, the
final image of the play, as dispossessed and possessing the closure—blankly
fixing the borders at her site as all there is of future, or promise.

Müller's spatial organization of what was once "character" thus
desubjectifies the performance space, as Deleuze and Guattari describe such
an operation in their notion of "nomadology": "Feelings become uprooted
from the interiority of a 'subject,' to be projected violently outward into a
milieu of pure exteriority . . . no longer feelings but affects. . . . The
deterritorialization velocity of affect" (356). In this way, such sites denoted as
"character" deterritorialize while they occupy, take performance space. In

their insistent exteriority, they play against the interiorizing capitalist state.

The organization of such sites also institutes heterosexist assumptions. As the strategy moves from one against capitalism to one against the regime of gender and heterosexism, its identification changes from "blind metaphor" to what, in lesbian and gay theory, Jonathan Dollimore terms "blind mimicry." Through camp, which Dollimore asserts "undermines the depth model of identity. . . . hollows out from within, making depth recede into its surfaces," "blank mimicry" creates a performative space that is anti-normal, but which produces nothing as an alternative mode (310). Dollimore uses Joe Orton's *What the Butler Saw* to identify the operations of such mimicry. In Orton's play, Dollimore discovers that the madcap drive from any domain of "normalcy" in gender codes, sexual codes, legal codes, or the medical codes of insanity leads to a "blank mimicry"—one which does not imitate the dominant in its parody of it, but creates a blindness to it. "Blank mimicry" thus claims the space the dominant would hold, but apes it, blankly producing what Dollimore understands as perversion. Dollimore's blank space-out resists the occupation of gender and sexual practices. Perversion is its form of deterritorialization.

Recalling the screen blanker, where corporate logos claim space on the screen, an adaptation of such strategies may be deployed to deterritorialize the billboard effect by offering a design of fields which betray no alliances, but instead organize a deterritorializing logo. They might claim space, but for no perceptible owner. "Saving" the screen then takes on a different set of implications. The screen, as territory, is being claimed every three to five minutes, across all texts. For whom? By what? Guerrilla graphics might help to promote the space wars initiated by the hacker's cry *"information wants to be free."* Yet beyond the hacker's anarchism, the composition of these deterritorializing spaces would specifically breach national structures of ownership alongside hierarchical structures of gender and sexual practice. As inhabiters of space, they would suggest, as they disavow, the exact limits of corporate, nationalist space claims on the screen of cultural production. Blind, flat, signifying spaces would also contrast to Microsoft's perspectival conceit of "deep space." The perspective embedded in the Windows logo, as old as the king's Gaze, hurls the Windows logo outward toward the computer operator, creating the graphic suggestion of an "origin" of the flying icons—they come from Microsoft to you. Let, instead, a blind Tiresias dance across the corporate screen, prophesying the destruction of the values of ownership in a language and choreography that no one can translate. As Hakim Bey's "voluntary illiteracy" offers a practice that would break all codes of translation, these performances of deterritorialization are the interrupt signal of the screen's own organization of space—the already occupied territories of the future.

IVD. PLAYING THE CYBERSTREET: HAMLET REVERSED

At the computer screen, writing is stretched thin across the modem highway, out into the new virtual world. The process of writing is vulnerable to outside infection from a computer virus; shopping could split its screen; the arrival of email could flash at the top corner; sex lines are calling; people of all sorts are masquerading through loops of false addresses, cavorting about in the same space as my writing. I'm writing out on the screen-street, thinking on my cyberfeet.

Recalling Hamlet, once again, as the door to the play of interiority on the stage, the character from the era of the formation of the capitalist, bourgeois self, stepping downstage off the court plenum to ponder a new, private "within," imagine performance across the computer screen as "going through Hamlet backwards." The long, three-century reign of the capitalist project of interiority and private ownership, concomitant with the creation of the author and the privileging of print, is drawing to a close. Production on the corporate, global screen is more consonant with the emblematic stage that preceded Hamlet than with his recession from it. Critics such as Francis Barker in *The Tremulous Private Body* and Catherine Belsey in *The Subject of Tragedy* have sketched the emblematic stage as world, or court, where the players strut out their meanings across a space that was defined by location. Before Hamlet, Barker argues, the stage operated as an image of "the indivisibility of the plenum":

> The keynote is the very visibility with which the space is delineated: it is the pertinent metaphor, as concrete as any could be, for the indivisibility of the plenum. . . . This is why so many stand around, paying attention or not, near the action of the throne, in the center of the kingdom and of the family. They and we are attentive or indifferent, but *necessary* spectators here . . . because no other conditions are extant. (34)

There is nowhere else to "be" than somewhere on the plenum. Barker conjures up the sense that any position or "cross" onstage is in direct relation to the seat of power. Every gesture, every instance of blocking performs what there is of knowledge and experience by its location. Proximity to, or distance from, the throne or the Hellmouth produces meaning and value by its location. Exterior relations across space constitute the workings of power, thought, and feeling. As Belsey points out, Knowledge is an actor in *Everyman*. The computer screen as cyberstreet is homologous to Barker's notion of the indivisible plenum. The scrim of text or image across the screen is "standing around" in the indivisible cyberspace of information, communication, commerce, and entertainment. What remains of the former bourgeois interior subjectivity, emulating print and authorship, nostalgic for focus, privacy, and the remove of concentration, operates as a website, or an address, on the techno-stage of interactive functions. The key difference is the absence of a throne or any site as source of value. The sense of Mosaic, the name of one navigating system on the World Wide Web, better captures the accretional process of value. Value on the cyberstreet is a side effect of where one has traveled, or who or what has made an appearance on the screen, or a kind of acceleration through different sites. Knowledge is not an actor but an effect of locations. The distinction among erstwhile interior processes and exterior effects has been subsumed by the morphing, traveling, simultaneously appearing screenic processes. Hence, the cyberpunk graffiti mix of genres, genders, and identities, biting philosophy and feelings alongside comix and digital sound, is out on the street—a mosaic of cultural production. Knowledge, or self, is "where you're at" and "what you do."

This exteriorizing process of the cyberstreet seems suspiciously similar to those strategies currently perceived as subversive. Unfortunately, as we have seen in section Ia, "Queer Performativity," polemics organized as seeming contradictions to the dominant order, claiming a subversive status, actually emulate these structures of global capitalism and its screen. Take, for instance, the influential notion of "nomadology" cited above. This is a strategy reproduced and appropriated by a variety of feminist and cultural studies critics for seemingly subversive ends. From Rosi Braidotti's use of it in understanding a global, "nomadic" feminist subject, to Elizabeth Grosz's adoption of it as the correction to her earlier psychoanalytic approach to a feminist and lesbian political critique, nomadology is received as an effective move out of the State, or the dominant order. Yet nomadology's strategy of exteriority as the subversion of the State's interiority emulates new corporate global screen practices. Regard this example that Deleuze and Guattari proffer as the rules of the game:

> A Go piece has only a milieu of exteriority, or extrinsic relations . . . according to which it fulfills functions of insertion or situation. . . . In chess it is a question of arranging a closed space for oneself . . . of going from one point to another. . . . Go proceeds altogether differently: . . . make the outside a territory in space . . . deterritorialize the enemy by shattering his territory from within, deterritorialize oneself by . . . going elsewhere. (353)

Does this process describe the workings of the screen of email, shopping, quick-time movies, computer games, sound bites, and writing? The net, the network, the superhighway, the hacker, the cyberpunk, the gopher all operate as exteriorities busily inserting, morphing, entering stealthily by windows, being entered, perforated, permeated, and moving on. The throne is nearby,

DOMAIN-MATRIX

82
PAGE

PREV

NEXT

OPEN

PRINT

FIND

HELP

MENU

the Hellmouth constructed down the superhighway in some MUD, and all the men and women, if you can imagine them as that, or whatever they choose to sign on as, are merely strutting players signifying through entrances and exits.

Going through Hamlet backward to the emblematic stage, or to the indivisible plenum, is what this new era of the computer screen establishes as the performative space. Writing as linked to interiority is merely playing out its final act as a tragic obsession. Subverting the State by exteriority is playing onto its screen. What, then, is politics? Is it really the melodrama of hegemony against diversity, as the last decade has insisted? What if diversity is the mode of screenic performance, yet its ground is a corporate one? The subversive potential, then, is clearly not the practice of exteriority—screen as Go. However, the specificity of exteriority's oxymoronic blank identity adds the subversive spice to its global stew. Ophelia, as dispossessed, is still "woman." How is a screenic space anything like "woman"?

IVE. TURBO-LESBO

Much of the writing of this text occurred in the midst of major software problems for me, which caused a deep level of panic about "saving" my writing, "finding" it again, and being able to "print it out." Technological decisions consumed most of my time and anxiety, which occasioned email queries to help lines and a performance of crisis across several bulletin boards. A butch lesbian, secure in performances of drag, I was regendered into the helpless, feminized role of petitioning young men who could drive the hot rods of software to scale my 486 turbo tower and rescue me from its failure to open my files. As I proceeded out into the world of software and even hardware, I discovered a world almost completely dominated by young men, who replicated their gender and sexual performance anxieties in the functions they created as well as in their modes of problem solving. Wandering through various sources on computer lore, I found my solutions to the problems of producing this text nested alongside new developments in software pornography, and vicious interactive games with racist and misogynist narratives. I sought refuge along the way in electronic communities which promised shelter from that world, such as the cyber-reconstruction of Sappho—a bulletin board of writing lesbian.

Online, one lesbian body takes space as Sappho, reconstructed as scrim, interpenetrated by communal messages, traveling through the Internet, "bundles," and "branches," creates a "Screen Skin Utopia" out into global dimensions. As Sappho, that lesbian is an island, once known as Lesbos—the root of the term. Judy Grahn, the lesbian feminist poet, wrote Sappho as an island: "Everything she represents lives on an island. . . . an island of appar- ent safety for women. . . . The love bonds established between her and other women were open. . . . She lived on an island of women in the company of women" (6). Grahn's 1970s separatist space of women's bookstores and presses, where the lesbian body was "safely" produced, lingers still in the 1990s cyberbody of Sappho.

Sappho's Electronic Body

Sappho is an electronic bulletin board focused on lesbian issues and iden- tities. "Women" from around the world participate in this virtual commu- nity, primarily, it seems, through the Internet, which includes university cam- puses in the United States and Europe, but also NASA and the Jet Propulsion Lab. Some members, who work for companies such as municipal utilities, sign on from commercial nets. Others may join through their subscriptions to CompuServe or MCImail. Sappho evidences the new cybercommunity, or social "body," now possible for lesbians. Access to the bulletin board is par- ticularly useful for the lesbian isolated, perhaps even closeted, at her job, or one geographically isolated from lesbian communal activities. On Sappho she finds an ongoing conversation about current concerns at her fingertips. She "meets" other lesbians, thus able to keep "abreast" of activist projects, subcultural fashions, and sex-radical pleasure practices on the "privacy" of her own screen. However, in contrast to Grahn's earlier community, writing across computer networks requires a privilege of access. Whereas early les- bian feminist publishing might have been produced by a mimeograph ma- chine in the basement, these women write from within positions at institu- tions which can afford the massive computer hardware to make the Internet available to their workers. One might argue that access to reading and writ- ing and the technologies of cultural production have always required privi- lege, such as education, leisure time, and the material means of distribution. Yet the concentration of capital required for the computer "banks" out into the Internet makes a sharper distinction between economic classes than the mimeograph machine might. Access to these secured pools of capital/infor- mation requires the advanced education, the disciplined personality, and the consequent lifestyle that permits integration into complex bureaucratic, hier- archical institutions. "Sappho," then, is partially an effect of the profes- sionalization of many of its subscribers.

This Sappho tirelessly composes herself twenty-four hours a day, seven days a week. Daily, approximately 75 to 125 new messages arrive onscreen, with topics ranging from discussions of a lesbian character on a TV show, to "outing" closeted performers, to debates over racism in the movement, to providing advice on sex toys, narratives of breakups and meetings, confer- ence announcements, requests for bibliographies of lesbian books, notices of

D O M A I N - M A T R I X

84
PAGE

 PREV

 NEXT

 OPEN

 PRINT

 FIND

 HELP

 MENU

public demonstrations, calls for email protests of various issues, news items, and reports on local social activities. Because the bulletin board community, out of concern for the safety of its space, refused several requests to quote its writing, or to report specifically on its composition and members, I will refrain from any actual quotations from the board, and only generally discuss its profile. My interest in it is not to create a specific study, but to consider it as an example of a cyberlesbian body.

"Performing lesbian," in this instance, signifies the composition of Sappho's virtual body/community in its dialogic, electronic space. The virtual nature of this body, however, has inspired anxieties about the eligibility of its membership. Constituted as lesbian, but identified only by electronic address, how can the members be certain that no man is online with them? No heterosexuals? Defining itself as a kind of separatist community, in the specificity of its denotation, the problem of membership on Sappho resides in determining who is behind the words onscreen. How to screen the lesbian? How to deny access—to protect against the voyeur? In this case, masquerading as lesbian requires only a fabricated address and an imitation of lesbian concerns and issues. On the other side of the issue, when a specifically "lesbian" address does cross the lines, it requires a certain protection when traveling through generally accessible nets. For while Sappho's serene isle may exist, it floats within a wide sexist sea. Sappho's body, traveling down the information highway, is surrounded by the hot rod bodies of racist, sexist cyberporn. Moreover, right-wing Fundamentalists, already organized on Christian bulletin boards, may, in different ways, abuse the knowledge of lesbian dialogue and address. While a certain postmodern lesbian critique applauds the destabilized condition of this identity, and the primary status of masquerade, the spread of the anti-homosexual Right agenda makes masquerade a potentially dangerous, violent act.

If, in the world of electronic communities, masquerade provides not only pleasure, but also the opportunity for a kind of invasive terrorism, then perhaps a different kind of encrypting the lesbian address might better serve as a security system. Now, there are encrypting programs available that scramble messages. "Cyberpunks," a group in Silicon Valley, has produced cryptography freeware that it has distributed over the Internet. Yet the federal government has already suggested something called the "Clipper chip" that would be installed in computers to open a back door to all data sent and received. It is, in other words, an inbuilt scrambler that acts like the old phone taps. This means that scrambling messages may likely be too simple to break.

Looking once more to performance texts for a model of subversive screenic practices, certain operations in the inventions of Gertrude Stein may be identified as pertinent. Although Stein was not strictly cyber, the Cubist element in her experiments made spatial organization central to her writing. These spatial subversions were not mere formal folly to Stein, but a component of her lesbian security system. In Stein's script, the spatial traditions of meaning inscribe not so much the problem of late capitalism as high heterosexism, which is laid, like land mines, within the linear prescriptions of grammatical conventions. The one-way street of print grammar terrifies Stein, who, according to the lore, when she did not know how to put her new car in reverse, rather than ask for help (probably from a man, who could drive the machine) abandoned the car and walked home. Spatial reorganizations divert this drive to heterosexist coupling, helping to create an encrypted lesbian address. Along with textual choreography, Stein's performance texts vociferously and repetitively circulate meaning in the system of representation while keeping its denotation unavailable. Stein does not want to give out her address, for the production of meaning in print grammar depends upon the reproduction of heterosexual mating rituals Stein calls "dating."

In her manual *How to Write*, Stein notes the mandate, in grammar, to "arrive at a meaning." Sentences make "dates," as Stein calls it, with signification. Stein: "Grammar makes dates. Dates are a fruit that may be pressed together or may be lain [*sic*] in a box regularly still attached to a stem. In this way they think" (57). In an act of deep compression, Stein has conflated traveling down the print highway to meaning with grammar, dating, and, suggestively, lying in a box together. Later in her "manual," Stein further develops the notion of grammar as the print highway: "Two nuns inside a motor omnibus and a nun driving it that is it. They got out before they came to their destination" (313). You can't get a date with Gertrude Stein. She's around, but she's impervious. Like the nuns in the bus, she keeps circulating, but she exits before you can open the door.

Subverting this "dating" game, Stein encrypts the address to which her meanings are sent by complex assignations of dialogue to character and scattershot repetitions of signs throughout the texts. Like her Cubist counterparts, Stein invents a syntax which points to the spatial organization of its production. Complex assignations of dialogue to characters, syncopated through repetitions, not only disrupt the organization of print space on the page, but successfully hijack the "omnibus" grammar that would send along its narrow streets. Consider the following example from her play *Pink Melon Joy*:

> Come in.
> I don't mean to antagonize the present aged parent.
> That is a strong present leaf.
> Line.
>
> Line line line away.
> Line.
> Lining.

DOMAIN-MATRIX

86
PAGE
PREV
NEXT

OPEN

PRINT

FIND

HELP

MENU

> I don't care what she mentions.
> It will be very funny when I don't mean to say it.
> I can forgive that is to say chopping.
> Not any more.
> Will I be surprised with Jane Singleton. I will not if I meet her. I will not yet. I will say that. I am determined. It is so much. Good bye.
>
> I did do it then.
> Come back to me Fanny.
>
> Oh dear.
> Come back to me Fanny.
>
> That's a picture.
> When I remember how surprised I was at certain places which were nearly in the way I cannot doubt that more accumulation is needed. I cannot doubt it. (351–352)

Stein has used what spacing she can to break with the hold of the print text: indentation seems to suggest a swerve in the direction of meaning; double spacing may suggest change of character, or of scene. Space signifies alteration—intervention in the linear print production of meaning. The volume from which the text is taken is titled *Geography and Plays,* articulating the consonance between the terms as spatial.

Stein brings her experiments with print space together with encryptions of address. How many different "I" speakers are there? To whom are they speaking? What is a character, when no names may be found in their traditional position, along the left margin? Yet, seemingly out of nowhere, formal names are invoked. Jane Singleton and Fanny seem to be the objects of some action, and Fanny, explicitly, of desire. Of course, the name Fanny could also suggest a certain part of the anatomy. The "I" is presumably the author, but is actually located in a play as a character. The character is simply the position she takes in regard to others—a position that is not long maintained.

The rules of print are invoked in the section on lining—as if to interrupt any reading that would overlook their structure. The structure, then, determines how the position of the character "I" and the others, Jane and Fanny, must be organized on the page. Lining perseveres even when distributed in fanciful ways within the spaces of the page. It continues to organize even the "freest" of spaces. Although it is possibly a pun on "pining" away—particularly for Fanny (someone's). All of the elements somehow combine to complete the "picture" Stein is here relegating to the page, but suggesting as performance by writing it in the format of a play. What stage space and the blocking of characters within this play may be is up to the associative and imaginative powers of the players. **(See the discussion of Müller's** *Hamletmachine* **in the section of "Bringing Home the Meat"** subtitled "From Collective to Commodity" for some similar relations between text and performance.) Playful signals of lesbian desire are strewn across the spaces in an encrypted way. One might well imagine, for example, what places were "in the way" during her "accumulation." The indirect reference makes it all the more titillating to do so. A Fanny certainly is an object of her longing, and something has transpired with Jane. "It will be very funny if I don't mean to say it" as well as very funny if I mean not to say it provides keys to the encryption.

Much critical energy has been expended in tracking the lesbian in Stein's writing. I would suggest that "lesbian" is performed here as both a spatial intervention into "dating" practices and a certain figure of address that both traces and erases a complex return to referent. The encrypting process measures a distance from hetero-"dating" practices by refusing to "show up" for the denotation. In combination with playful teasing, this distance suggests that perhaps a specific address is located "elsewhere," within the spaces of the unsaid. The Gertrude lover sometimes peeks out, as she does, hidden behind Alice's skirts, in the autobiography. The foreplay, or report of sexual excursions, is available only to the reader who "knows" Stein as a lesbian and can read the intimations.

How might the cyberlesbian borrow this strategy from Stein? Perhaps rather than imagining encrypting her address as a masquerade of personae, she might, like Stein's Cubist counterparts, "sign" the screen by her organization of space on it, and the indirect way in which meanings are assigned upon it. Her visual writing style, then, like Stein's, would in this case "screen" the lesbian and make it more difficult for others to simply masquerade through a fake address. This strategy suggests a style of screen composition that would break with the nineteenth-century realist conventions that hold to the present sense of images onscreen. Writing would not conform to the pressures to "data," or information, but would tease "out" lesbian as embedded in spatial encryption. Is this strategy merely a mode of modernist practices writ large on the postmodern screen? Perhaps. But consider the appearance of screen icons as they are now conceived. Consider also the pressure to "data." Has the old regime of realism found a new performance, bearing, once again, the status quo? Were not those modernist "abstractions" or "detractions"—the spaces of Cubism or even Abstract Expressionism—shifting the social screen? If, as we have noted, Dollimore makes camp into a hollowing, flattening process, masquerade, illumination, interpermeable skin/screens abound in subcultural practices, then Steining the screen, Sapphing the net is the lesbian's signature two-step—her body.

Some will ask, "What about lesbians on welfare who can't afford computers?" "What about lesbians in the so-called third world?" Assuredly, as Kroker

D O M A I N — M A T R I X

88
PAGE

PREV

NEXT

OPEN

PRINT

FIND

HELP

MENU

and Weinstein put it, virtual is a class. But what class is television? What is its role in the third world? The aim of globalization, by definition, is to assimilate everyone. These are strategies for those already online to reorganize the future screen. What is lesbian, then, in this screenic worlding? Look at the icons of lesbian. Click on them and morph across their spaces: Sappho, Gertrude Stein, Judy Grahn, Nicole Brossard. . . .

IVF. THE HOT ROD BODIES OF CYBERSEX

In the chat room for new members on America Online, the conversation soon turned to the password for a certain porn bulletin board. Upon receipt of the password, half the people exited. I followed them, to find myself in a world of sexist remarks and the kind of talk that reminded me of dirty phone calls. I remembered reading about the first "rape" in cyberspace, where a woman was accosted by a violent, sadistic scenario someone sent to her before asking her permission. I looked up at the menu, where I saw the button that would censor incoming data, in case I had children in my house with access to the computer.

While Sappho's body is being reconstituted on a bulletin board, and spatial/address encryption may be suggested indirectly in feminist/lesbian theories and modernist writings, the hot rod cybersex body is already in full production. A multitude of porn bulletin boards already exist. One called "Chicago's Windy City Freedom Fortress" serves up pictorial displays of "everything from a woman going down on a dog, to up close and personal action potty shots to fisting the next door neighbor" (79). "Hot chatting," online flirtation, and sex cover more territory. Suddenly the bulletin boards begin to reveal the profiles of those who run them and those who subscribe. Some few are run by women, and many maintain an interesting, even high quality of "chat." For example, the book *The Joy of Cybersex* identifies Stacy Horn, the woman who runs ECHO, one of the large, arty boards, as "a stylish avenger to the prototypical computer nerd, [who] commands ECHO with grace, and a distinct and welcoming literary bent." Horn refers to her own board as an "electronic salon" (104). Women are in the minority, however, online. According to *Boardwatch Magazine,* only 10 percent of bulletin board callers are female (86).

Online activities often follow those of the first computer games. The games were composed of two genres: violence and sex. *The Joy of Cybersex* notes that the first "dirty" computer game was *Softporn Adventure,* published in 1980 by Chuck Benton. Fifty thousand copies were sold at the time, when there were fewer than 400,000 Apple computers. A new version of the game is now available on CompuServe as donationware (23). In 1983, Leather Goddesses of Phobos appeared, which had three "filth levels" and in which gender-switching was possible, but the book identifies 1984 as the turning point. In Leisure Suit Larry in the Land of Lounge Lizards, animated graphics, stories, a central character, and graphic anatomy are portrayed. The success of this game, reviewed positively in major newspapers and presses, encouraged the growth of the industry (23–27). Then came Macplaymate—eventually with a button that allowed the player to return to text immediately, in order to play at the work site and avoid surveillance. The electronic bunny, the Macplaymate, is available for the insertion of dildo icons, moved by the mouse into her orifice, exacting moans and groans. Penetration fantasies reached new depths with the release in CD-ROM of Virtual Valerie, in 1990. In full-color graphics, the player can enter her apartment, play her CDs, and enter her with a full regalia of sex toys. Macfoxes offers Misty, the cheerleader: "Across the top of the screen is a selection of tools: a vibrator, a cucumber, an inanimate object, which the program calls a 'dick,' a telescoping dildo," and you get a score for how hot you make her on the meter (61).

Unfortunately, sex games do not seem to be produced by or for women. Nor do women seem to buy them. Larry Miller of Interotica stresses that "regardless of the content, it's men who buy it [the software]. Men are more voyeuristic. . . . Generally, nothing is being done by and for women" (31). So cybersex reiterates the old sexist structures of the passive female and the active male, who literally "scores" when he penetrates her. The Adult Reference Library on CD-ROM offers these possibilities: "Do you like young love? You'll find it here. Do you like. . . . Your women pregnant, or lactating? There are Oriental women and women who aren't women at all. . . . You'll see both-sex folks, same-sex folks disporting, contortionists contorting" (55–56). The "you" emerges as pretty gender-specific, appealing to the traditional mix of racism and sexism.

In 1993, at the Comdex Fall Trade Show in Las Vegas, where leading hardware and software producers gather, CD-ROM sales hit new heights. The mobbed booths were selling porn. CD-ROM, as it turns out, is the best way to ship or carry porn into countries or states with strict laws, for the mirror-like disks offer no clue as to their contents and can be carried in an audio CD case. So what difference does it make? In one of the fastest-growing industries in the world, owned, operated, and produced primarily by men, the center of entertainment is in sexist porn. And the future for women online?

Certainly, the chat rooms on America Online are humming with lesbian encounters. The lesbian or queer dyke sex-radical project of the last decade or so has been to write sex. An interactive sex-writing site promises the pleasures of fantasy scenarios, roles, and appearances. Online sex seems to provide much of the pleasure that the sex-radical movement seeks. Group sex takes on a whole new dimension. A friend of mine reported having online sex with someone who was in her office in Hong Kong, before the work day began, and at the same time with another who was enjoying a break in Australia. Writing sex can happen anywhere the computer can be set up: the workplace, the private office at home, the jacked-in laptop in the lonely hotel room, etc. Sex may turn into relationships. One colleague has flown to several distant cities to meet her online sex partners in the flesh. The first divorce case has been filed against a wife who was having sexual relations online. The status of the virtual is tested by online sex. The regime of the flesh is tested as well. Writing sex finds a lively format.

The promise, problems, and possible threats inherent in online sex have already raised a number of familiar issues. Should the "hot" lines be censored? We have just witnessed a self-censoring shutdown of such lines by CompuServe, in compliance with the wishes of its German members. In December 1995, CompuServe denied access to two hundred Internet newsgroups because their communication was deemed indecent and offensive, in violation of German obscenity laws. Several issues arose. The international membership of the service was, in effect, legislated by one nation's influence. Cyberspace is already the global space that many economies and political structures seem to foreshadow. There are no international tribunes for its management. Nevertheless, the United States has just passed the Telecommunications Reform Act (February 1996), which includes a Communications Decency Act. The law bans materials considered "obscene" as well as making it illegal to display "patently offensive" material in a manner in which it could be seen by children. The ACLU has already filed a suit against the act, but President Clinton has already signed it. The frontier phase of the net may be over—its very organization tried through considerations of writing sex.

Feminists will recall the anti-porn debates that raged throughout the 1980s and into the 1990s. On one side were Andrea Dworkin and Catherine MacKinnon, who would pass legislation against pornographic materials in support of victims of sexual violence and of the porn industry; on the other were those who would protect freedom of communication between consenting adults and provide lesbians, who were historically denied access to writing their sex, the freedom to do so. The ferocity of the sex-radical position within lesbian political circles was fueled by Dworkin's and MacKinnon's censoring ordinances. As the ACLU had foreseen, the materials to be censored were not only those produced by the familiar porn industry, but, in the case of Canadian laws, the photographs of the lesbian/queer dyke subculture shot by Della Grace and the photo/theory books published by the lesbian collective called Kiss and Tell. The historical irony of laws encouraged by feminists shutting down lesbian sexual discourse still guides debates in the 1990s.

In the case of CompuServe, the censorship was based upon words that seemed to suggest pornographic exchanges. For this reason, they denied access to the women's newsgroup dedicated to discussions of breast cancer. These sad ironies occasion a series of questions. How does one constitute pornography? How does one create a safe space on the net? How define the space of consenting adults around a screen in the home where children may live? How contemplate the various cultural contexts for explicit sexual materials in different nations, within different subcultures? The latter question reminds me of a debate I witnessed on a panel dedicated to writing sex in an international festival for women playwrights. The playwright from Sweden reported that children saw so much sex on TV that, ironically, it affected the girls' ability to discover their own pleasure. For the boys, the graphic depiction encouraged copulation. The girls had less a sense of their pleasure, but found themselves, early on, caught up in the most traditional sexual scenarios. The playwright from Argentina felt that any representation of sex on the stage would be liberating within their repressive regime. The lesbian playwright from London reported that their concern was in depicting lesbian sexual acts, not to provide titillating porn for voyeuristic straight male audience members.

Trouble, the protagonist of *Trouble and Her Friends,* who launched us into the Domain-Matrix at the end of the section on "Cruising/Surfing the Matrix," was driven underground by a similar international law that legislated and thus delimited the net. The lesbian couple in the novel illustrate the two choices remaining after such legislation: Trouble drops out, withdrawing into a small artists' commune, and abandoning her expertise in hacking; Cerise joins a global corporation, where she uses her expertise to develop programs designed to keep hackers out. Trouble lives on the brink of poverty and Cerise in the luxury that global corporations can provide. The novel concludes within the last outlaw village on the net. The lesbian couple reunites by cleaning up the town, where the outlaw Trouble will become the next mayor.

IVG. DRIVING MY MOUSE

While I cannot yet drive the hot rod computers on the fast track, I have learned to drive a mouse. My hand on the back of the beast, scooting around the space of the desk, clicking on the icons, navigating cyberspace, is the site where my "meat" melds with the machine. I'm wired, "jacked-in" through my mouse to the organizing functions of my writing and my modem receiving.

Raymond Barglow, both a computer analyst and a psychological analyst, writes the relationship between human and computer as *The Crisis of the Self in the Age of Information.* Barglow reports that the "metaphorical talk" that

D O M A I N – M A T R I X

92
PAGE

 PREV
 NEXT
 OPEN
 PRINT
 FIND
 HELP
 MENU

has developed around computers is qualitatively different from that surrounding earlier technologies. Employing the example of driving a car, he notes that our sense of earlier technologies presupposed human agency (14). He chooses the example of driving a car because of its status as one of the central male fantasies in the culture. The fantasy of penetration, hurtling through space, and willful stopping and starting composes a relationship to the machine as an instrument, a servant. Feminists have noted how, in advertisements addressed to the male driver, the car is either feminized, in terms of the masculinized driver of it, or portrayed as a dildo. The language around computers, however, is about interface and feedback, indicating a more relational mode than driving. The move away from the sense of the machine as a tool marks the beginnings of cyberspace, where the machine produces sociality and something like intersubjective responses—what Scott Bukatman terms "terminal identity."

While the new sense of interface does reconfigure the relationship between the human and the machine, certain legacies from the earlier sense of it as tool, specifically as car, remain. The most crucial of these is the sense of speed or acceleration. The increasingly turbo-charged machines have quickly accelerated up through the 386, 486, Pentium 75, 100, 120. The computer may be the only product that changes more often than the automobile. Along with faster chips, immense software programs also promise speed. Leaving behind sequential lines of text which had emulated print in interfacing with software functions, the effect of Windows, and now Windows 95, promises faster access to more files at once through the icon, or the image. Designing the space of the screen, rather than the sequences of commands, streamlines the interface. For the user, the mouse is what "drives" the fast interface. It connects the body to the speed of the software, rendering the perception of the machine as what Virilio has termed the "static audiovisual vehicle." To drive it is to speed along on "the information highway" at such a speed that arrival is almost immediate. The transmission to Beijing, then, requires no arduous, lengthy travel, but appears almost immediately upon the "static vehicle's" windshield. In fact, the nature of "telepresence," argues Virilio, is constructed through a "general arrival," in which no sense of travel or distance is marked by passing time. Thus, to be "telepresent" is to be "here and elsewhere at the same time" (1993, 4). The requirement of speed, a notion of acceleration, supports this electronic transmission that arrives in the split second. Virilio has extended this drive for acceleration to associations with seduction and war. Looking back through the twentieth century, we find the famous Futurist Marinetti creating one of his first performances by driving through Europe in a fast car. Futurist speed and fascist war became good bedfellows. Yet, ironically, Virilio does not perceive this drive as encoded with masculinity; instead, he associates it with the "destructive" results of the "Women's Liberation Movement" and "homosexuals in the U.S." (1991, 80).

One might imagine Virilio's displacement of this drive's signification to signal his own anxiety in the move from tool, or prosthesis, to interface. For him, women and homosexuals haunt the new relationship with the "static vehicle"—no doubt because of its ultimately "static" presence that engulfs him. Barglow reports a similar anxiety in his patients, who panic in the interface at the feeling of the loss of individuation, (s)mothering in the continuing embrace the intricate lacings of the web provide (38). The mouse negotiates the ambivalence of that interface—providing something to drive that controls the machine as well as the tactile surface the machine provides for its massage. Ads for the mouse often promise both functions, as in Microsoft's phrase "it connects your mind to the machine," advertised in the computer culture journal *Wired*:

> An idea
> is followed by an impulse
> that shoots down your arm.
> Your fingers move
> across a keyboard.
> Words appear
> upon a screen.
> This is how we work,
> how we think,
> *how we are.* (*Wired*, June 1995, 35)

Several pages later, Microsoft continues, with another two-page spread:

> The machine is
> nothing
> but nuts, bolts and chips
> until infused with ideas,
> thoughts,
> notions,
> that come to it
> through a keyboard.
> Together with a Microsoft Mouse
> that *instinctively* slows the cursor
> when near an icon,
> that *knows* when to double-click,
> you have extensions of the machine,
> of the software . . .
> That connect you
> to a *mean, lean,*
> *thinking* machine. (67)

D O M A I N - M A T R I X

94
PAGE

 PREV

 NEXT

 OPEN

 PRINT

 FIND

 HELP

 MENU

I have italicized words that purposely combine the representation of both interface and a driving machine. The first ad is reminiscent of Oskar Schlemmer's Bauhaus experiments, in which the human body, costumed in geometric designs, extends its gestures outward, through poles. Within that kind of convention, the mouse is pictured as an extension of the arm, producing text. The final line, however, summing up the movement of ideas, exchanges the instrumental notions of work to the shared ontological sense of "how we are." Together, the mouse and the human constitute an entity. The second ad seems to make the traditional human/machine dichotomy explicit in its beginning, assuring "us" that a machine is nuts and bolts, but then ascribes "instinct" and "knowing" to the mouse, until it is the machine that is doing the thinking. A careful melding of human and machine is thus produced, beginning with a clear distinction that later confuses the terms. The mouse, then, is portrayed as the middle-"man" in a new cyborgean interface that the industry encourages between humans and machines—"us" and "them" are categories that begin to blur.

In science fiction and in the critique of science, this sense of the machine has produced a recurring image of the cyborg. One predominant image of the cyborg is the type produced in the *Terminator* movies, in which the cyborg is a masculinized killing machine, out to destroy (or protect) human life. This cyborg is the sublation of fascist regimes of the body, "smart" military weaponry, and patriarchal power. The narratives often pose the dilemma "If a cyborg can think, is it human?" The legacy of scientism and Enlightenment thinking ascribes "coldness" to pure rationality, or objective thought. Thus, ultimate rationality is similar to steel, the metal of machines, which also promises strength and endurance. The only "heat" such cold, resistant, tough material produces is violence. The sense of the machine's armor has been produced, argues Sandy Stone, since the 1930s, when "the guts of things . . . began to recede inward and the skin of devices such as toasters and vacuum cleaners became smooth and shiny" (1995, 398). Commodity fetishism offered up the machine as a gleaming spectacle of the commodity—a thing in shining armor. Several critics, using Klaus Theweleit's study of the fascist *Freikorps*, presume that "armor substitutes for the 'desiring machine' of a functional self: the armor of these men can be seen as constituting their ego" (Bukatman, 303) . Alternatively, as Hal Foster phrases it: "armored figures of commercial culture symbolically treat fantasmatic threats to the normative social ego" (Bukatman, 304). The conflation of armor with ego seems a familiar logic that offers a credible explanation, within Freudian assumptions. While the relations to the machine offer images of human functions, they do not produce a dynamic sense of the machine. The machine, as in the oft-employed notions of Deleuze and Guattari, remains a stable referent. Its seductive quality is an exclusively exterior one. It acquires complexity and interest only when it becomes a metaphor for human, generally psychological processes. Driving inward, the machine as "man" claims powers of revelation about individual and social processes, whereas the link to actual machines remains simplistic. **(See section IVa, "A Revision of the Gaze,"** for a similar treatment of technology situated as a "given" to reveal the complexity of psychological dynamics.) In such paradigms, machine is generally set against notions of "warm," "organic," and "emotional," which seem to signify positive, well-adjusted "human" attributes. Moreover, these dichotomies generally run along the gender divide. Machine is masculine and "warmth" is feminine. The false Maria, the "female" robot in *Metropolis,* illustrates how woman-as-machine represents social, emotional treachery. The machine has no compassion, while the woman Maria brings laborers unto her as unto a mother.

However, as Jonathan Goldberg has illustrated in his study of Arnold Schwarzenegger's *Terminator* image, the hypermasculinity of these cyborg representations may not enforce notions of sexual difference so much as suggest attributes assigned to the gay man. First the Terminator is portrayed as "anti-reproductive" in order to "ensure the end of the human race" (243). As anti-reproductive, the Terminator suggests the heteronormative image of the gay man. Goldberg notes that the cyborg body "like the bodybuilder's body is grown" (244). He then likens the Terminator to the gay leather man: "he embodies—or bears the image of—leather culture, displaying machismo with a difference" (246). Goldberg is able to see Schwarzenegger's Terminator as "pure Tom of Finland" (well-known drawings of super-leather-men) (247). Whether Goldberg is describing Schwarzenegger's performance or performing gay male spectatorship, the point is the same—that hypermasculinity may be read as gay, making that kind of cyborg an image to disorient gender roles along the axis of sexual performance. Goldberg's reading suggests the point this book entertained in the discussions of queer performativity **(see section Ia, "Queer Performativity").** Contemporary images of the melding of, specifically, man with machine may indicate the kind of queer crisis figure that has accompanied this transition from print culture into the new cyberworld. In fact, Goldberg uses the Terminator image to press the argument for queer sex, that breaks down traditional lesbian and gay practices, asking, "what form of sex is it when a gay man and a lesbian have sex?" He concludes that "these questions take us back to the cyborg" (245). Queer and cyborg make good bedfellows, Goldberg argues, in imagining "a possibility for the future" (249).

In contrast, in spite of its title, Marge Piercy's novel *He, She and It* (1991) retains the traditional gendering of the cyborg, along with its killing intent. Situating the cyborg next to the Jewish *golem,* Piercy breaks the unmarked status of cyborg as part of the white, dominant culture. Associating the cyborg with an ethnic community, Piercy poses the problems of what, exactly, constitutes "live" or "human" as different from machine, alongside what consequences imagining the need "to protect the community" produces. Traditionally, the cyborg has begged the human/machine divide in terms of knowledge and rationality. In setting the question alongside endangered communities, either the Jewish ghetto or a sci-fi version of it, Piercy asks, "If the cyborg wishes to please, how is that different from love?" Unlike Goldberg's Terminator leather-man, Piercy portrays a heterosexual cyborg, whose violent strength is tested in combination with compassion and love. Piercy's cyborg carries on a rather lengthy affair with one of the women in the community. Sex with cyborgs, who are produced to please, takes up the pages of not only feminist writers such as Piercy, but also short stories in 'zines such as *boing boing* and *Mondo 2000,* where they fulsomely fill out male adolescent fantasies. Piercy, like the 'zines, keeps this sexual servitude in consonance with a violent one, but her narrative is more critical. Yes, in the familiar heterosexist paradigm, sex with the cyborg means intercourse. So, does that make the cyborg a sophisticated version of a dildo with software? Is it, like the Microsoft mouse, a combination of prosthesis and interface? Piercy's link between the role that the cyborg plays of service and satisfaction in bed, and the violent protector of borders runs counter to the sex-radical proffering of sex toys as political critique. **(See "Commodity Dildoism" in "Bringing Home the Meat.")** In her narrative, instrumentalizing relationships through notions of service and performance continue to retain violence at the borders of individual relationships and those among communities. The cyborg must be exiled or destroyed in order to cleanse the community of its tendency toward violent protectionism. Cyborg is tested against ethnic community, rather than queer subculture, offering a critique of violent separatism as a way to continue in the process of creating community.

The cyborg has a tradition of representing the positive prosthesis as well. Cyborgean meldings that improve damaged or limited bodies may represent positive couplings. Anne McCaffrey's *The Ship Who Sang* (1969) portrays the melding of a machine with a handicapped girl, who becomes an ace pilot of the ship she partially "is." The notion of cyborg aids the constitution of human, amplifying its possibilities. Other postmechanical meldings between human and machine may break with masculinized, violent narratives, while retaining other stereotypical constraints on the composition of the "organic." In the work of Octavia Butler, the "machine," the spaceship, may be a complex of organic materials. Butler breaks with the metallic and thus the mechanical tradition of machine. Yet, in Butler, this new recombinant cyborgean sense runs along narratives that privilege heterosexual and reproductive contact. Butler successfully extends a kind of ecosystem through the technological. Hers is a kinder, gentler future, in that sense. Consequently, the prior sense of the mechanistic haunts her texts as the "unnatural," which, unfortunately, also seems to apply to sexual orientation that is not heterosexual and reproductive. The latent bond between these two traditionally linked uses of the "unnatural" is worrisome in her work. Whereas Goldberg would celebrate the break that cyborgs produce with heteronormativity, Butler would realign the organic with the reproductive. The trace of ethnicity in Butler's world, as in Piercy's, operates alongside a critical intervention into the tradition privileging cyborg/machine as violent. Yet they also privilege heteronormative sexuality. Goldberg offers a queer reading of the cyborg, associating the violence with an s/m sexual practice that breaks with heteronormativity but is also anti-community, in the individualist tradition of the Terminator, and unmarked as "white."

Anxieties of gender and sexual practice accompany anxieties around the move from the mechanistic to the electronic world. As Barglow noted in the beginning of this section, how one imagines the human position in the new, postmechanical age recalls performance anixeties, penetration metaphors, and phobias of the womb. In this sense, the cyborg is the "uncanny," as Freud established it, in reference to the engulfing cybersphere. Octavia Butler emphasizes a neo-organic world, in contrast to the passing mechanistic one, while others inflate masculinist, cyborgean machines to maintain it. Claudia Springer, in "Muscular Circuitry," suggests that the ever more grandiose version of man/machine may signify the obsolescence of both the mechanical and the masculine in the era of the electronic: "it is this feminization of electronic technology and the passivity of human interaction with computers that the hypermasculine cyborg in films resists" (Springer, in Bukatman, 306). Like the ads for the Microsoft mouse, a transitional phase is marked, from mechanical tool to electronic interface, but in "muscular circuitry" it is marked by resisting becoming "how we are." Springer notes that the anxiety may be prompted by an association with the masculine as external hardware and the feminine as internal circuitry. In other words, being drawn "into" a relationship with internal circuitry is imagined as relating to the feminine. In such a relationship, an anxiety similar to that of castration is produced, as registered above in the work of Virilio. Thus, Springer perceives the hypermasculinity not as transgressive (as in Goldberg) but as reactionary. In associating this armored effect with commodity fetishism, with the gleaming surface of the thing in shining armor, one could also read the hyperarmored cyborg as retaining the sense of commodity as thing against its passing into cybercirculation within the screen. **(See a discussion of this process in the section entitled "The Flowing Locks of TV.")**

> *I was seeing my mind as a vast empty space, subdivided by an interface or membrane. The dividing surface was absolutely still, still as ice and hard, like the surface of a pond in the dead of winter. I felt trapped. I had to break through, or suffocate and die.*

Barglow records this dream, which his patient Robert, a programmer, related to him. Barglow reports that Robert had a compulsion to log into his email multiple times during the day, especially after completing an "outside" activity. In tracing *The Crisis of the Self in the Age of Information*, Barglow includes this dream as an example of the peculiarly current anxiety around individuation and agency that the computer has prompted (38). Like Springer, he sees the move to relation with "internal" circuitry as different from the external, mechanistic image of the machine. Moreover, Barglow emphasizes that the relationship with computers is one of connection, rather than the traditional association of tools with agency, or domination. He concludes that the recurring association with connection rather than separation promotes an anxiety of sovereignty and self (6). Barglow retains the traditional psychological concepts into which he reads the interface with the computer, once more evacuating a study of the experience of computers in terms of technology, for the metaphorizing of technology into stable psychological constructs. Nevertheless, Barglow creates a record of impressions of the move into interface—the fear of the cyborgean relationship which might promote the fantasy of the menacing, dangerous cyborg.

In contrast to the murderous images of cyborgs, or their psychoanalytic metaphorization, Donna Haraway's "A Cyborg Manifesto: Science, Technology and Socialist Feminism in the 1980s" proposes the cyborg as "an argument for *pleasure* in the confusion of boundaries." But pleasure, in Haraway's system, is not isolated into sexual functions. Haraway's cyborg is poised to make a critical intervention into systems of gender, class, and race. Her strategic utopianism sets the cyborg in "a post-gender world" (150) where it represents a "myth," as she calls it, of "transgressed boundaries, potent fusions, and dangerous possibilities" (154). Haraway proposes the cyborg as the solution to the problem of "warranting" posed by Stone, through which a unitary subject is enforced by the assignation of citizenship to a single body.

(See section IIc, "Getting the Point.") For Haraway, "the cyborg skips the step of original unity," offering a ludic, ironic, excessive strategy to deploy against both instrumentality and unity (151). She wants to encourage the partial, the part of something in place of totalizing systems and images—both in struggles with the subject position and in the locus of machines. Haraway's cyborg conforms to the new computer "world" by crossing a multitude of the borders patrolled by institutional and ideological guards.

Although Haraway openly desires a utopic vision in her cyborg article, in a later interview she qualifies the location from which she imagined it:

> What I was trying to do in the cyborg piece . . . is locate myself and us in the belly of the monster, in a technostrategic discourse within a heavily militarized technology. . . . At an extremely deep level, nature for us has been reconstructed in the belly of a heavily militarized, communications-systems-based technoscience in its late capitalist and imperialist forms. (1991, 6)

Her cyborg is part of a resistance against giving in, against despair at the military and "worlding" projects that technology actually brings with it. Socialist feminism offered her the tools for building this imaginary, strategic cyborg. She wants to contest not only commodity fetishism, with her cyborg, but its collusion with the military compound. Resistant to social norms, this cyborg is also resistant to capitalism.

Yet Haraway's cyborg, imagined as part of the feminist agenda, with its resistance to masculinist projects, is "a girl." Haraway describes how the cyborg's imagined gender works:

> Yeah, it is a polychromatic girl . . . the cyborg is a bad girl, she really is not a boy. Maybe she is not so much bad as a shape changer, whose dislocations are never free. She is a girl who is trying not to become a Woman, but remain responsible to women of many colors and positions that makes the necessary articulations with the boys who are your allies. It's undone work. (1991, 20)

Haraway's context of socialist feminism allows her to bring together the Marxist sense of modes of production and issues of ownership along with those of gender oppression. Her cyborg is, in fact, a metadiscourse for imagining that union in regard to technology. Haraway would wrest the interface from its violent associations with seduction and war to deploy it for the preservation and building of the habitat. The cyborg is not the inflated individual of global capitalist systems, but the feminist "bad girl" in coalition with the oppressed. Processes of territorialization, commodification, and capitalist labor inequities are built into this resistant cyborg.

Imagining the cyborg as sexy not only registers gender anxieties at the dawning of cyberspace, but also introduces a sense of the ludic in the consideration of the machine. As long as technology was perceived as a tool, its association with work was a simple one to maintain. Consequently, serious attitudes prevailed in its production and use. Not only was human posited as agency and technology as machine, but the human was sober and rational in the interface with it. Instrumental human agency has posed in dark, serious lifewear since the inception of the move to the interior space, as Barker describes with Pepys's diary—a record of hidden desire receding from the social space of spectacle. **(See section IVc, "Blanking Out.")** Puritans and Calvinists linked serious work to promises of eternal profit and all-black wardrobes (ironically now preferred in urban, underground circles). The development of computer software and the use of computers has defied this traditional sense, combining the ludic with work in a way that confounds earlier forms of development and research. In *The War of Desire and Technology*, Allucquere Rosanne Stone relates the demise of Atari as a narrative that illustrates how the role of the ludic has confounded traditional business practices. The suc-

D O M A I N - M A T R I X

100
PAGE

 PREV

 NEXT

 OPEN

 PRINT

 FIND

 HELP

 MENU

cessful programmers refused to distinguish between play and work—they were, after all, creating computer games (for great profit). Their work habits were unorthodox. They stayed up all night, playing at the machines, inventing new aspects of the programs as puzzles, mazes, entrances, and escapes. When new management brought the old style of working with technology, the serious, disciplined, product-oriented manner, into the firm, the profits declined (Stone 1995, 123–155).

In section IVb, "Out of Focus," the move away from focus in computer or screenic culture is sketched as a break with traditional structures of learning, seeing, and thinking. The notion of "work" shares many of the attendant notions to focus, such as preparation, concentration, and a strict division between "work" and "play." "Voluntary illiteracy," the strategy proposed by Hakim Bey (in "Out of Focus"), suggests a deeper sense of anti-authoritarianism than the so-called subversive strategies concocted by academics. Remaining outside the strictures and traditions of focus and work, obsessively playing outside the rules, is a model that confounds not only traditional business and academic practices, but even the political systems, such as feminism or Marxism, that would imagine alternative social organizations. Does this mean that the interface with the computer is an interface with a toy, rather than a tool? Is this what the narratives that imagine sex with cyborgs act out? In other words, are these sexy cyborgs a way to reimagine the machine as neither a tool nor a killing machine, but a site for pleasure?

At present, the huge conglomerates forming among computer technology, communications, and entertainment are raising the capital to produce the screen that melds these various functions into one. Called "synergies" in the 1980s, several media buyout/consolidations made dramatic news. For example, both the media and the stock market looked on as the long duel between Viacom and QVC to purchase Paramount Communications played out. Two cable companies struggled with one another to buy the Paramount conglomerate, which consisted of professional sports teams, book publishing, and the last independent movie studio in the U.S. Would QVC, the shopping channel, merge with the movie studio? In 1988 Sony bought CBS records, and in 1989 Columbia Pictures. Microsoft has bought a money-management system in preparation for its offer of online banking and, at the same time, secured the digital rights to the art in the National Gallery. During the late 1980s and early 1990s, some of the world's largest, most powerful corporations staked their claims to the ground for the cyberspace they were beginning to organize. Far-reaching plans are being made to consolidate all work and play into the single screen.

Computers are already equipped with rudimentary mixtures of work and play, sending them out into classrooms. The encyclopedia, one of the first Enlightenment projects that sought to encompass knowledge, is now interactive. Its appearance signals the new age of learning as interactive work/play, subsumed by the screen. Taking the market by force, Compton's Interactive Encyclopedia reconfigured serious Enlightenment imperial factuality into fun-filled factoids. It introduces itself by running a clip of Patrick Stewart in his costume as Captain Picard on *Star Trek: The Next Generation*. He explains how to access the short video clips, musical offerings, and traditional encyclopedic text for the student's perusal. Watching Captain Picard in this context prompts the kind of question the future will not even pose: When are you watching television, or a movie, and when are you studying? Is a figure about, say, the exports of Peru of the same order as Captain Picard?

The evacuation of the category of work complicates political critiques. What, then, is labor, so central to the Marxist analysis? How does the cyborg fit into socialist feminism? For Haraway, the category of labor still works in the equation—not necessarily in the traditional sense of it, but something she calls "the ontological structure of labor" (1989, 158). I'm not clear about what that means, but in her section "The 'Homework Economy' outside 'the Home'" she discusses labor in the familiar sense. Apparently, borders are not so easily crossed in considerations of production—particularly for women working in microchip factories in the third world, or reduced to unemployment or low-paying jobs assigned to them during the "New Industrial Revolution" (166). Haraway's point is well taken. Most of the "players" in software concerns are, after all, white men. Perhaps "work" is something that will be assigned to the "third world" as it is imagined by the first, and to poor women, while "play" will become, increasingly, the mode of the privileged media class. Understanding the distinction between work and play is as old as the notion of an aristocracy dedicated to leisured pursuits. While it is helpful in one way, to remind us that there is blinding, dull work in microchip factories, there is something else at "play" in this new set of attitudes that requires a new conceptual and political model.

Within considerations of online functions, however, I want to pose the following questions: How do you determine the value of play in the market? What constitutes oppression within such conditions? Is obsession, in this regime, oppression? Are the addicts of the computer, who ruin marriages and careers with their online addictions, the oppressed of play? A new character emerges in the 'zines, on TV, and in movie representations of these online addicts: the nerd has few friends and no social life, works alone at the terminal at home, "lives" online. Such a woman has been depicted in the TV series *VR 5* and in the movie *The Net*. I became acquainted with one while writing this book. This woman, who lives in Berkeley, makes her living as a software consultant. She tests new versions of software for "bugs," etc. She lives alone in an apartment which is also her workplace. She has covered the windows with aluminum foil. She has no fleshly friends to visit her, and leaves her

DOMAIN-MATRIX

102
PAGE

 PREV

 NEXT

 OPEN

 PRINT

 FIND

 HELP

 MENU

apartment only to accomplish the necessary domestic chores. Does she signify the future normative lifestyle? Is she having a good time yet?

Certainly, play has changed the parameters of how the screen is imagined in the social, the ideological, and the economic. Remember how, in *1984*, it was the screen of "Big Brother Watching You"? Now the question is, "Do you want to be constantly watching Big Brother?" Are you one of the soporific housewives, then, in Bradbury's *Fahrenheit 451*, who have simply "checked out"? Or is that the old, organicist notion—doesn't Bradbury imagine that, instead, the alert and alive are reading books somewhere out in nature? Will the machine actually perform the old Marxist dream of "fishing in the morning, ..."? In a world of play, what constitutes a plan of resistance? Against what? Online living prompts a new configuration of materialism. It also challenges images of the interface. Isn't the mouse, after all, something like a joystick—the interface with the video game?

A new complex is opening in Irvine. The intention is to construct "the jewel in the crown" of Edwards's Cinema. The immense complex contains restaurants, a large bookstore, a virtual-reality game center, a coffeehouse, and twenty-one screens. The twenty-first screen will be the first six-story 3-D IMAX theater on the West Coast. Here's an entertainment complex, then, which combines the culture of print, with its bookstore and coffeehouse, with twenty-one screens, virtual reality, and a six-story projection of 3-D. Las Vegas, once the home of stray gamblers, has refashioned itself to appeal to families by constructing fantasy environments in the giant casino-hotel complexes. Pick the fantasy you wish to inhabit for three days: the Luxor for the Egyptian pyramid; the ride down the Nile in the lobby; the Mirage for plots of natural plantings and "live" animal shows run by two "flaming" men, Siegfried and Roy; the MGM Grand, where the lobby offers you a full trip through Oz, with a changing sky across the massive ceiling, across which the witch sometimes rides; or the Excalibur for the medieval touch. Las Vegas has grown into a city, where you might also sleep in the pyramid, among *faux* Egyptian furniture, or shop, stroll, and eat along the Forum in Caesar's Palace, where fountains play beneath the sunny skies of Rome and exclusive Italian restaurants offer a fine fare. All of these landscapes are dotted with various sorts of gambling opportunities, so the patron may while away her money along with her time. The fantasy of getting rich accompanies the fantasy of getting away. The canned music and rolling images of slot machines accompany every tree, glitter beneath every projection of a sunny sky, intrude upon every set dressing of a period, or of nature itself. Money is an illusion, like any other. The screen is a surround—one is actually on the set itself—in the movie.

The new entertainment concept at Las Vegas is the virtual rides: "static audiovisual vehicles" as Virilio has foreseen, into which one is strapped, which bump along on their little hydraulic feet, emulating a roller coaster ride, while going nowhere. The ride is in the visual projection—the screen, to which the little bumps are tied. The sometimes 3-D illusion provides the thrill of space—dropping hundreds of feet in a fantasy about a pyramid, within the glass pyramid of the Luxor itself. Back home, the patron switches on the computer, where files, documents which contain "serious" information, come up on the same screen, where a game of Solitaire is available when one is bored, or Tetris, or Myst. The interface is no longer a cyborgean one, in the sense of a single meshing with the machine—it is in the surround. A screenic landscape locates the viewer. Ludic processes are everywhere—even money is fun. One can live in the screen, onscreen, in a movie set. What, then, is the "live" and, in conjunction, the body? Are they relegated to the realm of the "serious"? Is that why "live" performance is losing its allure? Why "live" performance is alluring only with special effects, such as those in *Cats*? Is it too slow—unable to meet the acceleration requirements of the screenic? Do robots already look antiquated in their emulation of bodies? Are gender and sex attributes of the live body, or its virtual representative, the subject? Is there any way out of the interface? Why would anyone want to exit the program? Isn't the Microsoft mouse ad correct in its phrasing—this is now the "way we are"?

IVH. TRIPPING INTO CYBER-REVOLUTION

If the interface with machine and tool is coded as masculine and that with "interior" electronic surround as feminine, perhaps the play of proximity might be deployed in ways suggested by earlier feminist critics, such as Kristeva in her notion of the semiotic, or Irigaray's and Cixous's notions of contiguity and proximity **(see section Id, "The End of Print Culture")**. Something like the 1970s feminist project of imagining a matriarchal society anterior to the patriarchal one, in order to displace its single power and to open another space for imagining social relations, might be used here to posit a "feminine" construction of an interface as *posterior* to the masculinist, mechanical one. Could the strategies for women writing be deployed within the screenic culture?

Constructing cyberspace foregrounds social space as a shared one. Only the pooling of vast resources can construct the superhighway. Its production and use are nothing if not crowded. Individualism, the individual subject, single units of private property are already merely citations of an earlier capitalist mode. On *Star Trek,* a collective cyborg has already made an appearance: the Borg is represented as an integrated system rather than individualist cyborgs. On the web, the individual is represented, perhaps, by a web page—a billboard for one's own persona **(see "Death of the Author/Birth of the Persona" in "Bringing Home the Meat")**. Moreover, the pleasure in the

DOMAIN-MATRIX

104 PAGE

 PREV

 NEXT

 OPEN

 PRINT

 FIND

 HELP

 MENU

process is in inhabiting multiple personae. Now, as a corporate structure, all of these multiple, proximate aspects of the new space are aimed toward profit. But profit is merely something imagined to found the value of the space. If debts can be forgiven, if bankruptcy can be filed by individuals, corporations, and even nations, if the world bank can "forgive," say, Brazil's debt and movement within the system can restore its health, what is profit? If the nature of focus, the structures of learning, and the role of work can be challenged; if play can make major "profits"; if space is collectively produced; if the interface "feels" contiguous; why imagine it as a realm aimed in any direction, why imagine it as having "owners" who identify by corporate logos, or national ones?

One day (and night), the poet Allen Ginsberg and several hundred thousand other people collected around the outside of the Pentagon, meditating and chanting in an effort to make it levitate. That effort, along with several thousand other such performances, what the underground terrorist Abbie Hoffman called politics that are "shouting theater in a fire," resulted in the end of the Vietnam War. People imagined that the streets were theirs, marching in Lesbian and Gay Pride parades down the major avenues of the urban centers, founding People's Park as a collectively owned space in Berkeley; they imagined that the institutions were theirs, inaugurating ethnic studies and women's studies into the universities and colleges; they imagined that jobs were theirs, inventing and supporting affirmative action, founding collectively owned food companies, bookstores—this on the heels of the Eisenhower era, the McCarthy witch-hunts—one of the most oppressive decades in U.S. history.

Looking back to the hippie era recalls an alternate consolidation of entertainment with work. Rather than synergies of suits, hippie communes, which dotted the landscape of New Mexico, Arizona, Oregon, Colorado, California, and other states, combined concerts, sex, and dancing with housebuilding. Making adobe bricks, de- and reterritorializing the land and its buildings, accompanied a style of music, clothing, graphic arts, hairstyles, dancing, and hallucinating. LSD rearranged the perception of space through hallucination. The "user" could, through a chemical interface, redesign the colors, proportions, and significations of space. It is no accident that one of the pioneers of cyberspace, Jaron Lanier, was also involved in experimenting with LSD. Through that interface, hippies deterritorialized urban and rural environments by wandering (unlike Benjamin's flâneur, somewhat like the Situationists' dérive) through them, settling upon them, playing their music where they would, etc. These were experiments in redesigning social space. Buckminster Fuller invented the geodesic dome for affordable living in another shape of space; the Whole Earth Catalog gave instructions for alternative constructions (now available on the web). How much easier to redesign a space that foregrounds itself as a fiction. Hackers are hackers because they are isolated in their attempts—together it would be a form of social sculpture.

Combining hippie and underground tactics with feminist ones in imagining the redesign of cyberspace may be a way in which to secure the coming millennial space as habitat rather than as the playground of the virtual class.

Body as Flesh Zone

The body appears at various sites in this text, within different contexts, making it at the same time too simple to isolate it out as an address, and crucial enough to warrant a consolidation of considerations. In Section IIc, "Getting the Point," the body is situated as an effect of the Euclidean definition of space and, following, through the semiotic sign of the icon. In Section IVg, "Driving my Mouse," the body is treated as a mode of production, either of labor or of pleasure. As cyborg, the body becomes fused with postmechanical technology. In Section IId, "Voudou," the body dances and sweats, opening a window into another space. As lesbian bodies, they represent a pleasure-produced collective space that contradicts the exclusionary, difference-laden Euclidean point. Here I want to invoke the body as it has been traditionally configured—as flesh, but rather than the fleshly integer it once was, as a zone of flesh—a fleshly space.

The attempt to attend to the "fleshly" body is promptly thwarted by the obdurate body of print. The print body persists and persistently consumes the fleshly one, even as the technology of the screen revolutionizes its production. The "body of the text" has become ever more insistent upon its exchange for that of the flesh, as it nears the demise of its dominance. The first sections of "The Domain-Matrix" set out the attempt by poststructuralists to continue print's allure through self-referential writing. Yet another tradition central to Western thought, the Protestant tradition, also proffers the body of the text through the narrative of the fleshly body as that of "the Word became flesh," while actually producing the opposite: the flesh as word. The Protestant tradition, aided by the invention of the printing press, took the book, the Bible, as the body of its faith. Finding the Gideon Bible in a motel room proposes the exchange of flesh into word at a site which might promote the lascivious practices of the flesh. The vulgar Protestant tradition suggests that there is a body, but it is the Word, or, if not precisely the Word, just like the Word. Here, the Fundamentalists are caught in a contradiction that they rabidly insist upon—Bible in hand, they argue for family relations constructed by sexual intercourse and bloodlines, as if those practices of the flesh are produced by the print—emulate its order. The rise of virtual systems has produced a panic among the Fundamentalists around the retention of print. As we have seen in other sections, the theoretical discourses around the sexual liberation movement have become more and more in line with the rise of technological and late capitalist virtual systems. One might read the present attack by Christian Fundamentalists upon lesbians and gays as partially determined by the virtual relations the sexual liberation movement has organized: sex as pleasure, but worse, sex without genital contact, transmitted through pornography, s/m scenarios, or phone sex; families constructed solely through social relations, and finally, "lesbian" as a sign circulating through late capitalist marketing structures. All of these virtual relations that do not "go by the book" create a location for the eddying of the new virtual—a site (sight) the Fundamentalists can attack. Fundament is the root notion, and that fundament is the book, the Word made manifest in print, along with its earlier form of capital that still, as agents such as Ross Perot and Newt Gingrich insist, pays the bills in "real" money. These systems relegate the flesh as a poor emulation of print—the Word.

Yet, in the academic theories these Fundamentalists oppose, the fleshly body is also disciplined through the order of print. Rather than an imitation of the Word, it becomes the blank space that print writes upon. The body is imagined as inscribed, or written upon—the page of the law and social institutions. Elizabeth Grosz succinctly describes this current role in her book *Volatile Bodies:*

> Nietzsche, Foucault, Deleuze, Lingis, and others whose work I will analyze, focus on the body as a social object, *a text to be marked*, traced, *written upon* by various regimes of institutional (discursive and nondiscursive) power . . . and as a receptive surface on which the body's boundaries and various parts or zones are constituted, always with other surfaces and planes. (116; italics mine)

The result is that agency resides in the institutions which write on the body, which in turn functions as a passive recipient. Inscription assimilates the agency of the fleshly body. Moreover, the body loses its fleshly integrity as it intertwines with other "surfaces and planes." The term "body" thus ascends into a trope for the matrix of social forces. Section Ib, "Burying the Live Body," develops this point at length.

Critics of the new technoculture have also cast the net of their critique across the traditional spaces that print has organized. Determined to oppose the sanitized, transcendent virtual space the new technologies proffer, these critics suggest a return to the word as the solution. Take, for instance, Verena Andermatt Conley's careful and brilliant notion of "Eco-Subjects." After care-

D O M A I N - M A T R I X

108
PAGE

 PREV

 NEXT

 OPEN

 PRINT

 FIND

 HELP

 MENU

fully working through a feminist critique to the revelation of how "Integrated World Capitalism" creates the spoiling of habitat, both social and ecological, Conley proposes that

> by way of feminists such as Hélène Cixous, through geographers, philosophers, and culture critics, time and again we hear the need for becoming in cultural contexts of resingularization through storytelling, narrative, or poetry. Through voice, storytelling brings the body, or one's own story, into History. And insofar as it reopens onto space in time, away from technological reduction onto grids, it does preserve linguistic diversity. (88)

Ironically, a feminist critique that once formed around a deconstruction of the genderizing effects of narrative now returns to it as a healing agent. Yet Conley and others want to imply the body in this return to the word—as a productive force in terms of it. She calls for the voice to imprint the agency of the flesh upon the word. Print may still wane, but the narrative and the word might persist through the oral tradition. In Section Ic, "Performing Reading," I attempt to draw a relationship between the academic practice of reading a paper and the ways in which theorists imagine performance. Here I want to suggest that acting, or performance, might provide a fuller fleshly model than storytelling—one that does not necessarily rely upon the word for its constitution. In the same spirit as Conley's critique, I want to reimagine the fleshly zone of performance as a corrective to transubstantiation.

VA. THE BODY ACTS

The actor, like the dancer, like most people—even critical theorists—assumes the body in its traditional form. The performer merely does so in a heightened, more narrowly focused state. The performer focuses on training the body, listening to the body, working with the body, and enjoying the body. The body is the performer's primary interface with the social. Breath control, voice technique, body training, choreography, techniques for handling props—all compose the interface. Words do not reign supreme; rather, they are only one kind of sound among many, sculpted by posture and by the breath: sometimes produced by exhaling, received as screaming, moaning, whispering, laughing, wailing, panting, gnawing, "coming," and sometimes by sucking in the breath, received as surprise, fear, desire. The actor, as is often repeated in acting classes, is supported by the column of breath and the way the position of the body molds it.

Bodily movement when organized in this interface is termed "gesture." The training and study of gesture has a long, distinguished tradition in theater training and criticism. In contemporary performance, Robert Wilson's technique of slowing the gesture down has brought back its performance power, in a social and economic environment that privileges acceleration **(see section IVd, "Playing the Cyberstreet,"** for a discussion of acceleration/ capitalism/performance). The performer brings on a chair, each step requiring minutes to accomplish, and sets it down. The action is simple, unadorned, and without narrative "meaning." The physical control required to perform it requires practice and "focus" on movement. How to set one foot exactly in front of the other; to move across a large space with gestures proceeding at an even rate; to walk the straight line without looking down; to keep both arms at the same height; to keep the head straight forward; to release the shoulders; and to maintain even breathing.

As demonstrated in section Ib, "Burying the Live Body," accounts of such movement are generally developed from the perspective of the audience. Hence they are about the meaning and text such movements imply—how they are to be received. But what of the performer's processes in moving through space, and adjusting the body to its particular dimensions? Bertolt Brecht, author of the notion of the *gestus*, or the social gest(ure), said, near the end of his life, that his *Lehrstück, The Measures Taken* would be the "theater of the future." He was adamant that that performance should never have an audience, but remain for the exclusive benefit of the actors. He wanted to remove performance from any context of reception. In other words, he meant to design an actor's theater in which the performance would be in the making of it. Brecht's intent, followed by the German Democratic Republic, was to move this kind of performance out of the theater space and into, say, workplaces such as factories. The government allowed workers to use part of their work time for the exploration of such performances that might encourage new, inventive forms of collective living in the acting of them. Heiner Müller describes this tradition as "theater as social laboratory." Corporeal action, then, is considered a way to create social reality, rather than to be inscribed by it.

Now, within the Marxist Leninism of his time, Brecht's sense of bodily movement aligned performance with the "working" class. The association of labor with the acting body allowed a focus on theater to align with one on economic conditions. Similarly, in his work on painting, Norman Bryson retrieves the performing body from the Gaze through a notion of its labor in the artist's studio:

> It is this other space of the studio, of the body of labour, which Western painting negates; we are *given* the body with an intensity of disclosure and publicity . . . the body in a different guise, as picture, to be apprehended simultaneously by the Gaze. . . . Compensating this impoverishment of the body, this tradition rewards it with all the pleasures of seduction, for the body of the Gaze is nothing other than a sexual mask. (164)

> Let us be clear: we are speaking of a seductive illusion. If, in the general concealment of the body of labour, painting of the Gaze accords an acute a privileged position to sexuality. . . . The body of labour, in its studio space, is hidden by the brilliance of the posture, the facial or bodily feature . . . it is through the mask of seduction that the scaena becomes most coherent and most opaque—through local and libidinal fusions that the image so-lidifies around the "this," this moment and this body of pleasure . . . the *durée* of labour gives way to the immediacy of appetitive time. (167)

(See section IVa, "A Revision of the Gaze.") Bryson recuperates the body not only from the perspective of the perceiver, but also from the discourse around sexuality and seduction that would, he argues, rob the body of its productive potential. Rather than desire, the term which often sets the other discourses into motion, Bryson would attend to the "work of the body on matter, transformation of matter through work" (150).

Both Brecht and Bryson address how bodies make change. Brecht's theater changes social conditions—it is an active theater of manual laborers. Bryson's move back to the artist's studio is calculated to retrieve the corporeal production of appearance, the "transformative capacity the body possesses through work." "Work" is the sign of the body, then, and its productive sense. Insisting on the body as agent is insisting upon its productivity—the residue of efficacious action. While the body is recuperated as agent, once more, the ludic process is omitted from consideration. The body as agent, it seems, is serious business. Brecht's suture of the player to the social seems to result in a degradation of playing. In spite of the seriousness of production, however, Brecht and Bryson do manage to reinstate the sweating, breathing, blood-coursing, heart-thumping, bowel-moving body as agent.

In spite of their good "work," these critical guidelines back to the body as agent do not test the referent of "body." Difficult as it is to imagine such an easy recognition of the body in these times of the poststructuralist de-composition of its traditional meaning, most of us do operate upon similar simple assumptions in our daily lives. We dress, exercise, and involve ourselves in physical play as if the body were an integrated, recognizable whole. These quotidian uses of the body are the precise targets at which Brecht would aim his "theater of the future." His tradition is one of changing the body, changing how the body acts in order to change its environment. For him, social conditions are manually operated. Brecht would have the body matter.

Typically, neither Bryson nor Brecht calculates the effects of gendering processes on the body. Current treatments of the body that account for the effects of gender, such as those by Elizabeth Grosz and Judith Butler, turn to phenomenology in order to recuperate some sense of physical agency. There, the tendentious notion of "work" in constituting the body's agency is replaced by the seemingly more neutral sense of "experience." As feminists, they would operate through this philosophical model to reinstate agency along with body. Grosz moves through phenomenology to tattoos in her development of *Volatile Bodies*. Yet, as signs of the body as agent, they return to the model of "The Body as Inscriptive Surface," as her chapter is called. And, though they break social taboos, tattoos admit no account of gender—in fact, historically they have been etched primarily on the bodies of men. Thus, body as agent becomes body as inscribed surface, which returns agency to institutions.

Fraught as the project proves to be, I want to likewise seek some way to posit the notion of an effective body of change that also addresses sex or gender. For this reason, I would like to turn to a consideration of the transsexual as a practice of the body *qua* body as agent of change. The transsexual body not only offers a model of a transforming, sexed body, but also situates the body in relation to technology. The transsexual performs the desire for medical technology in the body.

VB. THE TRANSSEXUAL BODY

The transsexual body offers a site for the convergence of the body, technology, and sex. Situating the transsexual body in the space of technology, imbued with corporeal agency, changes the critical perspective generally afforded it. Traditionally, this practice of changing the body has been treated as a marker of interior subjectivity. The body is made merely to register the "feeling" that one's "true" gender identity is trapped inside the wrong body. Rather than treating transsexuality as a performance in the body, such critics assess the discontinuity between "feeling" and "flesh." Marjorie Garber in *Vested Interests* promotes this attitude toward sex reassignment procedures by regarding them as the result of the intent "to refashion the body to suit the subjectivity" (102). While her work reflects a deep interaction with those transsexuals who articulate their intent in this "fashion," the effect of such a sympathetic move is to relegate the signature acts of the transsexual, to rearrange the flesh, lie beneath the knife, and/or inject the body, to an anterior position vis-à-vis interiority.

Bernice Hausman, in her book *Changing Sex*, treats the transsexual as a body rather than as a subjectivity, carefully tracing how medical discourses used the notion of gender and interiority to control the changing body. She notes how

> the demand for sex change may then serve to consolidate gender as the
> stabilizing force of subjectivity for these subjects. But if transsexual subjec-
> tivity is constituted through a demand for technological intervention on

DOMAIN-MATRIX

112
PAGE

PREV

NEXT

OPEN

PRINT

FIND

HELP

MENU

the body, then the nature of demanding influences the structure of this subjectivity. In other words, it is not only the notion of technology that is significant here, but the idea of subjectivity predicated through a demand. (136)

Hausman has already made clear that gender, as the primary term for entering the discourse of transsexuality, situates the debates on the plane of psychological subjectivity. As such, that very subjectivity hangs on a demand for medical intervention and for changing the body. The latter two forces remain outside the considerations, discounting the body. Hausman concludes by insisting that "what we must do is rethink the body as the site for sexual signification. Theorizing the body means taking it seriously as a material structure that exceeds the power of language to inscribe its functions" (200). With that mandate in mind, perhaps we could imagine the body of the transsexual and the bodily change vis-à-vis technology, rather than subjectivity, as the site of change.

In her novel *Stone Butch Blues*, Leslie Feinberg describes her body changing secondary sexual characteristics from female to male through testosterone injections:

> As I brushed my teeth, I glanced in the mirror and had to look a second time. Beard stubble roughed my cheeks. My face looked slimmer and more angular. I stripped off my T-shirt and my BVD's. My body was lean and hard. My hips had melted away. I could actually see muscles in my thighs and arms I never knew I had. . . . I had saved sixteen hundred dollars over the winter toward breast reduction surgery. (171)

Rather than scripting the changing body as an effect of an interior subjectivity, this passage registers the shock to the consciousness caused by the body's change. The body is the agent to which the consciousness reacts. Moreover, Feinberg sets this transsexual procedure in a working-class environment. S/he narrates her life as a manual laborer—one caught up in union organizing. The sense of the productive body, the body that could change its working conditions, carries over to the sense of a body that could also "manually" change its sex.

VC. SCREENIC INTERRUPT

Yet there is a screen lurking in this bodily agency. In the episode above, Feinberg is looking at herself in the mirror, regarding what she knows to be the characteristics of sex. Active as the body may be, it is perceived through the space of medical technologies—at this point, somewhere between testosterone injections and breast reduction surgery. The transsexual body is an active agent for change, but within a romance with medical technology. Thus, while representing the body *qua* body, in one sense, the practice literally inter-sects (from the Latin *secare*, to cut) with technology. In this way, the transsexual body is situated along an axis with that "body" which will somehow relate to, or inhabit, cyberspace. The medical screen has prepared the way for its sublation into the screen-of-screens.

Isolating one kind of screen to investigate its effect on the body, like any discussion of the body "itself," is reductive. The landscape of screens, including the movie screen and urban screening devices, produces a relationship between the body and the screen in an interplay with the computer and the imminent cyberscreen. The following Case Study of the screenic landscape develops this screenic topology alongside a discussion of several particular cultural artifacts that play out the circulation of the body among screens. Other sections relate the body to the computer screen, as in section IVg, "Driving My Mouse"— another convenient, if not entirely accurate, focus on a single screen's environment. Nevertheless, medical technologies have devised their own screens for the body, which have helped to configure how the body is screened, constituting one of the screenic traditions that will build cyberspace.

Lisa Cartwright, in *Screening the Body,* traces the project in medical science, in consonance with the cinema, to visualize the body—both its exterior and its interior appearance. Beginning in the nineteenth century, photography, cinema, scopes of various kinds, graphing instruments, and x-ray technologies, in a "frenzy of the visible," sought to record the body. She concludes that "rather than simply augmenting the senses of the scientific observer," these screening devices soon "replaced the sensory observations of the physician or technician." Quoting Jonathan Crary's *Techniques of the Observer,* she concludes that newer visual technologies, such as ultrasound, MRI, and PET scanning, supplant the old order of the "real":

> Most of the historically important functions of the human eye are being supplanted by practices in which visual images no longer have any reference to an observer in a "real," optically perceived world. If these images can be said to refer to anything, it is to millions of bits of electronic mathematical data. Increasingly, visuality will be situated on a cybernetic and electromagnetic terrain where abstract visual and linguistic elements coincide and are consumed, circulated and exchanged globally. (In Cartwright, 23)

Cartwright practices a politics of space, interrogating how the flat optical field is organized across the cultural imaginary, from microscopy to cubist painting. Her argument presumes the forces of discipline and surveillance that Foucault established in his studies of medical science. As in the context of "work" in "Driving My Mouse," Cartwright portrays the medical screen as set in Big Brother mode, watching the living, possibly subversive body.

D O M A I N - M A T R I X

114
PAGE
 PREV
 NEXT
 OPEN
 PRINT
 FIND
 HELP
 MENU

Cartwright establishes the familiar paradigm of screen/gaze with screened/object-of-gaze by cobbling the body to the subject. Her linchpin resides in the consideration of pain. The examples she offers of the screen's development illustrate how pain was induced in the body in order for the symptoms to be screened. In fact, some symptoms to be screened necessarily cause pain in the body exhibiting them. Marking the omission of any consideration of "pain" in the screening technologies provides Cartwright with the divide between the institutional, controlling, disciplining "eye" and a "feeling" constitution of a subject. The body as object is thus established by its representation (90–98). We return again to the question posed in "Driving My Mouse": What if the screen is not Big Brother surveying the organic and thus subversive body, but the doorway to the body's agency?

To aid in confusing traditional attitudes here, I want to recall another version of the screen that performs its enticement: Cocteau's film version of the Orpheus myth, *L'Orphée*. Like Feinberg, Cocteau's Orpheus turns to the mirror to register change. His mirror opens to allow him to step into the realm of the living dead. Whereas Feinberg's mirror registers the change from female to male, Orpheus's moves him from the realm of the living to that of the dead. Now, Orpheus loved Death, eagerly passing through the mirror to search for her body. In my article "Tracking the Vampire," I develop the complex relationship between the undead and the appearance of the queer, which pertains to Cocteau's work, but it suffices here to note its point that consorting with the undead results in gender inversion. So Cocteau's mirror is the passage to the pleasurable inversion of the natural—the live. Cocteau's film may be perceived as the ambivalent desire for the virtual screen that had begun to open in his time. Although television had not yet brought the screen home, Orpheus, in Cocteau's version, did acquire Death's car, which received radio signals from her domain. Like the computer nerd, Orpheus obsessively returns to the radio, where he listens, for hours, to the broadcast of death into his art. Recalling Cocteau's film in this discussion invites a recognition of desiring the screen—imagining it as lending ludic agency, sexual pleasure, and fulfillment, rather than as surveying, with a cold eye, the "hot" body. Screens and mirrors lead to another space.

Interestingly, Philip Glass, the contemporary "postmodern" composer, is currently creating a trilogy around three of Cocteau's films. In his production of *Beauty and the Beast,* he projects the original film behind "live" musicians, who play and sing Glass's version of the sound track. The play between the film and the "live" has caused much consternation among the reviewers, who insist that one must take precedence over the other. Using Cocteau's older film to recover the "live" performance of music, in front of the images, produces a contemporary interface with this pioneering imagination. If Cocteau represented screens as breaking through to another ludic order, Glass's production uses the strength of that order to come back again to the "live." Glass plays Orpheus to Cocteau—returning to his films which opened up the imagination of the screen as passage or icon into the "other" space, entering that space and bringing back, to set before it, in music, the "live" body.

Fig. 3 Loren Cameron, self-portrait: "God's Will."
Copyright Loren Cameron.

VD. THE ROMANCE OF THE KNIFE

In this context, the transsexual may be perceived as actively choosing medical intervention as a site of pleasure. Bodily change is the point, rather than gender play. Leslie Feinberg again:

> I drank a beer before I took out the syringes and looked at them. Needles scared me so much I couldn't believe I was about to stab myself with one. I examined the vials of hormones as though their mysteries would reveal themselves to me right there at the kitchen table. They didn't. I went to the bathroom, took off my chinos, and hung them on the bathroom door.

DOMAIN-MATRIX

116
PAGE

 PREV

 NEXT

 OPEN

 PRINT

 FIND

 HELP

 MENU

> I sat down on the toilet seat and prepared the syringe. . . . Would I ever lie
> in a woman's arms again? . . . I stabbed my thigh with the needle and
> injected the hormone. . . . I felt a wave of excitement—the possibility that
> something was going to change. (164)

The injection is preceded by the thought of lying in a woman's arms and succeeded by "a wave of excitement." Testosterone is portrayed as "mysterious," and the injection as "exciting." The scenario scripts the excitement experienced in a physical relationship with medical technology.

Loren Cameron's self-portrait, "shot" years later, when a transgender movement supports such changes, openly celebrates the needle (fig. 3). The injection seems to be the "point" of the picture, which was printed as the cover of the *Bay Times*. Cameron is nude, challenging the tradition of photographing the transsexual with the accessories of gender, such as, in the case of male to female, the hairdo, makeup, and frock that enable one to "pass." In that sense, becoming a man in the social sphere does not seem to be of interest in this particular photo. The charge is in the altered body itself—its sex rather than its gender. Cameron celebrates the changing body rather than the resulting gender. Moreover, he celebrates the technological moment—the medical intervention that promotes the change. Cameron's stance hides the reconstructed penis, or the lack of it. Perhaps his body is literally trans-sexual, in that it shares the attributes of both sexes. Currently, the practice in some circles is to retain the specifically trans-sexual body, rather than the body transformed from one sex to the other. The combination of female and male secondary sexual characteristics and genitals marks the flesh as changing. Agency is located in the changing body.

As celebratory as the changing body may be in relation to medical technology, economic access to its pleasures is restricted. Some transsexuals manage to accomplish this bodily transformation through certified medical facilities, but many cannot afford such luxuries and buy the hormones on the street, or across the border in Tijuana, where pharmaceuticals are sold in several venues, with little government regulation. Feinberg's protagonist buys her hormones from a doctor who displays no medical degrees on his walls. In the case of possibly impure hormones, it is not clear exactly what chemical changes may be occurring in the body—what the changed body will actually become. Even the licensed medical establishment is distributing estrogen to menopausal women, on the basis of minimal and short-term testing. This means that new bodies are being constructed for women by both estrogen and testosterone treatments, and no one knows exactly what results lie ahead. In the book *Horsexe,* Catherine Millot records a remark one of her transsexual patients made to her: "'With us, science fiction becomes reality'" (13).

VE. PERFORMING THE CUT: ORLAN AND KATE BORNSTEIN

(One could return here to the discussion of the cyborg in "Driving My Mouse.") Critics often move through implants and prostheses to the notion of the cyborg. But I want to stay with the changing body a little longer, to explore how the ludic pleasures it takes in the knife constitute a kind of fleshly agency. In 1990, the French multimedia artist Orlan began a series of plastic surgeries designed to progressively sculpt her face into a combination of the Mona Lisa, Diana, and Botticelli's Venus. Her seventh operation, titled "Omnipresence," was broadcast via satellite to thirteen galleries around the world, including the Pompidou Center in Paris, the Banff Center in Canada, and the Sandra Gering Gallery in SoHo (Manhattan). Under local anesthetic, with a woman surgeon, Orlan read aloud from a psychoanalytic text by Eugénie Lemoine Luccioni which posits, among other things, a notion of the body as obsolete. Orlan read before the knife cut into her face and two silicone implants were injected above her eyebrows to duplicate the Mona Lisa's brow. She calls the entire project "The Reincarnation of Saint Orlan," emphasizing, in a French Catholic way, the agency (saint) that resides in the changing body.

Orlan's performances lend new meaning to the term "operating theater," in which the patient is the performer rather than the doctor. Medical technology is her object, rather than vice versa. She is neither registering pain nor performing patient-as-object of the institution of medicine, as suggested in Cartwright's history of the medical screen. Orlan is making a "live" performance of her changing body, at the moment of intervention by medical technology, screened out through satellite transmissions to electronically constructed audiences in distant parts of the globe. The changing, live body is the node that connects the various technologies. Orlan performs a critique of the change while producing it. She is constructing a critical performance of the imperatives of the regime of beauty that cuts into the flesh of women. Titling her performance "Omnipresence," she plays on the broad scope of videoconferencing and faxing procedures that create the interface between her body and the audience in the art galleries around the world. Cutting change into her body, then, mobilizes not only a critical consciousness, but also a ludic entry into the burgeoning cyberspace. At one point, the Pompidou Center suggested that it was "surgery in virtual reality," but I would suggest that it was a critique of beauty produced through a live body which catalyzed the virtual systems into operation.

Orlan costumes herself and her doctors and nurses in *haute couture* outfits created by leading designers. The costumes lend visual interest to the sterile visual conditions of the operating room. More, they suggest the cost of cosmetic surgeries. The class implications of that surgery are not lost among the velvets and the glistening futuristic fabrics that surround the procedure. Likewise, the galleries that are connected to the operation represent leading cutting-edge (so to speak) art production, elevated far "above" the plane of popular culture. The first-world circulation of the requirements of beauty and the class-specific interventions to create its illusion in the body of women are critically performed by Orlan's "Omnipresence." The changing body acts on the procedure, sets up the technological web, activates the virtual, displaying class and first-world privilege and cut by the gendered regime of beauty.

Similarly, the performance artist Kate Bornstein stages the transsexual body. In her play *Hidden: A Gender,* she relates incidents from her own life as well as those from the records of Herculine Barbin. The play swings from the sadistic, ironic commentary of Doc Grinder, a "medicine man" in the older sense of the word, who sells gender the way such characters used to sell snake oil, and the romantic, wistful monologues of Barbin. The centerpiece of the action, however, resides in the portrayal of the operation. Introduced by Drs. Razor and Weener, greedy, sex-assignment surgeons played in high Marx Brothers slapstick style, the actual operation is performed by a cook. Emulating the style of Julia Child, she describes the operation as baking a cake. First, the dough is rolled into a penis, which is cut, squashed, and finally fashioned into a clitoris. A candle is placed on top of it, as an adornment on what is called a birthday cake. A positive "light" is lent to what at first seems the gruesome details of the surgery.

Bornstein's narrative seems distant from Cameron's naked celebration of the testosterone injection. Sadistic wit and lyric melancholy belong more to the subjectivity Garber ascribes to the transsexual project than to a celebration of bodily agency. It is Bornstein's own performing body that belies this impression. Entering as Doc Grinder, Bornstein wears tights that reveal the "lack" of the penis. Her low-cut, tight-fitting top also reveals fulsome, shapely breasts. Her alluring display of the transsexual body as performer distances the greedy and sadistic practices that surround the surgery. Instead, its success greets the viewer at every turn. As she puts it: "I'm real glad I had my surgery, and I'd do it again, just for the comfort I now feel with a constructed vagina. I *like* that thang!" (119–120). Appearing as a transsexual, rather than as a woman, a "gender outlaw" as she terms it, Bornstein plays the body, the cut, the "slice of life" for her own gain and for the support it lends to others like her. She displays the changing, changed body as alluring and successful.

Significantly, Bornstein also plays the Internet and computer games, and is completing a novel about an online relationship. Both Bornstein's and Orlan's postoperative or operative bodies coincide with cyberspace. When asked about the relationship between transsexuals and this new technology, Bornstein responded that so many are intensely involved with online functions that there is a joke implying that CRT rays make you have the operation. The example of Sandy Stone comes to mind along this axis. Writing on cyberspace under the name Allucquere Rosanne Stone and on "post-transsexual politics" under the name Sandy Stone, Stone stops the convergence of those two orders at her body. For some reason, she seems to divide the discussions of technology and those of transsexuality into two different discourses, employing two different authorial personae. Although Stone concludes her book on desire and technology with this intervention, it is the slight mention of transsexualism in the book:

> In cyberspace the transgendered body is the natural body. The nets are spaces of transformation, identity factories in which bodies are meaning machines, and transgender—identity as performance, as play, as a wrench in the smooth gears of the social apparatus of vision—is the ground state. . . . Conversely—and, I think, obviously—in physical space the transgendered body is the unnatural body. . . . *The transgendered body is a screen, upon which is projected the war between unnatural and natural.* (1995, 181; italics mine)

Stone still draws a significant difference in the way the body relates through screens and some "other" order of the body that remains undefined. Whereas Stone has moved from metaphors of inscription to those of the screen, the body retains the same receptive position it had in print culture. The body does not screen, but is a screen upon which the "unnatural and natural" are projected. The transgendered body swings between two orders, but one of them is still constituted as "natural." What does "nature" imply?

In another discussion in the book, where the transsexual body does not appear, Stone describes what she perceives as the traditional role the body plays in certifying subjects—perhaps this is what she means by "nature." She calls the process the "warranting" of the subject by the body. Stone argues that a subject position, or a position as citizen, one who has some rights to a domain, is established by referencing a body. The single body, the integer, thus warrants subjectivity and citizenship. Multiplicity is confounded simply by the practice of referencing the singleness of the body. The body acts as a location, and that location holds back the virtual play of multiple identities. Therefore, as she puts it, "We are no longer unproblematically secure within the nest of our location technologies" (182). The transsexual body may "throw a wrench" into the "smooth gears" of such operations, as Stone puts it, but is not in itself the sign of the body as a site of change. For Stone, the transsexual body points to the potential of subversion of the "natural" order, but not necessarily the site of dynamic change. For that, she goes to multiple personalities—multiple subject positions online rather than in the body. Stone's brilliant revelation of the body as the "warrant" of the citizen leads her to a dichotomy between virtual as mul-

D O M A I N - M A T R I X

120
PAGE

PREV

NEXT

OPEN

PRINT

FIND

HELP

MENU

tiple and fleshly as too singular. In this context, traversing the virtual seems privileged over inhabiting the material.

Considering Stone's critical strategy from another perspective, the move away from location may also be perceived as a move against the local. It could signify what Kroker and Weinstein describe as "a universal media class that is arrayed against local populations" (29). Constituting personae through the media, cut loose from the bodily referent, then, operates like a universal(izing) class, practicing the privilege of abandoning the local. The specifically first-world privilege of abandoning locales where, as Conley noted above, "Integrated World Capitalism" plunders ecological and social habitats through a "universalized" technospace of multiplicity does not seem like the practice of a new citizenship to which Stone would really want to subscribe. Nor is the abjuration of the local what is sought here, in positioning the transsexual body in terms of cyberspace. In fact, the hope of this particular section is in locating change in bodies rather than in that universalized space. Material change may be perceived in the sculpting of the flesh, by change in the flesh. The transsexual body produces change and multiplicity in the flesh. The body as actively inhabiting the position of "trans," in the flesh, performing rather than registering, is the necessary tie that binds accountability to play, labor to end product, and death to repetitive loops.

Yet the cybernetic circulation that Cartwright noted in her passage on the medical screen has imagined the medical body in its cellular units rather than in its several parts. The transsexual body, like the mechanical age, may still retain too much of the integer in its composition. Judith Shapiro, in her article on transsexualism, phrases it this way:

> Sex change surgery, for its part, belongs to the domain of heroic medicine, destined, however, to be left behind as science marches on. The prospects of such things as recombinant DNA technology already permit us to look ahead to a time when these operations would be viewed as a crude and primitive approach to transforming our natural endowments. (262)

Transsexualism still imagines a passing between two states, or retains, as residence, a notion of bounded states that may become antique as genetic and DNA research moves on. The silicon implants that Orlan had in her brows, that others have in their breasts, are, after all, the same material as the silicon chip. (Thanks to Jordy Jones for this tip.)

Does this mean that the body, then, is not an agent for change? Perhaps it is the mechanical nature of the change that is in question. Perhaps it is its tie to the retention of integers—the desire to make, whole, a transgender move. There is another lesbian model for such change that carries over, in a less mechanical, more screenic manner, into the new order of the material.

VF. *SCREEN/SKIN/UTOPIA*: THE LESBIAN BODY

Along the way of the twentieth century, there have been road signs of a homosexual break with the linear path of tropes of transformation. Proust's immense novel ushered in the century with a new narrative map of space and time, designed through homosexual encounters and tropes of the closet. Proust provided the mature matrix of his childhood nightshade, which spun colored images like screens, passing rapidly through paradigms of the urban, of class, of fantasy, of materiality, of sexuality—all caught on his night screen. Cocteau filmed an Orpheus who found mirrors to be windows into other systems, secured by lesbian bacchantes. Yet Proust's nightshade retains its cells of painted units, offering themselves up to the episodic, printed novel. Cocteau's world, likewise, retains the sense of passing from order to order, filming Orpheus, who must always go and return and who, although listening to a car radio for inspiration, still writes. Monique Wittig wrote an erotic journey into *The Lesbian Body,* which opened it up and splayed it out. The writing surveyed elemental modules such as: "NERVE NETWORKS THE NERVE- ROOTS THE BUNDLES THE BRANCHES THE PLEXUSES" (53). However, while the body parts are intruded, navigated by Wittig, they still retain their integrity as parts. Integers are invaded, passed through, spun on shades, and splayed out in the homosexual imagination of space and the desiring body. Yet they continue to play as integers.

Nicole Brossard provides a poetic meditation on the lesbian body that creates something like a "field theory" of lesbian as space. In her poetic novel *Mauve Desert,* Brossard names her protagonist Claire Dérive, after the Situationist notion of the "drift" through space. **(See the section "Cruis-ing/Surfing the Matrix.")** Dérive in the desert positions "lesbian" as a topographical figure, for whom seduction is something like "solicitations of the terrain." Drifting in the desert is desire, but it is bounded by a television set in a motel, a violent man, a scientist, who kills, suggesting, through images of the deadly detonating flash, the atomic bomb, developed by men in the desert, and the lesbian body of "tremors" and "illuminations" (10). Brossard sets out the lesbian protagonist to drift in the field of desire, but it is mined by military uses of technology.

The "field" of lesbian space dissolves, finally, the sheath of the body as integer—the skin. In her book *Picture Theory*—a term she borrowed from Wittgenstein—Brossard imagines holograms and skinscreens as the space of lesbian desire. The book is organized into sections such as "Screen Skin," "Screen Skin II," and "Screen Skin Utopia," concluding with "Hologram." Yet the screen is not something projected upon—it constitutes the image:

D O M A I N - M A T R I X

 PREV

 NEXT

 OPEN

 PRINT

 FIND

 HELP

 MENU

122 PAGE

"At the end of the patriarchal night the body anticipates on the horizon I have in front of me on the screen of skin, mine, whose resonance endures in what weaves the text/ure t/issue *the light*" (155). To Brossard, Eco's icon (point) as a sheath of correspondence opens out into the productive screen. The skin caught up in lesbian sex is not the sheath which encloses, or holds together. Nor is skin the inscriptive surface that attains permeability through scarification or tattoo, as Elizabeth Grosz suggests (140–141). Instead, Brossard imagines this skin as a screen, which both receives and projects at once. Skin is an interpermeable, virtual screen. Lesbian-specific in this interpermeability, Brossard's skin stretches from "virtual to infinity, form-ELLE in every dimension of understanding, method and memory" (153).

As Brossard imagines the simultaneous dissolve and constitution this screen effects, she begins her perception with skin as a linked system: "Skin/link: yes language could be reconstituted in three dimensions beginning with the part so-called pleasure where the lesbian body, language and energy fuse. In the first chapter, the book promised when she rubbed against tribade in the words of her tribe torrential torrere" (169). Rubbing in tribade lust, the skins produce a virtual link-up through a specifically lesbian sexual practice. Like the net, integers are retained as locations, but the link, through lesbian sex, is an "essential" way to fuse expression, transmission, and production. In other words, the net is produced through the sexual practice—the duopoly held by notions that locate the body on one side of the system and technology on the other is imagined away. There is, then, the possibility not to imagine body and technology across a divide, and that way is through ludic production of the virtual in the body. As we have seen in another section, voudou crosses this threshold as well.

Brossard also figures lesbian space and motility as hologram, where skin is virtualized, drawn into a homo space of coincidence, rather than located in the space of distance and difference. The hologram yields what, long ago, Rimbaud, another lyric theorist of the homosexual, called "illuminations."

> At certain moments we reach limits it's limit origin
> ex hausts 'story stele. In the crossing, smthg. is
> (can)celled where one believes grass such vertigo
> verre glass mirror image gradual lentissimo weaves
> the screen horizon light era scream aim(é) skin
> version where it works. (172)

At the limit of limits, leaving the space of story, the hologram crosses into a vertigo of screen/light/skin/horizon where the distinctions among the terms indissolubly weave together. The projected upon, screen, the projector, light, the producer, skin, and the limit of the field, horizon, weave together. In

Brossard, the screen/skin virtualizes in lesbian seduction, rather than, as in cyberspace, through a technological sublation.

As a lyric meditation, a compressed, rarefied theory of screening as lesbian, Brossard remains without the materialist concerns constitutive of any full consideration of cyber or lesbian-screened space. The notion is a utopian one, to set against other instrumental treatments and critical deconstructions. Together, these different functions may help to reimagine the coming screen, already being produced through the imagined utopias, dystopias, and critiques of those who are building it.

DOMAIN-MATRIX

124 PAGE

 PREV

 NEXT

 OPEN

 PRINT

 FIND

 HELP

 MENU

CASE STUDIES:
PERFORMANCE &
THE SCREEN

BRINGING HOME THE MEAT:
MATERIALIST SPATIAL DESIGNS
OF NATION AND STAGE

Angels in America: Perestroika begins with a monologue by the "World's Oldest Living Bolshevik":

> *(With sudden, violent passion)* And *Theory*? How are we supposed to proceed without *Theory*? What System of Thought have these Reformers to present to this mad swirling planetary disorganization. . . . Do they have, as we did, a beautiful Theory . . . ? You can't imagine, when we first read the Classic Texts . . . and shoved incomprehension aside . . . into Red Blooming [that] gave us Praxis, True Praxis, True Theory married to Actual Life. . . . And what have you to offer now, children of this Theory? What have you to offer in its place? Market incentives. . . . makeshift Capitalism. . . . We must change, only show me the Theory. . . . *(A tremendous tearing and crashing sound, the great red flag is flown out, and lights come up on . . . Prior cowering in his bed which is strewn with the wreckage of his bedroom ceiling; and the Angel . . . hovering in the air, facing him.)*

Marxist theory is evoked and evacuated as the beginning of the *Perestroika* process for the gay social fabric. Prior, the gay man with AIDS, is caught between the last vestiges of Marxist theory and the opening of the new space of the millennium. Nation, capitalism, and ethnic memory are major players in this staging of the formation of gay sexual discovery, the process of coming out of the closet, new forms of social bonding for gay men, and activist episodes around the medical treatment and funding for AIDS. The play begins as the nostalgia for and the need for a theory that could traverse a cultural landscape riven by the intrusion of mysterious images. It swings between traditional theatrical dialogue and imagistic representations of another order of beings living in the heaven of a devastated San Francisco—sex-mad angels who collectively try to govern the future. Gay and national issues move through dialogue and yet are riven by a window into an imagistic, different order. Similarly, David Henry Hwang's *M. Butterfly* plays the narrative of homosexual attraction and cross-gender acting across the backdrop of the Communist cultural revolution in China and even, in the film, the Maoist student movement in Paris. Homosexual desire is caught up in class attitudes, colonialist fictions, and capitalist projects. Likewise, *The Crying Game* opens with the taking of a British soldier as hostage by the Irish Republican Army, only to later disclose, as the major turn of events, that his cross-dressing lover is a man. Across contemporary stage and screen, a certain panic and intrigue play through the intersection of national, ethnic politics and issues of gendered sexual practices. This intersection of revolutionary processes, colonial market struggles, the performance of gender, state agendas, homosexual practices, and the binary of dialogue and image constitutes the location this chapter seeks to inhabit by virtue of some *"Theory"* that would be "other" than the call to an isolated sex-radical position. The project is to resituate the term "performing lesbian" within these considerations, constituting it in relation to the "meat" of materialist practices. It is hoped that these strategies, when brought to bear on "performing lesbian," may better focus the full context of the formulation, so that "lesbian" may once again go to bed with the "meat." In order to set up that particular use of "lesbian," however, uses of private property, state agendas, and the strategies of "live" performance need to be outlined as part of her meat's *mise-en-scène.*

STAGING INTELLECTUAL PROPERTY

As the "World's Oldest Living Bolshevik" opened *Angels in America*, this chapter opens with a critical examination of the work of Heiner Müller, the Communist playwright of the erstwhile German Democratic Republic and of the "new" united Germany. Certainly, Müller contributes nothing to the configuration of the term "lesbian," but then lesbian never appears in socialist state productions, nor, much, in the critical considerations of capitalism and state. Leaving, for a section, the discourse that would run "lesbian," an examination of Müller's materialist practices may inform "performing" (in contrast to the "performative") as a term that accounts for its participation in national agendas and economic structures.

A study of how Müller's early plays organize a relationship between performance and nation will be particularly helpful in creating a context for the later consideration of lesbian and gay community, or subculture, vis-à-vis performance, and to clarify, by contrast, the project of Queer Nation and its performance style of ACT UP! Müller's early work contrives a key relationship between the elements of the traditional stage and the dynamics of the collective. If identity politics, visibility, and collectivity, the remnants of lesbian feminist practices, may be reconfigured as grounds for contradiction and coalition, rather than perceived as calls to stable ontology, they may find a retrofitted recuperation through these operations—particularly when they are compounded with issues of property, sexuality, and systems of value. Set within the notion of a collective, Müller's construction of agency also seems particularly acute within current debates. Agency, as a potential site for collective decision making, arises amid the contradictions inherent in a collective process of imagining. Müller's early works enact a notion of agency, complicated by both historical legacies and collective contradictions, which circulates between those two forces like a bargaining chip, to open up a dialogue among peoples and conditions. "Communism," in early Müller, is the operative term for collective improvisation, with the Epic form as its agent of cultural production that would stage its dialogue. Characters are positions in the collective process, anchored by the ground of the state territory. Formal stage space and national space similarly represent a base for the development of these positions. Both realms share borders established by public decree: the proscenium arch mimics national borders. In its official building, the theater offers a monument of national processes—the "real estate" of the state stage.

If the early plays characterize the interrelationship between play and nation, the later performance scripts structure a consonance between global capitalist projects and postmodern performance practices. The distribution of property focuses, increasingly, on the conditions of intellectual property and, finally, on the system of representation itself. In the early plays, Müller's drama of intellectual property begins with situating the book—the function of print—within the state agenda. The later scripts perform the shrinking of the text within a proliferation of images. A complete disjunction between the print text and its performance reveals the alignment of the two orders of representation with those of the two major economic systems, capitalism and communism, to act out their agon. Rather than suturing the orders of the visible and writing by intervening through a free-floating practice of subversion, as in Butler, or by positing a mediating subjective realm, as Hart accomplishes through affixing Lacanian strategies to the Butlerian model, Müller sets print and performance against one another to run on entirely separate tracks. **(See section Ib, "Burying the Live Body," in "The Domain-Matrix.")**

Observing Müller's shift from verse to mute images traces the shift in cultural production from the collective to the commodified. Yet, in Müller, even the commodified proceeds from the collective—a process important for those who would account for lesbian as proceeding from lesbian feminism and its collective practices. General perceptions aside, Müller's contribution to this project is in specifying precisely how these performance structures operate.

THE BOOK OF STATE

Müller's pre-1968 plays demonstrate how the project of state socialism (termed "communism" in his texts) in the German Democratic Republic encouraged him to assume that cultural production was allied with state production. His play *Die Korrektur (The Correction)* (1959) underwent several revisions to correct what an audience of workers perceived to be the problems in the play. HM: "The new literature can only be developed together with our new audience" (Müller 1984, 32). The hope was that critical experiments on what he perceived as the social laboratory of the stage would produce an interactive dialogue with the collective creation of a state ideology. Müller's scripting of Epic plays in the Shakespearean and Brechtian tradition created what he considered to be a formal consonance between theatrical representations of the state and the actual conditions of state—dependent upon the hopes and plans embedded in the Marxist-Leninist critique as well as its failures. Müller's Epic dramaturgy operated within the comfortable equation that early GDR Marxist ideology encouraged of representational and political systems—that they co-determined one another through their interactive functions as outside, determining referents. Although art and politics were not the same thing, as in later notions of the system of representation, neither were the two systems closed and self-referential. They remained open to one another as long as certain conditions prevailed. Primarily, the open state of the systems was secured by a homologous "open" future, invented by the people who would populate it.

One play in particular seemed to stage, for the audience and the author, both the promise and the problems of the GDR and its theatrical tradition. From 1956 to 1964, Müller wrote and revised *Die Umsiedlerin oder das Leben auf dem Lande* (*The Resettler, or Life on the Land*), later entitled *Die Bauern* (*The Peasants*, or *Farmers*). The play opens with the founding of the GDR in 1949. Its revisions, produced both before and after the erection of the wall, register the changing role that Müller's critique played in this period. Unlike the collective revisions practiced on *The Correction,* these revisions were Müller's own, increasingly critical of the political direction that official decisions were legislating. In fact, the critical elements in the play ultimately caused it to be recalled by the Party as an "inadequate portrayal of realism and the formal use of dialectics" (Huettich, 134–136), for the GDR had adopted Soviet Socialist Realism as its sanctioned form of theatrical production. Soviet Socialist Realism mandated a narrative of change that ultimately resolved into a better life, concluding with a political happy ending. Müller's rolling dialectic was at odds with such a conclusion, never coming to rest, but continuing to critique each moment of the collective process, encouraging further improvisations of inclusion. In spite of these differences, Müller's critique literally resided in the GDR until its end. His criticism was positioned within the communist system, as long as one existed. The intent of the criticism was to spur the dialectic forward, as if the state were the protagonist and Müller's dramaturgy the antagonist in GDR development. His theater was addressed directly to the state, situating the audience as citizens. Looking back at this play now, when the GDR no longer exists, the image of the resettler still provides a vivid testimony to how political geographies are carried on the backs of such people, who are forced to leave and found new, often impoverished lives. While Müller's *The Resettler* narrativized the fascist diaspora and the founding of the communist state, the current migration might be termed the communist diaspora, accompanied by the reclaiming of the capitalist territories. The once-official "communist" theatrical inventions have been thrown out onto "foreign" streets. Bankrupting the communist state, as we will see, capitalizes the virtual nations of commodification, such as Queer Nation.

Life on the Land is literalized in the opening stage picture of the play as a stretch of land, of space open to claim. The end of private property is signaled by the initial collectivization of labor and the land. Several characters populate the landscape: a farmer with a hand-pulled wagon full of borderstones, another with the red flag, a beggar, and an accordionist. They speak of their Nazi past, the end of the war, sexuality, and women as wounds driven into their bodies. HM: "This is indeed my theatrical point: the thrusting onstage of bodies, and their conflict with ideas. As long as there are ideas, there are wounds. Ideas are inflicting wounds on the body" (Müller 1982, 65). Perforated by experience and ideologies, these are the characters who are creating the land reform as they distribute the borderstones. Space is divided and held by the stones: will they serve to "cement" social relations along with redistributing space, or will they stand as ossifications of Party principles? The play tests these possibilities in a landscape laid with leftover mines from the final Nazi withdrawal into Berlin and prepared for the coming of tractors from the USSR.

Verse or dialogue serves as the motor of social change, registering the human conflicts occasioned by the redistribution of land, the remains of traditional class hierarchies, and of the new possibilities for the formerly dispossessed. HM: "It [verse] depends on the material and the material is very historical. . . . When there is stagnation you have prose. When the process has a more violent rhythm you have verse" (Müller 1979, 69). Dialogue represents how a new ideology is improvised through the dialectic. Characters assume the discursive positions that, in contradiction to one another, create social change. Enter the Party secretary—the character who officially represents the site where ideology and experience confront one another. He is riding a bicycle. The farmers ask him for a horse to pull the plow, but he answers with only the promise of tractors. Both his bicycle and his promise of tractors represent the possibilities of new technology that collective ownership can provide, but these farmers are still standing in the mud of past inequities and present starvation. To them, considerations of the future seem like privilege. Enter a farmer with his arms full of books. The Party secretary asks him where he got them. He replies that he took them from the now-abandoned local castle. The Party secretary tells him to return them. The farmer replies:

> Why? Even before the cock crow that followed the exit of the masters, half the village cooked its watery soup and wiped its ass with the castle books. Why should I be the exception, with 8 mouths to feed . . . 8 asses and no paper? . . . The best one is *Mein Kampf.* The Americans are buying it in Berlin. (*attempts to exit*)

The Party secretary counters with the ideology of the collective, proletarian appropriation of the mode of cultural production:

> SchillerandGoethe, who filled his belly with them? Homer, who dressed in him?
> No alphabet without you and no thoughts.
> Your crooked hunchback, your crooked hand.
> And to you they're for cigarettes and backsides.
> The books are collective property.
> Take them back to the castle, tomorrow's common house of culture.
> Farmer: Do it yourself, Jesus. I have other problems.

> *He drops the books and leaves. Flint picks them up and attempts to exit on his bicycle, with flag, signpost, and books. Enter Hitler, with Eva Braun breasts . . . followed by Frederick II of Prussia. . . . Hitler jumps on Flint's back, Frederick II on Hitler's. Flint continually tries to go, but they all fall in a heap, along with the flag, signpost and books. End of scene one.* (25; translation mine)

The first scene of the play yokes the redistribution of land to that of intellectual property rights. The limits of private property are tested by divisions of space and the uses of books. Print culture has produced thought as private property, which, in the new state, must also find a place within collective ownership. Those who own the books also own the ideas. Concluding with a set of images animated by books, the scene represents the complex set of negotiations required by the appropriation of culture. The scene thus offers several contradictory positions on the process of appropriation. First, from the simple materialist perspective, books are paper, which, after all, is useful for cigarettes and cleaning up in a time of shortages. As the dialectic holds, the idea of books as paper is both correct and correctable: correct in the old Brechtian formulation "Erst kommt das Fressen, dann die Moral" (First comes eating, then morals) posited by the farmer; correctable by the Party secretary as to the definition of the material.

There is something in this simple materialist formulation of books as paper that seems almost antique or nostalgic within the current critical atmosphere, with the exception, perhaps, of those who consider the production of books from the ecological perspective, concerned that trees (rain forests) might be felled for paper. Is it that ownership is figured as individual, or as individual in contradiction to collective? Perhaps private ownership, in that sense, seems outdated by the new forms of institutional, foundational, and corporate ownership of cultural artifacts. As universities and entertainment conglomerates burgeon in the size of their capital investment, work force, and client base, individual ownership spreads out over a wider network of acquisition. How can the value of a book be determined when it was produced on time secured by grant monies, yielded low royalties, but earned tenure and perhaps a tour on the academic circuit? Corporate and institutional structures mesh in organizing a complex economic location for a book, somewhere between the private castle and the common house of culture.

Or perhaps the formation of books as paper seems antiquated in its closed utilitarian format, seemingly without broader social or cultural ramifications. The notions of "use" are dull in the current critical climate of "seduction" theories. Yet, as James Scott emphasizes in *Weapons of the Weak:* "The intrinsic nature and, in one sense, the 'beauty' of much peasant resistance is that it often confers immediate and concrete advantages . . . and that it requires little or no manifest organization." From Scott's perspective, the correction offered by the Party secretary is "utopian and a slander" because fundamental "bread and butter issues are the essence of lower class politics and resistance. Consumption, from this perspective, is both the goal and the result of resistance and counterresistance" (296). As we shall see, the way in which consumption is defined may constitute the difference between colonial and revolutionary practices. More pertinent here is the operating logic of consumption within current critical reception.

Müller's setting for the book, as contesting individual ownership with collective utility, casts the critique more in the direction of earlier class practices than as a vanguard idea for the "classless" or corporate future. What complicates this orientation is the way in which the earlier, elitist past which that scene would correct has been recuperated within the current political critique. If, as history has shown, individual ownership of the GDR land never really disappeared, but merely lay dormant to be resurrected by the fall of the wall, prior forms of cultural ownership persevered as well, only to be recuperated within current critical practices. This may be taken as a description of the ground of political theory as well. If later theory purports to correct earlier "private" interests, how may those elements be seen to persevere? In critical theory, this process is exemplified in the recuperation of earlier proto-Marxist writings that embed the materialist critique within structures that would maintain a sense of private ownership and commodification. In this regard, Walter Benjamin's 1931 essay "Unpacking My Library" may be read against Müller's later scenario. Benjamin's work is particularly significant to test this matter because of the central role his opus has played in considerations of the interrelated processes of commodification, print, and technology. Benjamin on books represents both an earlier order that Müller would correct and a nonperishable celebration of private property.

Benjamin set out a kind of materialist base for books, not as vehicles for ideas, but as things to be collected. Benjamin's sense of books as property reflects classist, elitist attitudes seemingly corrected by the later Marxist scenario, yet his position is ultimately more recuperable by current theorists of the performative than is the Marxist notion. His ambivalent relationship to commodities recommends him to both early and late forms of capitalism. He has also served to solve a historical problem with the Marxist critique. As Yosek Hayim Yerushalmi testifies: "Benjamin is today an international icon of high culture" filling a need for a "Neo-Marxist critique of modern culture and society untainted by Stalinism" within which a "certain nostalgia also played a role" (*New York Times Book Review*, July 13, 1994, 13–14). In fact, both the recent events in the East bloc and current critical strategies would seem to affirm Benjamin's sense of books and deny the Marxist correction. A consideration of Benjamin's sensibility in light of Müller's scene might suggest just what is implied in the adoption of either position and begin to establish the role they play in twentieth-century critical theories.

BENJAMIN'S LIBRARY AND THE PERFORMATIVE

Benjamin begins by describing some images and sensations around owning books: "the air saturated with the dust of wood, the floor covered with torn paper." These sensations inspire a mood: "not an elegaic mood, but, rather, one of anticipation— which these books arouse in a genuine collector" (59). This mood is an important foil to the notion of utility. In fact, indulgence in such moods induces, in Benjamin "a very mysterious relationship to ownership" that leads him to eschew the utilitarian role that books might proffer for a consideration of them as "the scene, the stage, of their fate" (60). Here Benjamin verges on contemporary notions of performativity. Something in the "mysterious" relationship between ownership and books produces books as "scene" or "stage." Looking back to section Ia, "Queer Performativity," in "The Domain-Matrix," Benjamin's operation is reminiscent of the way in which Sedgwick reads James's Prefaces as performative, with the Prefaces as "spectacle," the readers as "audience," and James's inscribed relation to his past as "gestural" (Sedgwick, 7). Müller's farmer fails to serve this sense of performativity. He wants a book to wipe his asshole, not, as Sedgwick would have it, for James to write his out.

Nevertheless, in both Benjamin and Sedgwick, books are cast as the stage for performing certain structures of subjectivity. Benjamin's is not played out in the reading or writing of books—in fact, he notes, the collector is, in a way, a nonreader (62). Benjamin is invested in books as paper, as original illustrations, as in good condition, and finally, as in their market scarcity. He both affirms books as paper and identifies precisely those material properties as that which transforms them into catalysts for internal, subjective processes. It is the ownership of books, the regard for their physical properties, that produces his subjectivity—his profound "enchantment" produced by "locking individual items within a magic circle in which they are fixed as the final thrill . . . of acquisition" (60). Thus, the "mysterious" element in Benjamin's ownership is the way in which it causes him to perform his own subjectivity through the purchasing of books. Buying and keeping provoke the sensual, the pleasurable (particularly, as he notes, in attaining a good price), and the subjective.

If Müller associates the redistribution of land, its appropriation by the dispossessed, with the farmer's acquisition of books from the castle, Benjamin associates the experience of purchasing books as an imperialist mapping of territories:

> Property and possession belong to the tactile sphere. Collectors are people with a tactile instinct; their instinct tells them that when they capture a strange city, the smallest antique shop can be a fortress, the most remote stationery store a key position. How many cities have revealed themselves to me in the marches I undertook in pursuit of books. (63)

Müller would resituate books from this traditional association of private ownership with imperialist projects. In *The Resettler,* books are dropped on the redistributed land that charts its new social geography by the flight of such collectors. Caught between farmers who put private property to their backsides and Party secretaries who would collectivize it, owners can only take their valuables and flee: "In a military vehicle, sat the Junker, drove, fear in his neck, without chauffeur, weak in the knees, with his bankbook and his wife, westwards" (50). Throughout *The Resettler*, such "owners" steal off to the West. They are cowardly figures, running from those whose depreciated labor produced their wealth. With no useful skills, they pay their way across a hungry, impoverished landscape. The busy farmers, who are trying to grow new crops, find them unremarkable—take little note of them. Imperialism relocates "elsewhere" in the West. The land of Müller's play closes its borders behind them. East and West become the two poles of rival economic systems.

In comparing the episode in *The Resettler* to "Unpacking My Library," the urgent need of farmers' bowels plays as theater to Benjamin's performativity. Benjamin's hermetic closet performativity is broken open, like the castle, to yield to a collective dialogue catalyzed by need. Books, rather than prompting memory, retaining the past, and providing the sensual pleasures of shopping, must find a place in the new landscape that verges on their destruction in the service of corporeal need. "Shit," the word Jarry flung into the underground, subversive theater tradition that opened the century, threatens once again to smear the "dusty" preciosity of culture. Benjamin's staging of book ownership as subjective performativity actually emulates the properties of the bourgeois stage. The *Trauerspiel* that so compelled his critical interest, which invested the private properties of the bourgeois individual with the emotional gestures of the internal psychological realm, is here refined into a consideration of his own library. He has invested the private realm of individual ownership with all the seductive powers of moods, memories, and abstruse pleasures. Private ownership is represented as an engaging, "performative" experience.

CONTRADICTING THE BOOK: DIALOGUE

Keeping in mind the enduring structures of individual ownership celebrated by Benjamin and latent in contemporary recuperations of individual ownership in the system of representation, let us return to the contradictions Müller sets up for the uses and proprietary structures of intellectual property within the collective, to see how they will respond to the shifts in economic ideologies. What has been proposed as the simple, materialist argument in the first scene of *The Resettler* does not rest the matter of ownership and property with utility. The Party Secretary blocks the farmer's way to the toilet by deploying "SchillerandGoethe" as canon fodder. He complicates the notion of the material by arguing that, as ideas, not paper, books challenge the new citizens to appropriate them for the construction of a new culture, better living conditions, and a new ideology. As culture meets hunger, the debate over what constitutes the material breaks out. Ideas and skills are material as well as paper, the Party Secretary teaches. Yet ideas also summon the ghosts of idealism, who haunt utopian projects and are historically resident in the material of ideas. They appear at the end of the scene to leap onto the back of the present. The Party Secretary is literally weighed down with the baggage of the German tradition of Idealism. This dumb show of Idealism is prescient with Müller's later strategies. Before tracing its dynamics, however, I want to follow the itinerary of the book throughout the play.

Toward evening, the farmland of furrows and borderstones gives way to the more lyrical meadow. Couples lie in the meadows, exploring sexual and emotional relationships on the land of the new nation. Typical, as Müller would have it, is a scene between a man whose belief in communism prompts him to read its books and a woman who wants, at that moment, to act spontaneously:

> Schmulka: Do you love me, Siegfried?
>
> Siegfried: Why do you ask, Schmulka? I have given you the COMMUNIST MORALS
> as gifts for women's day, and for your birthday
> Bebel. I have taught you the three principles
> two you can do already, out of love, and still you ask.
>
> *Siegfried throws the books.*
>
> Schmulka, the literature! (67)

In this scene, books no longer represent the appropriation and endurance of the German Idealist tradition, but the stru(i)ctures of Party ideology. Literally bound to the intractable quality of print, books, in this scene, comically signify the attempt to render the spontaneous as policy. But Schmulka runs off without the literature. The book, as an ossified set of moral prescriptions, is also gendered as masculine—it falls short of the fleeing woman. To make this point, Müller casts Schmulka in the traditional role of "woman"—as the spontaneous and the emotional that constitute the border of ossified processes. Hers is only one of the multiple exits that women will make in Müller's dramatization of the new GDR. After 1968, the exits become exile as Dascha, the heroine of *Cement,* exits, never to reappear. Müller noted that after a certain point in the constitution of the Soviet Union, women who had notions of "free love," as spontaneous, improvised, and outside the realm of private property, were exiled from the scene. They could no longer take the stage. They are made to represent the omission of those values from the Party agenda. Books and the Party became the property of men who would deploy them against the spontaneous. Benjamin might have found a stage for subjectivity in books, but Müller treats them as subjectivity bound. Thus, even when books no longer signify the Idealist traditions, are no longer representative of private property, their conditions as bound and as print align them with the destructive processes of the immutable—the site where the improvised collective imagination becomes policy rather than dialogue. The scene with Schmulka is another scene that concludes with the drop of a book. Farmers and women leave them behind.

As books become cast aside, Müller's later work takes its cue from the dumb show of Hitler and Frederick II that concludes scene one. The mute clown show marks the distinction between what may be represented by words and what by images. While the redistribution of land, the new national space, is portrayed through the verse and within the narrative, the Idealist past is represented through stage images. The scene concludes in a wordless play of images that stand outside the narrative. A mute clown play enacts just how the techno-cycling Party Secretary breaks down on his way into the future. Why does wordless image interrupt such verse? What does the interruption signal? After all, the critical communist play, according to Müller, is written as verse, in the tradition of critical Epic theater. This single episode gathers even more significance when considered in regard to Müller's later texts, in which the wordless image will take over the writing and verse will shrink back into single lines quoted from earlier scripts. The image intrudes as outside the collective process. Wordless play does not engage in the dialectic, but stands, like private property, as a clown show on its borders.

FROM COLLECTIVE TO COMMODITY: POSTMODERN PERFORMANCE

The news images of Russian tanks and soldiers entering Czechoslovakia in 1968 irrevocably altered the terms of representation in the GDR. The perception was that the Russian military apparatus was literally taking over the collective decision-making process in the USSR. What had been considered an alternative state, though admittedly the object of an imported revolution, now clearly became a colonized one. The ironic exchange of roles from revolutionary to colonized nation complicated the GDR's status in relation to the USSR. At the same time, the advance of global capitalism permeated its borders—primarily, in East Berlin, through television reception, which brought to the GDR citizens the narrated pleasures of capitalism through the broadcast of West German and U.S. TV series, along with the playing of Hollywood films. Two forms of colonization, then, intersected in the GDR: Russian colonial practices cynically filtered through a communist ideology and Western capitalist colonization through alluring images of consumerism and the pleasures of mass culture.

By 1972, Müller's play *Cement*, taken off the stage of the Berliner Ensemble, stood as his final example of Epic verse. When the alternative experiment of communism seemed to be failing, Epic verse and the state stage could no longer support the theatrical enterprise. When the "open" future was shut down by the use of military force, the consonance between collective dialogue onstage and the discourse of the state no longer held. Consequently, Müller began to stage the impossible stage—the disjunction between performance and that which supports its production. Writing performance scripts, rather than plays, he sought to tune his form to the more dominant processes of commodification and state repression, generally charting the imbalance of power rather than its dialectical swings.

Müller's later scripts have been received as examples of "postmodern" performance—a term that overwrites specific national and communist performance practices with a more indefinite, global style. "Postmodern," in part, suggests remove from a specific, aligned political agenda, substituting a free-floating signification of the subversive (as we have seen in section Ia, "Queer Performativity") for representational strategies tied to activist agendas. Attached to Müller's works as a style, postmodernism did not draw the historical situation of postmodernity to its process of signification. It is the aspect of the postmodern as style that recommended Müller's later scripts to Western stages which have remained uninterested in the earlier plays. From the perspective of Müller's dramaturgy, however, the move into postmodernism performs the global expansion of first-world high capitalism. His late works both comply with the structural consonance between high capitalism and postmodern performance scripts and promise some violent agitation against it. Fredric Jameson in *Postmodernism or The Cultural Logic of Late Capitalism* positions the uses of postmodernism within a similar political ambivalence:

> For political groups which seek actively to intervene in history and modify its otherwise passive momentum. . . . there cannot but be much that is deplorable and reprehensible in a cultural form which . . . effectively abolishes any practical sense of the future and of the collective project. . . . Yet . . . the attempt to conceptualize it in terms of moral or moralizing judgments must finally be identified as a category mistake. . . . The luxury of the old-fashioned ideological critique . . . becomes unavailable. . . . Still, the urgency of the subject demands that we make

at least some effort to think the cultural evolution of late capitalism dialectically, as catastrophe and progress all together. (46–47)

[For] postmodern space is not merely a cultural ideology or fantasy but has genuine historical (and socioeconomic) reality as a third great original expansion of capitalism around the globe. (49)

The move from theater to performance is an adjustment to the conditions of successful global capitalism. Abandoning the state stage for an indefinite arena, formed by the specific practices in the script, rather than any formal "real estate" of the stage, emulates the growth into a global system of what had previously been produced as part of national contests. Performance, like global capitalism, appropriates space wherever it occurs. The national redistribution of land represented in *The Resettler* becomes *DESPOILED SHORE MEDEAMATERIAL LANDSCAPE WITH ARGONAUTS*. This is the shore where Jason, the colonizer of lands, women, and children landed and

> watched the images crash into each other
> The forests burned in EASTMAN COLOR. . . .
> Our port was a dead movie house
> On the screen the stars rotted in competition
> In the lobby Fritz Lang strangled Boris Karloff (135)

Colonized space is represented as the screen of the most successful cultural export of the capitalist West: movies. The landscape is swallowed up and spit back out by Eastman color, and the people are competing actors on the screen. Land, territory, as the space of the screen represents the commodification of it. Elegant, insulated images trail across this space, emulating the commercial packaging of things on the "despoiled shore" of global capitalism. The despoiling of the habitat is represented by movies that subsume its relations into a purely commodified space (see Conley's notion of "habitat" in section V, "Body as Flesh Zone"). In Müller's late texts, the reign of images follows Guy Debord's notion that "the image has become the final form of commodity reification" (in Jameson, 18). The cultural and literal landscapes are completely commodified and available only as screened. The verse play is supplanted by the image play—more like high-budget, special-effect movies in its interest in the visible and its dis-investment in the discursive: more like *Cats* than *Hamlet*. Screening is the process of exporting capitalism. What role can communist performance or intellectual production play within high commodification?

Two performance scripts by Müller focus on the condition of the intellectual and of books in these altered territories: *Hamletmaschine* (*Hamletmachine,* 1977) and *Leben Gundling's Friedrich von Preussen Lessings Schlaf Traum Schrei* (*GUNDLING'S LIFE FREDERICK OF PRUSSIA LESSING'S SLEEP DREAM SCREAM, 1979*). The former title is agglutinative, melding the intellectual function with the notion of the desiring "machine," borrowed from Deleuze and Guattari. The latter title, like DESPOILED SHORE, is shredded into isolated captions, separated by empty space, moving through history and literature into the horrific. Both plays are short and scrappy—*Hamlet* only eight pages. HM: "there was no historical substance for real dialogues, it turned into separate monologues of Hamlet and Ophelia. . . . It is the description of a petrified hope, an effort to articulate a despair. . . . It certainly is a terminal point" (Müller 1984, 50). *GUNDLING* still retains a few conventions of a play. Some scenes relate sequentially, and some characters suffer narrative development, but dialogue and character soon give way to long, imagistic stage directions and ungrammatical collections of capitalized words.

Intellectual and sexual proclivities are conflated as impossible operations within the commodified, fascist state. This assumption contradicts the later one posed by Queer Nation that sexual practice can found an alternative "state" in the midst of commodification. The intellectual, Gundling, is sequestered in the court of Frederick I as the tutor of young Frederick II. Gundling is mocked and abused by gruff courtiers for his intellectual proclivities; Frederick II is likewise mocked and abused for his sexual ones. In one scene, the young Frederick II appears in drag, playing Phedre to his lover Katte's Hippolytus. Katte is then executed by Frederick I, in order to "teach" his son "to fuck assholes and to prattle in French" (65). Compulsory masculinity, heterosexuality, and nationality are compounded in an aggressive, sadistic practice of state torture. The action moves to a scene with professor and students in a madhouse, where he introduces them to virtues of the straitjacket:

> An instrument of dialectics, as my colleague on the faculty of Philosophy would conclude. A school of freedom indeed. . . . The more the patient struggles, the tighter he straps himself . . . into his own destiny. Everyone is his own Prussian, to use a popular phrase. Here lies the educational value, the humanism so to speak. . . . The philosopher would conclude that true freedom is based on catatonia. . . . The ideal state founded on the stupor of its populace, eternal peace on the global stoppage of the bowels. The physician knows: states are based on the sweat of their peoples, the temple of reason on pillars of feces. (72)

This passage reflects that there is no longer any sense of the GDR as the setting for an alternative state. Statehood constrains, dialectics constrain, and local change has become "global stoppage." International capitalism and, after 1968, imperialism seem to be the practices of states both East and West. Following the straitjacket, the masturbation bandage is introduced as a way to bind citizens from the pleasure manipulation of their genitals. Sexual activity only increases the ba(o)ndage. There is no possibility for an "anti-normal" or "queer" sexuality in the state. If there is, performing it only tightens the bonds of constraint.

The "ground" of cultural production appears in a section entitled ET IN ARCADIA EGO: THE INSPECTION. The scene is a turnip field, where land is linked once again to intellectual property. Frederick II presides over the scene populated by (unlanded) working peasants, a boys' choir, a flock of painters, Schiller, and Voltaire. The land, the people, and the arts produce for the monarch's pleasure. The idea of books as paper is reversed: material conditions are defined by despotic whim. The peasants pull turnips, which Frederick calls "oranges," and his vocabulary prevails. He then requires the peasants to exhibit a folk dance. Cultural production is now a requirement of the state, rather than in dialogue with it. Those of a different class—the un-landed—are required to produce "folk" arts for the reception of the tyrant. "Tyrant" might here be read as the colonial aspect of either the "first world," the U.S., or the USSR. The farmer's resistance practiced by stealing books for toilet paper, represented in *The Resettler*, is no longer possible in this order. "The peasant," the "farmer," and even the "worker," those who produce, either material or cultural goods, are already a fiction of the state. So, "self-interest," in the sense of using the books, has already been colonized by an outside demand for production. Notably, cultural and agrarian production is on the same "land." When there is no alternative nation, or division of property, there is no alternative culture. Frederick, as the benevolent despot, represents not only a legacy of Prussian history, but also the legacy of contemporary "tyrants" who would import "foreign" cultures into the field. Frederick's penchant for the French is a structural homology of global capitalism that exports cultural goods from the U.S. into other local spaces that would Americanize, in this case, German taste.

In the final scene of *GUNDLING'S LIFE,* the United States provides the stage, the land for culture as an automobile junkyard. Enter Nathan the Wise and Emilia Galotti. She cries, "Force! Force! Who can resist force?" (78). Projections and voice-overs overcome the characters. Lessing is fit (over) with a bronze bust. The play closes as he screams beneath it. "Taste" is unmasked as the forceful exportation of ideology through culture. Bourgeois theatrical forms, represented by Nathan and Emilia, are on the consumerist junk stage of the U.S. Their interiority is out of style. Art is monumentalized as spectacle and as consumer item—in one sense, Lessing becomes a car. Or perhaps he has become a television—a movie—the "canned" product of his theatrical voice. There is no other way for him to appear. In one sense, this setting of the junkyard seems Romantic—as if there were authenticity and "art," in the traditional meaning of the term. The resonances are more specific than that, however. While in the U.S. the television or movie appears to be "within" the culture, from the perspective of a nation that has long been the target of Voice of America broadcasts, rock concerts staged just on the other side of the wall (produced in "sympathy" with the GDR youth), and television broadcasts increasingly consumed by U.S. productions, the ideological intent of cultural export/importation is nakedly colonizing in intent, junking all other uses of production in service to national agendas and international markets.

One might continue to read arresting connotations into such scenes, as when Nathan, the Jew, collides with Emilia, the woman—both the victims of their own "bourgeois tragedies." Yet to unpack all these images for their allusions would be to go against the text. Their impacted state, along with the acceleration of their accumulation, produces the performance. The critical practice of tracing images, isolating them, and explicating them pertains to a different order of performance:

HM: "When I write I feel the need to load people with so much that they don't know what to take on first. . . . Not to introduce one thing after another, which was still the law for Brecht. Now you have to bring in as many factors as possible at the same time so that people are forced to make choices. That is, maybe they can't choose anymore, but have to decide fast what they can assimilate first" (Fehervary, 81). The critic is situated similarly to those who perform the texts: forced to make local decisions within the maelstrom of images. The texts remain turgid and impenetrable through their accelerated accumulation of isolated effects. In contrast to the long, five-act Epics, which wrote out the dialectic in its full narrative effect, the compression of these images and phrases forestalls any discursive process. The act of interpretation manages, somehow, to create a relationship with the artifact—narrow the distance between the stage and the viewer. In contrast, these performances run loose, without a citizenry or collective body to create an audience and without the land that supports the stage; their dramatic action is, instead, a spectacular head-on collision.

The strategy intensifies in *Hamletmachine*—the eight-page fragmentary end of Hamlet (read European male intellectual). Hamlet is a cipher that signifies the end of the masculinist tradition of knowledge. While Hamlet's play no longer has a stage, Ophelia's has never been representable; therefore she provides the possibility for dramatic action. Without a land, or an audience, the performance text maps what is impossible to stage: *"The deep sea. Ophelia in a wheel chair. Fish, debris, dead bodies and limbs drift by"* (58); or, *"On a swing, the madonna with breast cancer"* (55). These suggestions are so technically absurd that they call for the performers to conceive of something quite different, but somehow appropriate. Through these kinds of decisions, the performance becomes more and more distant from the text. Yet, at the same time, the local is intensely produced. The author can no longer script the stage where the performance appears—the performance runs loose from the text. In the middle of *Hamletmachine*, the stage directions indicate that a picture of the author appears—only to be ripped apart. The last vestige of his agency remains shredded on the stage. The written, print text is thus distanced from the production. The words, the print run along their own, distant course while the sweating bodies of the actors find their own space—establish their own use for the images. They have no other choice.

Along with the intensification of the process of commodification, a resident terrorism is revealed in the way the images work. HM: "Ophelia has to do with Ulrike Meinhof and the problem of terrorism in Europe, a complex issue that was very much, and in an ambivalent way, on my mind when I wrote the piece" (Müller 1984, 50). It is important to understand the term "terrorism" in the sense it accrued in the 1970s, before it became a strategy of the Fundamentalist Right in the U.S. in the 1980s. By now, terrorism seems a double-edged sword, although some would contend that it always has been. Müller's sense of it was both a literal and a semiotic one, composed from the practice of Ulrike Meinhof and the semiotic terrorism suggested by eurocommunist authors such as Jean Baudrillard in his book on terrorism, *Kool Killer oder der Aufstand der Zeichen (Kool Killer or the Revolt of Signs)*. Müller's late plays incorporate two terrorist strategies that Baudrillard identifies as efficient within a high capitalist system: the reversibility of signs and semiotic implosion. Baudrillard notes, "Terrorism is everything ambivalent and reversible: death, the media, violence and victory" (10; translation mine). He asserts that the terrorist act is to make all values interchangeable so that no fixed value may be assigned to any one. The acts as signs are therefore not absorbed into the system of meaning, or the uses of that system. This is an anti-Enlightenment form of political writing and action— working in opposition to the process that would eradicate error, win victories, find absolute contradictions, or resolve them. Instead, the terrorist revolt of signs inscribes unclear distinctions, error, confusion, and failure. In this way, it is not a modernist terrorism, nor does it reinscribe the modernist subject as agent that had, for example, informed the founding of the GDR and the traditional meaning of revolution. Baudrillard: "the order of the real belongs to the expansionist system in which everything functions . . . to shut out the contradictory powers . . . in contradiction to this principle is the virulent implosion . . . the suppression of worth, sense . . . and thus a gigantic suction, a gigantic absorption" (14–15). However poststructuralist or postmodern this strategy may seem, when held up against the practice of 1970s terrorism, it confounds a purely discursive use of it.

Terrorism, in the Meinhof-Baader practice of it, was anticonsumerist, in the bombing of a seemingly uninhabited department store; class-conscious, in its terrorizing of a wealthy banker; and directly involved in struggles for alternative nations, in its association with the Palestine Liberation Army (the PLO). From one perspective, such terrorism could be perceived as isolated revolutionary acts without a popular movement. Ophelia is "on" the stage—one run amok by Hamlets and Poloniuses— where she flickers between debris and destruction (breast cancer) and terrorist action. Ironically, in 1989, those few women terrorists who had been offered protection by the GDR, where they established useful lives in communities and workplaces, were turned in by the Stasi for reward money when the state collapsed.

Ophelia's terrorism is set against Hamlet's spin of empty reversibility. Beginning with the first line of the play, "I was Hamlet," some position, no longer held, is nevertheless taken. **(See section IVc, "Blanking Out," for the computer uses of these performance strategies.)** Hamlet continues to speak, but it is self-admitted nonsense, as he reports that he "talked with the surf BLABLA." Capitalized segments resembling verse are montages of quotations, either from Shakespeare (IM GOOD HAMLET GI'ME A CAUSE FOR GRIEF) or from other works by Müller himself (CLOWN NUMBER TWO IN THE SPRING OF COMMUNISM). Authors are dead quotations, snipped out of their Epic possibilities for action, or dialogue. The actor playing Hamlet insists, "I'm not Hamlet. I don't take part anymore," and the author's photo is ripped up, as the script nevertheless continues. A run on reversibility is made through the script. The exchangeability of meanings is kept spinning. A continual revolt of the signs is under way, in which the axes of referents sway this way and that. If there is no collective, and if hierarchical forces seek to everywhere oppress, then the dialectic exchange of meanings cannot take place in dialogue; instead, reversibility replaces contradiction. Strike the pos(e)ition and the other way. Nevertheless, the script closes on the promise of terrorist activity:

> This is Electra speaking. In the heart of darkness. Under the sun of torture. To the capitals of the world. In the names of the victims. I eject all the sperm I have

received. . . . Down with the happiness of submission. Long live hate and contempt, rebellion and death. When she walks through your bedrooms carrying butcher knives you'll know the truth. (58)

If the GDR provides no other space of operations from which or in collusion with which a movement may be launched, then the revolt must be buried within the burgeoning, tumescent capitalist system itself. Impossible images and the undermined text compose the script that would perform the terrorism. What was once an alternative space is now the space embedded in the packaging. Terrorism, then, is performed at the same time, and through the same means, as the complete commodification of the system. Text and image are isolated into commercial-like fragments of packaging. The image takes over as the sight of commodification in the stead of dialogue. The consummate site of terrorism is the final moment in *Hamletmachine*. The terrorist Ophelia is confined to a wheelchair, while "fish, debris, dead bodies float by." She is lodged within the swollen, dead image. HM: "It is a time when one must bury the lesson, as Brecht would say, as deep as possible, so that the dogs won't come upon it. Until the time when it can be dug up, and a new, altered reality can be proposed" (Müller 1990, 24). But she will walk through bedrooms with her knife. Note once again how the subversive element is located in the spoken text, while the image bears the weight of commodifying pressure.

Text and image are at odds with one another. Robert Wilson's production of *Hamletmachine* or Johannes Birringer's of *Explosion of a Memory* celebrates the distance of physical action and images of the performance from the text. By running Müller's text on tape, or in Birringer's case through a digital sampler, in a loop separate from the performance of images, they create an "elsewhere" that no longer exists in any site other than an authorial one. In their scenario, Müller the author functions as the GDR once did, to signify the space of the now-dead dialogue—to run a monologue of political impulse. From the perspective of the performance of commodification, the author regains the spotlight as commodity, and the terrorist potential is defused by the box office success of spectacle. What *Cats* did for T. S. Eliot, Wilson's productions can do for Müller.

Nevertheless, unhinging performance from text continues to play the disjunction that performs both the commodification of practices and the resident terrorism. Separating the two orders operates in direct opposition to the aims of performativity that would somehow ally text and performance, either by lending the performative to writing, or by affirming writing about performance. Adding a consideration of economic forces in addition to those of gender and sexual practice has encouraged a style of performance that would stage the very schism that notions of performativity seek to heal. When the politics of sexual practice and gender insubordination are cut loose from their economic bearings, then, their operations find a shelter in subversion, a quiet lea of consonance that, through a notion of subjectivities, sutures the orders of text/action/visible to a discursive, critical mode. These performance strategies of disjunction enact a screening that doesn't suture. The disjunction is both the motor and the endpoint of the performance.

DEATH OF THE AUTHOR/BIRTH OF THE PERSONA

Ironically, the much-touted death of the author heralded by postmodern critics has made celebrities of the messengers. Earlier we observed how the fanzine *Judy!* accompanied the rise of Butler's writing of "queer performativity." There, the critical withdrawal from answerability to activist movements and any representative role they might play in the discourse allowed a swift commodification of the author herself as a "star." At this point, we may consider how Müller, the scribe of terrorism, became first the national "character" of the GDR, and later the celebrity of the two Germanies. While he may share in the process of postmodern commodity fetishism with Butler and others, his case also illustrates the specific formation that turned communism into a character.

Ever since the Greek tragedies served civic holidays, or Shakespeare staged the succession of kings, the playwright has scripted the state—even, as in the above practice of guerrilla graphics, in the nature of his formal distance from it. Yet, traditionally, the margins of theater were prescribed by the head of state: Louis assigned Molière his role at Versailles, the Party assigned Brecht to the Berliner Ensemble. In recent years, the hierarchy of power between playwright and state has been reversed—particularly in the East bloc: Havel was elected president to literally script the state, and Heiner Müller garnered the role of the "national character" of the GDR. Indeed, this slippage between script and state, the power of strategies in representation to suffuse social life, operates as a central concept in the field of cultural studies. "Performance" and "spectacle" have become the catchwords for power relations in the public arena. The case of Heiner Müller provides an opportunity to demonstrate just how a playwright, through his dramatic, theatrical, and personal production, has emerged as a representative of the state. The case of Müller may be employed to organize a specific contemporary cooperation between cultural and social operations of power, which may imply a more prevailing practice of state and cultural assignment of value. First, just how has Müller been cast in the role of the "national character?"

In Germany, the format of a trial became the first postwar form to morally debate political issues. The Nuremberg Trials proceeded by individual case histories to create the sense that there was something like a fascist character. Through the legal processes of interrogation and punishment, state crimes were assigned to individuals—as if fascism lurked within a certain type of character. The drama of these trials found a long tradition in Germany's sense of the stage as "a moral institution" to test character and the decision-making process. Thus, subsequent to the actual trials, the dramatic form of the docudrama produced a literal staging of the discovery of fascism in the drawing of a character. Interrogation was "fleshed out" by biographical and psychological attributes of a personality that led to the development of fascism as a dramatic persona. Later plays such as Thomas Bernhard's *Eve of Retirement* abandoned the context of factual evidence altogether to draw the character of fascism as an ahistorical attribute, lingering on within certain types of personalities. In some docudramas, the audience was literally positioned as the jury, although this role was already implied in the form itself. Thus, in postwar Germany, the theater itself and the media served to create an audience of judges, positioned morally to establish political and historical verities through the analysis of character.

Cold War discourse cast the economic and ideological differences between the two Germanies in a melodramatic conflict of the "evil East" against the "heroic West." This time, a "communist" character emerged, whose insights and images could be interrogated. The "fall of the wall" provided the perfect sense of a climactic ending to this narrative. The familiar form of casting winners and losers as moral positions accompanied capitalism's "victory." The high moral ground of the victor was secured by the participation of the Church, which led the final strike against the state. Once again, the trial emerged as the major dramatic form. "Communists" were to be tried for their participation in the failed system. The economics of the situation were solved within the melodramatic form: the GDR was guilty of state socialism, and the punishment was the "restitution" of private property to those who owned it before the rise of the state.

On the moral plane, while some literal trials did occur, most of the evidence of "character" was established in the arena of the media. Who was guilty of being a communist, and how was that to be established? Denunciation became the glue of "unity." With much ado in the press and in the magazines, the files of the secret police were made public (somehow overlooking the retention of secret files in the BRG). The Stasi were most certainly guilty, and former citizens who had "cooperated" with them (which seemed to imply anything from meeting with one of them to actual files) were tried in the media and among themselves for that cooperation. The GDR Academy of the Arts was tried for authentic artistic production. The West did not consider the GDR members to be artists, but merely Party functionaries. (Interestingly, the BRG presumed no such contradiction within its membership.) They were guilty of producing propaganda rather than art. Within this spectacle, Müller became one of the central players in the finale. He headed the GDR Academy during its final months of existence. His photograph filled TV and magazine formats as he was charged with cooperation with the Stasi, producing propaganda for the state and enjoying, as such, illicit freedoms that were denied to other citizens. Yet, in spite of such charges, he retained a central role in the new state theater. He was made one of the Intendants of the Berliner Ensemble, a director at Bayreuth, and multiple productions of his plays filled the theaters.

Charges of communism announced the death of the final GDR "character," as well as its appropriated new birth in the capitalist West. That Müller would be cast in this role was no surprise. He had, for decades, given countless interviews that set him up as the "native informant" of GDR ideological practices. His plays had staged the history of the GDR and the merging role of the intellectual. He had put the media and the entire system of representation on trial in his own works. He had corrected the role of Brecht, who had hidden inside his theater in order to escape the strike of 1956. Brecht played the playwright who retreated into the state, as the state retreated into itself. Müller became the playwright to remain in the East, yet to be interviewed in the West about the values and practices of a communist existence. The interviews melded his own appearance with the character of the intellectual—the cultural producer. His impressions and reactions registered the character of the committed GDR intellectual, as in an interview in *Semiotext(e)*: "When I go from Friedrichstrasse checkpoint to the zoological garden in west Berlin, I feel a great difference, a difference in civilization, a difference of ages, of time"(36). Important here is the inscription of his own sensibility. "I feel"—appealing to his own perceptive powers as a subject of this historical divide, to register, from the side of the GDR, the experience of the two "cultures." He historicized the process of doing this, quoting himself as register, to make texts of his own earlier interviews and to conflate them with his work, with critical attention to his work. He described "the people" as a whole, and represented the Communist perspective on the West. He even framed it within psychoanalytic principles, as the following quotation exhibits:

> People brought up here have at least an image, or a hope, for another society, for another kind of living. This image is linked to the end of the commodity world. In the West, this world is in full bloom and you can never really get accustomed to that. Many of my friends moved to the West—writers especially. They tried to write there, but it's really a problem. You can never forget the image of another world. That becomes their schizophrenia. . . . Everything you write in the East is very important for the society or the society believes it's very important. You have a hard time being published here because it has such impact.

> SL: You mean that in West Germany you can publish almost anything because it has no impact?

> HM: It's an artificial freedom, an artificial space for ideology, for the arts and for literature. The artificiality of this freedom is based on the fact that West Germany couldn't function if foreigners, people from the south, from poor countries didn't do the dirty work or service work. In our countries, in our bloc, we are on the contrary in some sort of osmosis with the Third World. Russia is just a very small part of the Soviet Union. Its population is minimal in relation to the Asian provinces, the Asian regions. . . . The Third World is like a big waiting-room, waiting for history. There is a line by Jim Morrison: "Live with us in the forests of Asia. . . ." (37–39)

> SL: You actually mean that Western fantasies are a stabilizing factor in East Germany?

> HM: Yes.

> SL: Because they are produced on the other side of the wall?

> HM: Yes.

> SL: In psychoanalytic terms, fantasies are some sort of frame or window. Variations within the structure of the frame are virtually infinite, but if you go through the frame and act out your fantasy, you die. Is that what the wall is for East Germans: a window frame?

> HM: It's a good image for it. (43–44)

The idea of the wall as a frame, a fantasy, as screen, or as theater produces Müller as character—both the playwright and actor in the melodrama of East and West.

Müller uses the wall as a scrim, the (iron) curtain effect that with certain lighting reveals what is projected onto it from the audience side, and with backlighting reveals what it conceals on its other side. Walking from one side to the other, Müller lends the magic of theater to his persona. He commodifies his own persona. Drawing from the tradition of the communist character and the political playwright, he scripts himself as intellectual of the state—borrows from his own stage to enliven himself as persona. He travels back and forth, enthralled by the display and enabled to articulate its meanings. He is the roving communist character, the scripter of the deconstruction of the script— the very animation of the wall's graffiti. He circulates his own image while denying the author—like Butler, he quotes himself as an act of disabling the subject. He is the individualist end station of the collective—the new arena for staging the script.

What has happened to performance, as Müller becomes his own character? As we have seen, performance is tied to the establishment of another land, another kind of property. Within territories dedicated to another kind of ownership, the body could be productive. Processes of de- and re-territorialization provide a space for cultural production. When this space has been assimilated by colonialist or capitalist forces, there is no possibility for experimentation. Culture becomes commodification, local interest becomes folkloric apings of the indigenous, performance becomes part of an import-export structure. This is old stuff, traditional Marxist thought, seemingly corrected by postcolonialist or poststructuralist discourses. Debates over the uses of books in Müller's performance scripts are compacted into obscene citations of quotations that float free from characters and dramatic action. Instead, they stand like isolated columns remaining from the architecture of their production. In terms of Hamlets, like Müller, performance itself is compacted into the playwright's own persona, self-referentially exchanging interviews for performances, referring to the playwright without plays. The slight hope is in the Ophelia character, who has not lost her stage, but who has no stage—never had a stage. Her body, although infected by patriarchal sperm and breast cancer from the despoiled shore, is still capable of terrorist action, of producing contradiction, dialogue—performance.

During the final stages of this book's production, Heiner Müller died. The public and media reception of his death confirmed his role. The funeral was, in the words of many, the funeral for the GDR. Rites of Müller's demise served as ceremonies of mourning for the end of that particular brand of communist culture. The newspapers, magazines, and television talk shows presented the debates around Müller's position, from an excoriating review of his life and collusion with the Party by the GDR expatriate Wolf Biermann in *Der Spiegel,* to praise for his donation to pan-German theater by leading directors and actors. His plays were read aloud on Berlin stages in twenty-four-hour marathons, bygone productions were restaged within the month, a festival of videos of his interviews ran on one of the television stations, etc.

This complex relationship between persona, playwright, and political figure served to make Berlin the stage for Müller's passage from East to West as well as his passage into death. Berlin as stage is familiar to many since its postwar division and its reunification, but in this instance it became a kind of self-reflexive theater for the playwright himself. In the upcoming section on the lesbian stage, we will note a similar play between persona and stage in the productions of WOW. Without the formality and scope (and funding) that Müller and the state stage represent, the lesbian community's "open mike" and butch-femme role playing likewise conflate playwright, persona, and political figure. The issue of responsibility haunts these figures, dividing persona from star. In other words, as long as the persona remains responsible and responsive to the community she or he represents, the political affect remains. Charges against Müller as an informer for the Stasi question his loyalty and responsibility to the people of the state, while the early corrections to his work, his continuing citizenship in the GDR, and his final leadership of the Academy of the Arts and the Berliner Ensemble seem to signify his ongoing sense of responsibility as the character in the communist/capitalist melodrama. Likewise, the ongoing commitment of WOW, of Lois Weaver and Peggy Shaw, to the community will be tested by signs of commodification, both in their performance history and in the community's own dissolution into commodified subculture. Is the persona the last remnant of the socially responsible playwright, or scripter of performance within global capitalism? If persona and performativity represent the new theater-without-bounds that saturates social functions, do they install performance without dialogue, the finale of individualism and globalism?

The state funeral means to point to the final consideration of persona and state as something which has the potential to be alive and to die. Müller's own *Hamletmachine* opens with the state funeral set before the "ruins of Europe." Persona has, in one way, become a *tableau vivant* of a biography, signaling some kind of closure, even while living, within the signifying process. The question of the "live" comes back to haunt nation, then, at the site of the state funeral. Perhaps, in Müller's case, if the GDR was self-identified as the "worker's state," his funeral signified both the dying of a living man associated with performance and the dying of a state whose existence signified the visible properties of laboring.

QUEER PERESTROIKA

Perhaps it is no accident that the term "queer performativity" grew up around acts of dying. Many people who died because of untreated AIDS made a political spectacle of their dying acts—a state funeral in another sense of the term. Their deaths embodied the consequences of AIDS as an intervention into the abstracted practices of medical and state institutions, which would not account for their bodies. The body made a comeback in dying, and the mediating shell of a persona was perforated by "real" actions. At the same time, the necessary representation of (safe) sexual practices brought back the body along with an attention to the productive capabilities of action in the liveliest form since Existentialism. In the case of AIDS, the state funeral birthed the new state of Queer Nation. The point, as I embodied it in the fangs of the vampire (in "Tracking the Vampire"), was at the divide between life and death— necessarily an ontological consideration in the midst of its very deconstruction.

Both Müller and those who put their lives in the spectacle for the cause of AIDS self-consciously made of their bodies a persona that could be transmitted through virtual systems. ACT UP! deomonstrations were often created in order to garner media attention—they were aimed at the camera. Likewise, Müller mined the interview format to signal a communist character across the pages of magazines and through TV talk shows. He staged himself as the state. The crisis, then, in state systems of economic distribution, and the legislation of sexual practice converged in the persona, the virtual transmission of the "live" and the body. Unfortunately, as we shall see, the condition of the screen upon which they appeared overtook the representations it seemingly transmitted.

Returning to *Angels in America* after communism in the GDR renders a different perspective on its uses of socialism, nation, and gay identity. Ironic resonances are found in the use of the term "Perestroika," when one considers it from within an alternative, socialist nation. David Savran, in his forthcoming book, has made the astute point that the motif of the angel, derived from Benjamin's "Theses on the Philosophy of History," sutures "the Jewish notion of Messianic time . . . to the Marxist concept of revolution . . . not as the culmination of a conflict between classes . . . but as a 'blast[ing] open of the continuum of history'" (66). For the purposes of this work, I want to note also that the Angel in America blasts open history with a book—a book imbued with the power to fuse the alternative space of "heaven" with that of earth. It is as if Benjamin's performative library intercedes in history through the force of that blast. The book remains stable, then, as historical spaces are intersected. Messianic, in the promise of transformation, the book, print, takes its traditional position in relation to bodies in time and space. Print stands as the gateway to other spaces. If Müller has emptied *Hamlet*, the print text, out, Kushner reanimates it.

In *Angels*, the other space is "heaven"—an emulation of San Francisco after the earthquake. "Heaven," then, is the capital city of gay life, blasted by AIDS, disciplined by a closeted anticommunist homophobe (Roy Cohn), and haunted by the institutional murder of the communist revolution (Ethel Rosenberg's ghost). The millennium stands for hope—a second chance—a time to reconsider and repair. Yet the play seeks to establish neither an alternative nation nor an alternative economic system. The book remains a stable figure, the practice of private property goes untested, and individual relations find no collective possibility. Instead, the play represents the association between commodity fetishism and the politics of the gay subculture. David Savran sums it up:

> The Appearance of the Angels signals the degree to which utopia—and revolution!—have now become a product of commodity culture. Unlike earlier periods, when utopia tended to be imagined in terms of production (rather than consumption) . . . late capitalism envisions utopia through the lens of the commodity—and not unlike Walter Benjamin—projects it into a future and an elsewhere lit by that *"unearthly white light"* which seems to represent, among other things, the illimitable allure of the commodity form. (72)

Savran brings together the relations among Benjamin, the book, and commodity that were discussed in the section on Benjamin's library. This gay play, then, while signaling communism and socialism, actually proffers the performative link between commodity and individual subjectivity within the context of gay issues. As we will see, this form will constitute what the 1990s sexual movement imagined as its alternative space: Queer Nation.

America, then, is both de- and reconstituted as a liberal democratic nation of possibilities, knit together by individual loyalties and histories. In spite of the recurring mention of socialism in the play, collective experiments are omitted. Fragments of families, from mothers and grandmothers to wives, constitute central relationships. Finally, individual relationships overcome political differences. AIDS is presented without the backdrop of ACT UP! or other "community" organizations. Granted, the play is set in an earlier time period than the one of these organizations, but that choice offers the desired context within which AIDS politics may play. Jewish identity and Mormon identity are set within a historical past, but gay identity is not. Thus, sexual politics remain in consonance with notions of America, as it defines itself, of capitalism, as it is practiced, and of individualistic relationship, as they are privileged. *Angels in America* is the play of its time—judged not only by its success on Broadway, but by its staging of the contemporary trends in 1990s sexual politics.

Situating gay politics at the end of this section on communist practices begs the relation of sexual politics within its own historical context. How do these politics relate to the context of lesbian and gay movements? Certainly, the politics of *Angels* do not represent the entire movement—many critiques have circulated against them from other quarters. Nor would I set up a binary between gay and lesbian. Further, these politics seem more what I would define as "queer" rather than gay. They signify the 1990s. Just exactly what I mean by the 1990s can become clear only by returning to the 1970s and the development of notions of community and subculture within the lesbian political movement.

SEXUAL STAGES:
FROM LESBIAN COMMUNITY TO QUEER NATION

Initially, critics working on lesbian performance assumed the notion of community in order to identify what was "lesbian" onstage. Jill Dolan, in *The Feminist Spectator as Critic,* assumed a lesbian spectator who brought community values into the theater, and who perceived "lesbian" performance through the circulation of the signs of those values onstage. Kate Davy assumed that "the world as constituted by lesbians and inhabited by lesbians is the premise from which most WOW productions proceed," noting, then, that the performances actually proceeded out from community concerns and behaviors. Davy refined this notion into "lesbian spectatorial communities," to be more contingent on the performance itself, suggesting that community congealed around or during performance (Davy, 231). Central to my own earlier work was the notion of discursive practices that originated in the lesbian community, such as camp, or butch/femme role playing. The assumption of a lesbian community worked in performance criticism to produce a shared vocabulary of gesture, costume, language, and rules of the game which performance circulated or simulated, and was thus lesbian.

The performance pieces of Lois Weaver and Peggy Shaw became the icons of this relationship between performance and a sense of lesbian community. Writing on lesbian theater became writing on their work, as the ongoing articles by Kate Davy, Jill Dolan, Lynda Hart, and me illustrate. Their venue at WOW operated as an "open mike" into Manhattan's Lower East Side lesbian subculture. Their performances both moved out into political activism in the street and brought agitprop street slogans and poses onto the stage. The audience was composed of friends and other performers, who regarded WOW as a kind of clubhouse or alternate home. Through WOW, lesbian performance circulated within an urban community, formed, in part, by the performance space itself. Holly Hughes, now a performance artist of some note, describes the space:

> One day I was walking down East 11th Street and bumped into WOW . . . and started volunteering there. I had gone to WOW for a few events before that. They were having double XX-rated Christmas parties at Club 57. . . . It was *for* women. People would come in there and strip off their clothes and put on lingerie. It had a lot of the drag theatre flavor and permission. And everybody became a performer. . . . [with] "I Paid the Rent in My Maidenform Bra" parties. (174)

WOW's permission to performance, distributed across the stage, parties, and striptease acts, begged the notion of community in its shared camp sensibility in regard to gender and sexuality. Separatist in its all-women composition, WOW embodied several of the feminist social structures. Permission to wear male drag, to perform inversions of dominant sex show practices, and to perform a lusting lesbian audience both maintained and reconfigured traditional theatrical values. The roles of playwright, director, and actor were interchangeable. Writing was not the primary source of text. Lip-synching requires no original script, parties are improvisations, and even one-night acts leave little written record. There was no premium on originality, nor on intellectual property rights—everything was up for grabs, so to speak. In fact, the erotics of performance relied upon the canny use of floating signifiers, as Hughes's reference to "I paid the rent in my Maidenform Bra" illustrates. Economic and sexual fantasies intermingle in such "poor theater," where paying the rent, stripping for women, and emulating the effects of splendiferous spectacle combine to provide pleasure by circulating the pleasures of ownership through processes of deterritorialization. Likewise, the individual is merely a "flasher" among the collective—an appearance within the communal atmosphere. In its open-mike format, WOW invited an ongoing series of short acts that provided all present with their "fifteen minutes of fame," as Warhol had prophesied. In other words, the conditions of collective live performance determined the parameters of performance.

While WOW made performers of party-goers, it also created a performing audience. Of course, live performance in itself encourages a sense of community—a coherence among people. The audience coheres, for example, through spontaneous laughter at the same times during the performance, or the exhibition of other responses that produce the sense of shared values. This is particularly true when the production relies on agitprop elements that encourage catcalls, cheers, whistles, etc. The audience is active together—they become visible to one another—players in the performance. This is what Kate Davy theorized in the term "spectatorial community." And the audience is active in terms of the performers, who hold their next cue until the laughter subsides, or who milk the laughter by building on whatever occasioned it, or who hurry on to the next dramatic beat when the laughter fails to occur, altering their playing style or timing to secure the next laugh. Live performance enlivens both audience and performers in relation to one another. Venues such as WOW foreground this interchange of active roles between audience and performer, circulating the positions among the entire collected group. The circulation, as it accelerates through familiarity, encourages a feeling of cohesion—the glue of community.

Moreover, the audience has also attended the performance in some venue that feels appropriate and welcoming. In entering a performance space, the audience inhabits a particular vicinity within the urban landscape. By virtue of their location, venues draw regular audience members from a particular mix of gender, ethnicity and class affiliations. "Live" audiences create, then, if only nightly, a kind of community of people in regard to the mix of peoples and the location of the venue. In the case of WOW, its site in the East Village associated it with a class-specific tradition of underground performance. Like the clubs around the neighborhood, WOW participated in a certain style of dress, living, wage earning, and cultural production. The location itself served to invite and discourage certain audience members, infusing the performance conditions with the community values from the "Village" in which it resided. What made WOW distinctive, however, was that it was one of the only venues for lesbian performance in New York. Sarah Schulman, the novelist and playwright, related her early experiences with WOW, noting that almost no other space would produce specifically lesbian performance. Thus, the tightness of the WOW community and the intensity of relationships beyond the stage, as well as the commitment to political action, were partially mandated by the intolerant conditions surrounding lesbian performance in New York.

Putting it another way, the conditions of lesbian performance were ghettoized. With no stages or spaces open to specifically lesbian work, and with no reviews in the presses, part of WOW's agenda was to produce lesbian visibility—within the conditions of the ghetto. The performances also bore the historical markers of the broader ghettoization of social contacts. Emerging from an era of bars and other such separatist sites, lesbian performance inherited a commonality of signifying practices. The necessarily covert practices of lesbian social life produced specific, one might even say secret, codes of identification. The historical practice of this signification and even the lexicon of signs have been documented by several lesbian historians, such as Elizabeth Kennedy and Madeline Davis, Lillian Faderman, and Joan Nestle. Grassroots archives have been established to house the signs specific to lesbian commonality, in the separate space of lesbian herstory archives. Thus, one way of reading "lesbian" into a performance was by identifying those signs that referenced the vocabulary of ghettoization. "Community" was, in part, a positive term for "ghetto."

Beyond ghettoization, the sense of a community was a political goal. Lesbian feminists strove, as a political agenda, to imagine themselves together beyond the causes and even the sites designated by their oppression. The notion of community was part of a political enterprise and specific to a historical moment. Ti-Grace Atkinson in her resounding manifesto "Lesbianism and Feminism," produced in 1973, clarifies that "it is the commitment, by choice, full-time of one woman to others of her class that is called lesbianism. . . . The crucial features of lesbianism are the political and tactical significance of lesbianism to feminism. This involves both analysis and strategy" (12). Atkinson defines lesbian as the organization of community through commitment, political analysis, and tactical strategies. Atkinson is also describing a life—a full-time commitment that is more inclusive than a vocation, or a delimited, achievable goal.

Particularly crucial within the context of my argument is Atkinson's succeeding definition of lesbian through an analogy to trade unions and the Communist Party:

> The strategic importance of lesbianism to feminism can probably best be understood by analogy. . . . The Party was "political" in the sense of directly and publicly attacking class structure. It was "militant" socialism. . . . The witch hunt that followed, on the Communist Party ostensibly, was government terrorism aimed at the socialist principle. . . . Lesbianism is to feminism what the Communist Party was to the trade union movement. (13–14)

Some early formulations of lesbian feminist community, then, were along the axis of identification with the Communist Party, explicitly in this instance, and in others with at least some of its practices and ideology . In Atkinson, a simple notion of lesbian as class emerged as a way of transposing the communist critique to the lesbian one.

Later, groups such as the Combahee River Collective added race to the mixture, basing their identity in class politics and the radical materialist critique, while amplifying its application.

> We realize that the liberation of all oppressed peoples necessitates the destruction of the political-economic systems of capitalism and imperialism as well as patriarchy. We are socialists because we believe that work must be organized for the collective benefit of those who do work and create the products and not for the profit of the bosses. . . . We are not convinced, however, that a socialist revolution that is also not a feminist and antiracist revolution will guarantee our liberation. . . . Although we are in essential agreement with Marx's theory as it is applied to the very specific economic relationships he analyzed, we know that this analysis must be extended further in order for us to understand our specific economic situation as Black women. . . . As Black feminists and lesbians we know we have a very definite revolutionary task to perform and we are ready for the lifetime of work and struggle before us. (16–22)

The Combahee River Collective formed its collective and its sense of community in the call for a lifetime of work and struggle.

If the dominant culture had provided a lesbian community by enforcing separatism through ghettoization, early lesbian feminists made community out of a call for dedication to political analysis and activism. In sum, the relations between the notion of lesbian and that of community were a combination of the oppressive separatism shaped by dominant culture and a specific political analysis and sense of dedication within the lesbian feminist agenda. This production of community was both material and discursive, producing lesbian social practices as well as semiotic ones. Early analyses of lesbian performance relied upon the specific vocabulary of signs that constituted and represented this community in order to identify what was lesbian on the stage. Moreover, the stage itself, in its venue and live performance practices, also constituted itself as a community.

However, the notion of community later became problematic within critical circles. Deconstructive, poststructuralist strategies charged community with assumptions of presence and naive constructions of agency that rested upon a polluted, essentialist base. In contrast, celebrations of absence, through the application of Lacanian principles to performance, sought to correct any resident assumptions of presence in live performance (see section Ib, "Burying the Live Body"). Yet, reviewing these early manifestos, it seems a supreme irony to charge such socialist, Marxist formulations, deeply rooted in the materialist critique, with "essentialism." One can easily perceive why a sex-radical critique would seek to distance itself from this early lesbian feminism. The narrow emphasis on work and struggle, with no articulation of sexual pleasure, had unfortunate consequences for lesbians, particularly when the anti-porn movement grew in strength. But exactly how the charge of essentialism became the major deconstruction of this base for identity politics is "mystifying." Perhaps the later 1980s critique has more to do with the "witch hunt," as Atkinson phrased it in her moment, of the Reagan years and the institutional power of the Right in that decade, than with some inherent error in the formulation. While seeming to make a correction in the direction of material practices, it actually withdrew from them, in an era of privatization and profit taking. Nevertheless, the later construction of queer and queer nation proceeded from just such attacks on the resident notion of community. For this reason, it is important to note exactly how the critique works.

Iris Marion Young's influential essay, "The Ideal of Community and the Politics of Difference" exemplifies the typical charge. Asserting that community "privileges unity over difference" as her starting point, Young finds in community an ideal that "totalizes and detemporalizes its conception of social life by setting up an opposition between authentic and inauthentic social relations" (302). Read against Atkinson's emphasis on analysis and strategy, and the Combahee River Collective's amalgam of race, gender, class, and sexual practice, these accusations ring rather hollow. Young continues to allege that, by mapping an "opposition between individualism/community," one that is "homologous with masculine/feminine," community merely reverses the valuations of bourgeois culture without constituting "a genuine alternative to capitalist society" (306–307). Young deploys the "bad binary" in order to accomplish this—the notion that the second term is produced by the first, as surveyed earlier in Butler, Hart, et al. Young faults community as the second term produced by individualism and comparable to femininity, which in turn is produced by masculinity. Likewise, the fault with the communist or socialist position, it would seem, lies in its role as the single challenge to capitalism. As the only alternative, it sets up a binary.

Yet strangely, capitalist production and its alternatives, central to the earlier writings, fell out of the ensuing anti-essentialist theoretical work that would insist upon its altercations with the dominant system. As we will see, later political organizations, such as Queer Nation, would propose no alternative models of production.

Authors such as Young read models of community as more coherent and cohesive than the fragile, temporal collective of negotiated improvisations that Müller describes, or that the sometimes one-night character of lesbian communal associations has ever afforded. Nor does the shared send-up that produces community through the inauthentic seem to fit the description. A hope, caught in the spontaneous laughter at a performance, or in the whistle of desire at an entrance by Weaver, appears in these critiques as the nightmare of petrification. Perhaps the problem was that in spite of changing venues and fluid associations among lesbians, both Atkinson and the Combahee River Collective call for a lifetime commitment. The stability in the model is one of continual resistance. In contrast, the work in the late 1980s celebrates slippage, setting oscillation against full-time political struggle.

Young's pursuit of Derrida through a critical rehearsal of community is compelling, until her analysis yields its own historical moment—the specific dynamic of community she would undo—the one that has typically shaped much of the resistance to earlier lesbian feminist strategies:

> Many feminist groups, for example, have sought to foster relations of equality and reciprocity of understanding in such a way that disagreement, difference, and deviation have been interpreted as a breech of sisterhood. . . . Such pressure has often led to group and even more movement homogeneity—primarily straight, or primarily lesbian, or primarily white, or primarily academic. (312)

Atkinson's call to "commitment, by choice, full-time of one woman to others of her class" is understood here as "pressure" toward "homogeneity." Now, note that, in her sequence of examples, Young situates "lesbian" among "straight," "white," and "academic." Surely, the operations of "homogeneity" secured by dominant practices are of a different order from those of what was once termed "oppressed" groups. Not so in Young's analysis. Noting that "racism, ethnic chauvinism, and class devaluation . . . grow partly from a desire for community," Young insists, "I do not claim that appeal to community is itself racist" (311–312), while implying that, in its exclusivity it does, in fact, emulate racist structures.

The function of the charge of presence and exclusivity, then, is to detonate the bar of exclusion from the operations of community through a deconstruction of alternative ones. The dramatic dialogue of contradictions, set up among communities of difference, is emphasized as painful and negative, rather than necessary and productive. Why this emphasis? Perhaps Young smarts at the portals that would not invite access. The location of lesbian, lone among "straight" and "white," along with the deconstruction of ethnic communities hints that it is precisely these exclusions that are the problem, for the other homogeneities, such as white and straight, actually *demand* access—one is required to belong. Is one aim of this argument to open the portals of access to alternative communities, while not assuming any enduring commitment to "resettling"? One might argue that this petrification of the hope is also charted in Müller's *Resettler*—in fact, this has been the charge against the East bloc that helped to bring down the credibility of any critique proximate to the Marxist one as well as the feminist one. The "collective" or "community" wish, then, brings the Party? Hence, the emphasis in poststructuralist politics on "oscillation" or "hybridity," offered as corrections to earlier, stable models of community, may be perceived as opening the portals of access to multiple, alternative positions with no firm, "lifetime" in Ti-Grace Atkinson's words, commitment to any one of them.

For Müller, the solution was to maintain the rolling dialogue of contradictions—ossification occurred when the dialectic ceased. Lesbian feminist strategies of collectivity and coalition suggested a similar model in their insistence upon coalition politics. Each community was locked in the dialogue of coalition with another. There was no stable coalition, but there was a continuing call for the dialogue of contradiction. As Bernice Johnson Reagon once described the mandate: "The 'our' must include everybody you have to include in order for you to survive. . . . That's why we have to live in coalitions. 'Cause I ain't gonna let you live unless you let me live. Now there's danger in that, but there's also the possibility that we both can live—if you can stand it" (365). The dialogue is not an internal, subjective shifting among positions within the individual. It is among communities as political conduits for discourse.

In spite of this activist base for community, Young chooses to deconstruct operations as an "ideal," by insisting that the kind of "I" and "you" that resounded through manifestos such as Reagon's suggested intersubjectivity—a model of Derridean "presence." Young contradicts that base by proposing that subjects cannot totally comprehend themselves, therefore cannot be "wholly present to one another" (310). Community, in Young's analysis, operates in ways homologous to identity and visibility. However, presence, in Ti-Grace Atkinson's or Bernice Johnson Reagon's deployment of it, meant "showing up": "Anytime you find a person showing up at all those struggles . . . one, study them, and two, protect them. They're gonna be in trouble shortly because they are the most visible ones. . . . They can teach you how to cross cultures and not kill yourself" (363). Reagon forges an activist connection between presence and visibility that Young would represent as calling for a "whole" and "unified" subject position. Moreover, she suggests that coalition means showing up at more than one struggle. In spite of the vehemence in the tone of such writings, recording the lack of cohesion, and the urgency of the call for some coalition, Young finds in the earlier practices a fixed unity.

Young's ideal, in contrast to such a community, would be "an unoppressive city" that would remain "open" to "unassimilated otherness" (319). As an explicitly urban formation, with coalition iterated rather than built, Young's analysis is in consonance with "queer" notions beginning to be formulated around the same time period. Her notion of "unassimilated otherness," however, may free up individuals from exclusionary communities in order to assimilate them back into the dominant structures, for there is no "empty" social space. The term "unassimilated" stands like "subversion" as a faith in the planless negative—the signature move in these theories—what Verena Andermatt Conley proposes, in her article "Communal Crisis," as a "community of trembling people. . . . an agitation in the wind" (68–69). Both indicate how the attempt to incorporate difference produced a decaying resistance to the forces of assimilation—the other side of exclusion. What "wind" is blowing, and who is gentrifying the "city's" property? If the notion of community resonates through earlier lesbian feminist politics, this charge against it rings with the sore experience of exclusion, which, on the one hand, does not suit the project, but, which, on the other, reveals the privileged mandate for access. Inherent, then, in the charge of "presence" and the deconstruction of community and identity is the historical position of the postmodern critic in the 1980s who, to secure access to alternative positions, would move heterogeneity either into the internal arena of the individual, where one may move among a variety of positions within oneself, or into something like an "unassimilated otherness." The first solution reinstates traditional capitalist models, and the latter seems a kind of putting away of any hope for collective processes.

Both Young and Conley are among theorists who find themselves trying to accommodate "difference" as their sole or primary consideration. The priority of this concern overcame their own alliances with socialist-based lesbian feminism. Instead of seeking coalition, they sought oscillation and urban otherness. Other critics would not throw out the communist, feminist baby for the new poststructuralist bathwater. They search, instead, to clarify how a call for community might endure as an efficacious political concept. They reformulate identity after the poststructuralist critique as well as agency. The Miami Theory Collective (of which Conley is a member), bearing the collective signature in their work, edited a volume entitled *Community at Loose Ends*—also in 1991. Conley's article stands at one end of the critical spectrum the volume offers. Others trace a closer consonance with earlier feminist strategies. Chantal Mouffe reflects, without perhaps knowing it, or citing it, the feminist project of commonality, written out in the poetry of Adrienne Rich and Judy Grahn that underlay the 1970s sense of the term "community." Mouffe writes: "We need to conceive of a mode of political association that . . . implies commonality" (75). And Mouffe's "commonality," set within radical democracy, specifically entails identity: "The creation of political identities as radical democratic citizens depends . . . on a collective form of identification among the democratic demands found in a variety of movements: women, workers, black, gay" (79). Mouffe continues that such a process

> aims at constructing a "we," a chain of equivalence among their demands. . . .
> [that] is not a matter of establishing a mere alliance between given interests but
> of actually modifying the very identity of these forces. This is something many
> pluralist liberals do not understand because they are blind to relations of power.
> They agree on the need to extend the sphere of rights to include groups hitherto

> excluded . . . but ignore[s] the limits imposed on the extension of pluralism by
> the fact that some existing rights have been constituted on the very exclusion or
> subordination of the rights of other categories. (80)

Community, then, relies upon identity for its formulation because hegemonic forces
are explicit in their exclusions. Mouffe rehearses again the positive role that notions
of identity and community could play, which the poststructuralist critique "corrected."

In the same volume, Paul Smith rethinks Marxism in terms of Realpolitik, insisting upon a distinction between the fine points of theory and political exigency. Describing Gramsci's compromise in theorizing between a "theoretical position" and a
"pragmatic issue, " and noting the immense scale that state and economic organizations now reach (109), Smith concludes that

> poststructuralist accounts of the "subject" will have to be surpassed if we are to
> reach an adequate notion of, or explanation for, the place of the agent in relation
> to the manifold and variegated structures of power and resistance that we live in.
> . . . not a theoretical "subject" but an active actor, and crucially historical entity
> among historically laden discourses. (110)

Finally, Linda Singer's contribution closes the volume with a general discussion
of the contradictions raised around community. She concludes: "community is not
a referential sign but a call or appeal . . . [that] aims at response . . . a conversation.
. . . One reads the appeal to community in this way, as the call of something other
than presence" (125). This seems a precise recuperation of Müller's early position of
communism as an improvised dialogue of conflicting positions as well as an affirma-
tion of the performative exchange of audience/performer that WOW provided as
lesbian community.

Community as a political strategy is making a comeback in some critical circles
in the 1990s. These critics, admittedly thinking along a postMarxist axis, attempt to
recuperate many of the early tenets in spite of poststructuralist charges of presence
and essentialism. Between the notion of community and its retro fittings, other terms
arose to describe alternative positions in the culture. They reveal how economic forces
began to overwrite socialist ideals.

Community, then, becomes problematized, even while recuperated. In all of the
examples, from Müller to Reagon, that interior dialogue of contradictions is planted
within the community itself. Müller embraced the alternative nation through his critique—setting the stage at odds with the state as part of the health of its properties.
Reagon's quotations resonate with the raised voices at feminist gatherings, where
struggles over differences became the signature of the community. What Young situated as a call for cohesion, the negative appraisal of such dialogue, one might see as
the dialogue of difference which constitutes the very notion of community. Young's
"cool" notion of "unassimilated" others calmly passing one another on the city streets
seems a utopian balm to be applied to the site of struggle. In the upcoming section on
Queer Nation, Sarah Schulman describes the process of organizing ACT UP! as hur-
rying past such discussions, onto the streets, in order to work for the changes be-

tween life and death. Her history of the queer movement traces the way in which coalitional processes were abandoned for the presumption of cohesion. We can see the flight from the 1970s notion of community as the flight from debate, disagreement, and struggle. In the same way, performance, the site of dialogue on the ground of the collective, played before it, was abandoned for a solitary one-person show, or the solitary writing of it in academic theory.

Still untested, the city does seem to offer the only successful site for collectivity. WOW identifies its performance practice with a certain "Village" within Manhattan. Urban values accompany whatever sense of "lesbian" performance arose there. Young valorizes the city as *the* site for any potential community. Müller's script is finally animated by his own wandering persona, moving back and forth across the wall that divided Berlin. Benjamin's flâneur still haunts the streets—an individual who, while walking among the throngs drawn together by the spectacle of commodities, is both inspired by that condition and has privileged access to it. This urban sense, with its fetish magic of commodities, served eventually to overwrite the notion of community with what became subculture. Urban in its setting, subculture offers strategies of consumerism as politically efficacious. At the same time, a sense of territory, of land, recedes amid the space of shop windows. Both of these directions, set by the assumption of the urban as political ground, will define the direction of the critique of the 1980s. If the 1970s witnessed the formation of communal retreats in rural areas, the "lesbians on the land" movement, along with the hippie exodus into agraria, the 1980s presumed collectivity only within the city.

SLIPPING INTO SUBCULTURE

Since the lesbian feminist community was not strictly separate from the dominant system, their significations and performances seemed to straddle both systems at once. After all, the "Maidenform bra" parties at WOW rested on the push-up support of an ad campaign. So in the case of performances for targeted communities such as this lesbian one, the notion of a "subculture" as a specific, limited signifying system operating within or "sub" the dominant one articulated more accurately than community how the "recognition" that causes the common laughter is composed both in and apart from the system. A certain slippage operated, and still sometimes operates, between the terms "subculture" and "community," revealing an ambiguous sense of just how collective alterity is established in relation to a dominant system. Various adjectives served to delineate the terms more provisionally and locally, as in Davy's term "spectatorial community" cited above. The notions of community and subculture, not officially bounded by state borders or ideologies, were always unstable—part mythological, in the service of visibility politics, and part historical fact.

Dick Hebdige's influential book *Subculture: The Meaning of Style* appeared in 1979. Opening the 1980s, the book set the terms for much of the ensuing overwriting. Subculture, as Hebdige has defined it, tips the balance between cohesive and disjunctive forces in favor of the latter: "If we emphasize integration and coherence at the expense of dissonance and discontinuity, we are in danger of denying the very manner in which the subcultural form is made to crystallize, objectify and communicate group experience" (79). The ambivalence, then, between employing either "community" or "subculture" is one of privileging one of these forces over the other. "Community" emphasizes cohesion, whereas "subculture" charts the formation of a group as a process of discontinuity with the dominant. Community surveys those who would come together, while subculture registers the distance from the dominant. If performance critics use the notion of community to establish a referent for the lesbian gestural system, perhaps it is to posit, as the focal point of the study, a kind of collective agency in creating the signs, above a consideration of their determination by the dominant signifying field.

"Community" in the earlier work of lesbian performers and their critics may also have been enabled by the disinterest the market had in their subcultural signs, leaving them to the manipulations of those who created and bore them. In terms of later analyses that will illustrate how major ad campaigns deploy the sign of "lesbian" to sell their products, WOW party titles employing "Maidenform bras" remained in the hands of the lesbians who took them off. In the third-floor walk-up room where WOW performances occurred, before a small group of regulars who paid minimal prices for the tickets (if there were tickets) to see their friends perform a few lip-synched songs and scraps of dialogue, dressed in thrift-store clothes, "community" may, in fact, have better described the conditions of performance and lesbian than the disjunctions and determinations such a venue suffered under the dominant regime. If the camp discourse was subcultural in its significations, its venue operated more as a community house, where birthdays were celebrated, people "hung out," dances were given, and other occasions occurred alongside "performance" in the more traditional sense of the term. Later, when Shaw and Weaver garnered Obies, and Holly Hughes emerged as a major performance artist in venues across the country, their work became designated more as postmodern than as lesbian. In other words, the formal attributes set the subcultural signs in motion. Weaver now works as associate artistic director of the Gay Sweatshop in London, and Shaw and Hughes are touring with their one-woman shows. WOW is, at most, a touchstone to which they sometimes return. Subculture is the style of postmodernism, "acting out" within and against the culture—across its international face.

Remembering WOW, in one sense, is to remember that subcultural signs were produced within a collective. One seemingly forgotten signature of lesbian feminist culture was the widespread practice of collective labor and ownership. Living in collectives and working in them was the mark of lesbian feminist practice that was both social and material. Sharing labor and the profits of labor, cultural production and pleasure was about investing in and supporting one another. This collective practice might have signified community more than "sub" capitalist culture. Today, most of those collectives have disappeared, from theaters, to food cooperatives, to book publishers, to bookstores, to early articles written by such collectives. The disappearance of this practice seems to go without note. The new bookstore chain A Different Light testifies to the difference in private ownership and high capitalist practices around the distribution of "subcultural" materials; upscale restaurants to food collectives; series at major, commercial presses such as Routledge to collectively owned presses.

Apparently, once market forces and lucre more insistently entered those processes of production, an emphasis on the topography of signifying practices better represented the conditions of performance than a sense of collective agency. The turn to assimilated, capitalist organization brought a new sense of political activism as the manipulation of commodities. Hebdige, in linking the term "subculture" with style, hinges his article on the focus on commodities. Performance became a manipulation of the market forces—a bricolage—the alternative composition of commodities:

> Commodities can be symbolically "repossessed" in everyday life, and endowed
> with oppositional meanings. . . . The challenge to hegemony which subcultures
> represent is not issued directly by them. . . . The objections are lodged . . . at the
> profoundly superficial level of appearances: that is, at the level of signs. . . . the
> sign-community, the community of myth-consumers. (16–17)

Hebdige brings together a new conglomerate of forces: the market, the manipulation of commodity, and the production of style as subcultural.

The subtitle of Hebdige's *Subculture* asserts that the realm of the subcultural may be organized through style. Hebdige arrives at his final paradigm for subcultural style in the association between Jean Genet and George Jackson. The alliance between the homosexual/prisoner/writer and the Black nationalist best exemplifies, for Hebdige's sense of the term, the complex interweavings of subcultural practices. The site of confluence between the two subcultures of homosexual practices and ethnic ones, as Hebdige would have it, was through the graffiti on the prison walls—a graphic, guerrilla form of writing (136). The deconstructive nature of the subcultural act is exemplified by writing over, as in writing graffiti over a billboard, on the Berlin wall, or on the tidy, policed walls of prison. Graffiti foregrounds the "ghetto of signs" organized by the dominant organization of public space and breaks its laws through a "crime of style." Graffiti is writing in its appropriative, spatial mode. Anti-discursive, graffiti writing "means" through the territories it appropriates. Through such overwriting, Hebdige would argue, homosexual and ethnic subcultures may conjoin as disjunctive. The play over the material of commodities overwrites forces of community and coalition. But how do these strategies test out within ethnic practices?

QUEER AZTLÁN

In her book *The Last Generation,* Cherríe Moraga, the Chicana lesbian poet/performance writer, records driving down the road through the Anza Borrego desert, east of San Diego, rounding a curve to see, writ high on a rock: AZTLÁN—the mythical name of the Chicano homeland in the southwestern United States (151). Moraga sees in the graffiti a graphic reclamation of the landscape for the Chicano community. Her vision is not one of subcultural style, but one of an alternative "nation." Like Heiner Müller's, Moraga's foundation of an alternative nation rests on the redistribution of land. Moraga's account is of those who live as continual resettlers—the Chicano farmworkers. She recalls the annexation of southwestern territories in 1848 and the continuing force that those national borders levy on the Mexican/Chicano peoples (151). She imagines a dissolution of the United States through the activist movements of indigenous people, which would redistribute the land. The graffiti on the rock is a writing of territories. National borders are at issue in her political organization. No subculture could accept those legislated privileges.

Yet Moraga also rehearses the problems with her own form of nationalist politics, from "Lesbian Nation," through "Black Nationalism," to the atrocities in Bosnia (149). She responds to the charge from many quarters, both activist and academic, that such a movement is dead. She tentatively agrees, but insists that, on the other side of the issue, colonialist processes are not dead—in fact, they are very much alive in the oppressive conditions of the Chicano farm laborers and the chemical territorialization of their bodies. Moraga invokes the most recent ferocious expansionist move into Mexico through NAFTA. At the time of this writing, NAFTA has incurred an indigenous terrorist movement against it, which is struggling to reclaim the lands of the Indians. Once more, in this hemisphere, the struggle between capitalist expansion and terrorism is playing out. But, as Moraga mourns, without a movement to support the oppressed. Moraga clarifies that she would not revive the prior movement, with its sexism and homophobia; instead, she imagines a "Queer Aztlán":

> We discussed the limitations of "Queer Nation," whose leather-jacketed, shaved-headed white radicals and accompanying anglo-centricity were an "alien-nation" to most lesbians and gay men of color. We also spoke of Chicano Nationalism, which never accepted openly gay men and lesbians among its ranks. . . . What we need . . . is a Queer Aztlán. . . . A Chicano homeland that would embrace all [*sic*] its people. (147)

Outside the Anglo "Queer Nation" with her Chicana politics, and the traditional Chicano movement with her lesbian ones, Moraga imagines a melding of the two in a third term. The conditional mode of its existence leads Moraga to a formulation almost identical to the one Müller has suggested, in the burying of terrorism, until it is safe to be dug up again: "'El Movimiento'. . . has retreated into subterranean uncontaminated soils awaiting resurrection in a 'queerer,' more feminist generation" (148). With a "nationalist" (in the sense of territories and state borders) "movement" (in the sense of community) that would embrace "queer" (in the sense of embracing Chicana/o lesbians and gays), Moraga has positioned an amalgam of many of the above positions and tactics to confront what she calls the "mono-culture" of expansionist capitalism (168).

Moraga's stage version of these conditions is a play entitled *Heroes and Saints.* Unlike her earlier, much-celebrated lesbian play *Giving Up the Ghost,* which is written in an experimental poetic form, *Heroes and Saints* conforms to the more traditional requirements of characters and plotting. Perhaps the formal difference is, as we have seen, produced by the sense of community. Her Chicana lesbian play did not have a stage to play upon—the Chicano community, which is addressed in the play, initially did not stage it. *Heroes and Saints,* as the title implies, introduces "lead" dramatic characters that would also "lead" the community. While the play is traditional in many ways, the lead character, Cerezita, is only a head—the result of prenatal chemical contamination in the fields. The character is derived from a central issue of the Chicano activist community in its struggle against the chemical spraying of hand-picked crops that causes multiple birth defects among the Chicano workers. Cerezita, though only a head, is nonetheless sexual. In a scene that breaks multiple moral codes at once, she gives "head" to the local priest. She is also in support of her gay brother who must travel between the Chicano farm community and the San Francisco urban, gay one—split between his two different orders of political identity. At the end of the play, Cerezita's now-dead head is carried through the fields like the statue of a saint by militant organized farmworkers. Like the graffiti Aztlán on the rock, the head screens the space through which it travels, reterritorializing it through image. In its spectacle and through its elevation by the activist movement, it represents the drive to reclaim the land by the people who work it, the right to a whole, sexually active female body, and the right to community by the gay brother. Moraga's fulsome sense of community, as in Müller's early work, rests firmly on the stage peopled by its citizens, in the dialogical practice of characterization. Surely, the emphasis on "difference" that guides the later critiques is to ensure the embrace of such ethnic politics.

Yet, Moraga's project of imagining a consonance among community, land, nation, and lesbian/gay sexuality is received as "exclusive" by some of the notions that support "queer performativity." It seems the disjunction Moraga finds between Queer Nation and a Queer Aztlán runs both ways. As before, through the more general poststructuralist feminist critique, the explicitly "queer" one charges "community" with exclusivity. One such example may be found in Diana Fuss's introduction to the influential anthology *inside/out.* Fuss levels the charge that community is too stable a notion: "most of us are both inside and outside at the same time," she notes, affording us only partial and temporary membership in the community, or more likely, subculture. Fuss continues: "Any misplaced nostalgia for or romanticization of the outside as a privileged site of radicality immediately gives us away, for in order to idealize the outside we must already be, to some degree, comfortably entrenched on the inside" (5). Imagining community betrays a participation in the process of legitimization. Moreover, argues Fuss, what constitutes "in" and "out" either is always already determined by the dominant, or ignores the complex, multiple, and changing positions of the subjects involved. Thus, she would offer an inclusion of oscillation and mutability at the site of stability. Juxtaposing Moraga's Queer Aztlán with Fuss's charges incites a confusion of contexts and referents. As Fuss describes those whose status of "in" actually produces the location of "out," Moraga describes what constitutes citizenship "in" the alternative nation this way:

> A new generation of Chicanos arrives every day with every Mexican immigrant.
> . . . Certainly the Mexican women cannery workers of Watsonville who main-
> tained a two-year victorious strike against Green Giant, and . . . Mothers of East
> Los Angeles and the women of Kettleman City who have organized against the
> toxic contamination proposed for their communities. In the process, the Mexicana
> becomes a Chicana . . . a citizen of this country, not by virtue of a green card, but
> by virtue of the collective voice she assumes by staking her claim to this land
> and its resources. (156)

These cannery workers and farm laborers have not come to their sense of being "out"
by somehow being "in" the dominant culture. Nor are the indigenous peoples who
are forming the "Zapatista" terrorist groups in Mexico, in the face of NAFTA, "comfortably entrenched on the inside." Should Cerezita's dead, unchanging head, marched
around the fields by the farmworkers, be compared to Fuss's "Borromean knot"—an
"invertible, three dimensional four knot "(7–8)? Should the farmworkers abandon
their fields for what Fuss promotes as signified by the knot—the "undecidability of
this simple topology" as its "greatest appeal" (7)?

Clearly, these are not the contexts within which Fuss is writing her correction.
These are not her referents. A crucial difference in referents between the two positions is governing what seems to be a fierce and dismaying debate. Upon what group
of referents, what constituency, is it more critically accurate to emphasize fluctuation,
hesitance (undecidability), and changing positions (invertible) over inclusion, mutual history, and a shared signifying code? If notions of community are limited, are
there also limits to the application of the subcultural, poststructuralist model? Do the
two terms in fact belong to two different groups? Does Fuss's commentary belong to
an "unmarked" community? Is the debate actually about where one assigns fluctuation
and stability? In other words, are such "queer" strategies actually aimed at basically
white, basically middle-class urban activists and theorists? Can they structure a coalition with indigenous people's demands for redistributing the land? Should queer
notions, instead of claiming a general applicability, actually admit that they, too,
reside within a certain "identity" politics?

QUEER NATION

Retaining the sense of the end of lesbian feminist collective practice, with its
attendant call for women to invest in women as two of the several alternative socioeconomic experiments of collective material and cultural production, situating the
overwriting of such practices by the term "subculture" in the 1980s, and juxtaposing
ethnic models with new, queer ones, we can now turn to the rise of Queer Nation, and
the succeeding operations of the term "queer."

ACT UP! was formed in March 1987 in New York, calling itself "a diverse, non-
partisan group united in anger and committed to the AIDS crisis" (Smyth, 15). In
April 1990, Queer Nation was formed in New York in response to gay bashings in
the East Village. One simple comparison with Moraga's Queer Aztlán would cer-

tainly reside in the differences between an activist movement on the streets of an urban center and one addressed to farm workers. New York stands as both the referent of the sense of Nation and, in its centrist attitude, the means of securing its local strategies as transcendent representations.

A number of contradictory poses were immediately perceptible in Queer Nation's claims. Cherry Smyth, in *Lesbians Talk Queer Notions*, cites an early article in *Out/Look* as describing the new movement: "Queer Nationals are torn between affirming a new identity—'I am queer'—and rejecting restrictive identities—'I reject your categories'; between rejecting assimilation—'I don't need your approval, just get out of my face'—and wanting to be recognised by mainstream society—'we queers are gonna get in your face'" (17). Queer Nation defined itself as an anti-assimilationist strategy, reveling in transgression while also pleading for civil rights; eschewing identity while claiming it. These complex negotiations were acted out on the street—in the face of the media and the public.

For lesbians, as Smyth notes, the move to queer marks the split of sex radicals from feminism. The founding of Queer Nation supplanted the tradition of lesbian feminism. Although the critical moment came in the late 1980s, I would argue that the split actually began in 1982. The Barnard conference staged the outbreak of open conflict between the lesbian s/m community and the feminist anti-porn adherents—a conflict that never got resolved. The debates among lesbians and feminists were hot, and the rifts were deep. What later became the "sex radicals" tired of feminism's het "missionary position," while the feminist critique stalled out in its persistent blindness to heterosexism. Meanwhile, the AIDS crisis was beginning to forge new alliances between lesbians and gay men. Patriarchal privilege aside, the gay men were in a life-or-death discussion about sexual practices—sex was a given, open focus in their community, while the feminist community, where heterosexism forced a silencing of the debate they were afraid to continue, seemed to be formulating neo-puritanical prescriptions against erotic materials and the exploration of sexual pleasure.

The rise of the Fundamentalist Right demanded a new, more aggressive political activism. The failure of government institutions to respond to the need for AIDS treatment became more and more reactionary. Queer Nation consisted of agitprop street performances, along with what Douglas Crimp has called *AIDS DemoGraphics*—graphics and graphic writing as visual interventions. Queer Nation, then, invented itself through its own form of performance and of graffiti. Stickers pasted to newspaper stands, handed out at ballgames, stuck to billboards, on walls, on the sidewalk, deployed images and writing to turn the dominant representational strategies back on themselves. Thus, a nation was invented through performance and writing—a specifically subcultural nation that organized its borders through representational disjunction. This Queer Nation was composed of lesbians, gay men, bisexuals, people of color, and any concerned, to enact AIDS activism. For a while. While some ACT UP! organizations survived, others, such as the one in San Francisco and the one in Seattle, split into ACTS UPS, or whatever. Lesbians split from gay men over the focus of concern: Is AIDS a gay male disease, or how do we also address the problems of the category "women," straight or lesbian, of color who bear a high incidence of AIDS? Latent feminist coalitions with other women, particularly women of color, still haunted the new dyke.

Beyond its issues, the political enterprise of Queer Nation self-consciously over-wrote earlier formations of political aggregation—eschewing the identity politics represented by the terms "gay/lesbian/person of color." Thus, it set out to correct earlier notions of community, specifically adjusting the relation of the lesbian or gay critique to the ethnic one. Michael Warner, in his introduction to *Fear of a Queer Planet,* critiques the use of "community" in lesbian and gay practices as attempting to organize, by homology, as if ethnic: "gay and lesbian community" is "a notion generated in the tactics of Anglo-American identity politics and its liberal-national environment, where the buried model is racial and ethnic politics" (xxv). The homol-ogy does not hold, argues Warner, but has been borrowed and then buried. Warner, along with other queer theorists, rejects gay/lesbian politics as "liberal"—even assimilationist. Rather than emulate the specificity of the ethnic community model, Warner tenders the concept of Queer as sweeping up the messy, denotative border disputes of the more restricted terms. Its breadth is global—more, it is, if we take his title, "planetary."

> The preference for "queer" represents, among other things, an aggressive im-pulse for generalization; it rejects a minoritizing logic of . . . simple political-interest representation in favor of a more thorough resistance to regimes of the normal. . . . Lesbian feminism has made lesbian theorists more preoccupied with the theme of *identity* [*sic*]. . . . "A certain pressure is applied to the lesbian sub-ject," Fuss points out, "either to 'claim' or to 'discover' her true identity before she can elaborate a 'personal politics.'" For lesbian theorists, queer theory offers a way of basing politics in the personal *without* acceding to this pressure to clean up personal identity. (xxvi–xxvii)

Queer offers what Warner calls a "universalizing utopianism." Does this progres-sion, if a homology may be made from community politics to queer ones, bury the operations of global capitalism and then homologize them? Is the shift from emulat-ing ethnic politics to emulating market strategies? But before considering these ques-tions, let us pursue how the shift away from traditional, ethnic, lesbian feminist pat-terns of identity politics and notions of community is being performed.

Queer is construed as "anti-normal," in order to include a broad spectrum of eth-nic, gender, and sexual practices, linking them one to the other under its umbrella term. In this way, Queer Nation proposes to equalize what had been a hierarchy of differences. For example, Moraga's compound of "Queer Aztlán" actually subordi-nates queer to Aztlán—the queers in that nation are only Chicano ones. In the Queer Nation and its adjunct poststructuralist critique, ethnic identity no longer defines the political terrain, but is itself destabilized by processes such as "passing," or in condi-tions of "hybridity" or "hyphenation." Ethnicities are linked one to the other, as well as to other anti-normal categories such as transgendered people. Queer is thus multicultural rather than ethnic. In fact, for some, its potential for multicultural signification has been the specific allure of the term "Queer Nation." Phillip Brian Harper finds the "Queer" in "Queer Nation" to better beg the question of cultural difference than the terms "gay and lesbian," which, as he points out, articulate only one difference—that of gender (30). Fair enough—those politics specify no relation to the politics of "race." But confusingly, Harper argues the point "as a Black man," which grounds his argument for the multicultural "queer" within a traditional position of ethnic identity (29). "Multicultural," then, becomes an effect of ethnicity. Identity appears in its traditional form as the ground for its disappearance.

A similar slippage may be found in Lisa Duggan's "Making It Perfectly Queer." In arguing for the adoption of Queer Nation, Duggan defends her writing process in this way: "Because I am a Southern girl, I want to arrive at my discussion of these new meanings through a process of storytelling" (17). Duggan bases her writing process in a form produced by her regional identity in order to argue against identity politics. Nevertheless, she posits "nation" as a correction to the exclusivity enforced by those who practice identity politics as "self-appointed ayatollahs" who "suppress internal difference and political conflict" (17). Perhaps the broad, unspecific category of Queer Nation is welcome to both Harper and Duggan as accommodating this kind of ambivalence and self-contradiction. Yet claims to certain identities do seem to emerge, as if to suggest that one may have to ante up with an identity that one then may discard. This is an important point to note as the broad terrain is established. As the "ayatollahs" are invaded by more universal peacekeeping troops, how are "internal difference and political conflict" managed? Do they disappear in universalist aspiration? Are these metaphors of ayatollahs recording a relationship with national agendas—first-world attitudes?

Duggan's celebration of the inclusivity in Queer Nation, however, is not so much about ethnicity as about a variety of sexual practices. Duggan notes that the terms "lesbian and gay" exclude bisexuals, as well as the new practice of "gay sex" defined by Pat Califia as "sex between lesbians and gay men." Duggan celebrates how, upon the arrival of Queer Nation, the "notion of a fixed sexual identity determined by a firmly gendered desire began to slip quietly away" (21–22). If Moraga subordinates queer to Aztlán, critics such as Duggan make political aggregation an effect of pansexual behavior. Yet even Duggan in her fierce anti-ayatollah prescription finds the Queer Nation perhaps too vague a terrain, as she asks, "Can we avoid the dead end of various nationalisms and separatisms, without producing a bankrupt universalism?" (26). The positive aspect of the term "queer" is that it has no specific denotation. Unhinged by multiple sexual identities, operating as the equivalents of "hybridity" (bisexuality), "queer" may more freely constitute its constituents with, hopefully, the inclusion of broader differences. The negative import of the term is that it represents "the melting pot," as Charles Fernández has suggested, or an empty, "bankrupt universalism" (22). Such queer multiculturalism, or pan-sexuality, then, may signify the traditional way in which liberal democracy has "melted" differences together, or may emulate the new multinationalist form of differences.

Against such charges, however, Sarah Schulman, in *My American History,* argues that it was the sex wars that "saved the grass roots from total co-optation" (8). She portrays the lesbian feminist movement as retreating from activism into cultural production and 12 Step consciousness-raising ventures: "By the end of Reagan's first term, the women's movement was separating into identity groups which focused more on cultural expression and less on direct action" (5). In constructing "commonality" or "similarity" for coalition, the groups became bogged down in the preliminary process:

> So it is not identity politics, per se, that became an alternative to activism, but rather, the specific rhetoric of the seventies and early eighties which claimed that the process of social bonding on the basis of identity was a necessary "first step" before political action. . . . The second half of the eighties saw, instead, the evolution of movements more reliant on praxis. . . . For example, instead of stopping the activism of ACT UP! to do consciousness raising on sexism, or developing a women's caucus inside the organization principally to provide support (which would have been the old identity politics model) the question became one of application. (6)

Schulman admits that the sex wars, while offering a "revision," as she would put it, of earlier practices, played into an image "more fun" and "more palatable" to the dominant culture, that cast political activism in the role of "boring" (9). Queer Nation, she proffers, combines grassroots activism with sex-radical politics to correct the revision problem.

Schulman's portrayal of Queer Nation reinforces some of the distinctions above. An activist agenda was shared by people who had crucial social "differences" without any mechanism for dealing with them. Earlier coalitional discoveries were discarded in the rush onto the streets, impelled by the emergency of people dying. Activism was retrieved at the price of internal organization. If sexism did inform some of the discussions, there was no time to correct it. Schulman moves away from the internal theater, the investment in subjectivity, toward activism at the price of coalitional strategies. What remains puzzling is the notion of "grassroots"—a term from seventies politics. Community and grassroots were at one time connected in the discourse. In the context of sex-radicalism, it is difficult to imagine what grassroots might signify. Is it a term connoting class? Does it suggest community without asserting it? Is there some self-constituted raw, social material upon which such groups may act?

A series of Schulman's journalistic articles follow this cursory history of the movement. One article speaks directly to the context of this argument. Entitled "Low Marks for German Democracy," it chronicles her brief formal visit to the GDR in 1984. Guests of the government, a delegation of American feminists toured the nation. Schulman confidently draws conclusions from her few experiences, training the lens of her U.S. feminist ideology on what she encountered. As the title suggests, Schulman found the GDR to fail her tests of racism, sexism, and homophobia. Her disappointment or disapproval informs her own tenacious grasp of an activism that is unlike the so-called "communist" country. Another article, written the following year, is entitled "New York a Mass of Individually Beautiful Faces." Through this article,

Schulman guides the tourist through a lesbian bar, gay bookstores, and the endlessly fascinating cultural diversity of the city. Schulman's Queer Nation is situated between these territories: between the failure of communism and lesbian feminism and the promise of New York as a city. She, like Young before, finds the New York urban landscape to map out the "grassroots" where activism may be produced.

Schulman's disappointment with the women's movement that propelled her into the queer finds resonances with other accounts of Queer Nation's origins. Alexander Chee describes its beginnings this way:

> The name stuck simply for the sake of marketing. The original idea was this: choose a name around each action, keep responsibility with each individual and not with an institution. . . . People are tired of groups with egos, processes, personality cults, and politicking. So far Queer Nation is individuals confronting individuals. (15)

The interest, as Chee describes it, was not in collective agency, but in the individual. In fact, if Chee is correct, Queer Nation arose as a direct contradiction to collective, group-process-oriented politics. Instead it offered iteration, the discursive power of the term, to supplant the process of coalition. Individuals and change of tactics, venue, and organization invigorate those who are "tired" of group processes. The dialogue across communities gave way to individual confrontation. What was the ground of such organization, if not community? The key lies in Chee's claim that any practice of continuity was a marketing choice. Queer Nation, the subcultural writing and performance agency, rested firmly on the base of market interests.

"SUBVERSIVE" SHOPPING

In Cherríe Moraga's Queer Aztlán, ethnicity and sexual practice are class-specific. Her citizens are Chicano farmworkers, cannery workers, etc. From the perspective of underpaid agrarian labor, the workings of corporate capitalism and its ally national expansionism appear as negative forces. "Community" in such a paradigm connotes some alternative social and political structure that would vest the lesbian Chicana farmworker with property, the rights of citizenship, and community acceptance. Performances of "heroes and saints" act out the intense struggle and hope for victory in founding such an alternative. In contrast, Queer Nation is performed through a "subversive" reconstruction of the dominant formations of nation and the capitalist class system. "Queer Nationality," as Lauren Berlant and Elizabeth Freeman reveal, presumes a conflation of nation with capitalism:

> The Queer National corporate strategy—to reveal to the consumer desires he/ she didn't know he/she had, to make his/her identification with the product "homosexuality" both an unsettling and a pleasurable experience—makes consumer pleasure central to the transformation of public culture, thus linking the utopian promises of the commodity with those of the nation. (208)

The trafficking of nation and capitalism is run through the commodity. "Consumer pleasure" and "the utopian promises of the commodity" form the base for Queer National struggles. Berlant and Freeman continue, describing how the Queer Shopping Network of New York and the Queer Shoppers use ad formats for their own purposes, creating a "mock-twin" of "existing national corporate logos" (210). From this, they conclude that Queer Nation "embodies the corporation" as a way of revealing it (213). The site of Queer Nation is not a community, a region, or even a venue such as WOW; instead, it is embedded in ads, shopping strategies, mall demonstrations, and logos. Capitalism, corporate structures, and nationhood are resident in the basic unit of the commodity that functions as its strategy. No alternative to capitalism is imagined—only that its market forces would redirect their address toward the "Queer."

It is along this market axis that Michael Warner, who earlier eschewed an unwarranted homology of ethnic organization, argues that the reason "community" is not a useful term for "queers" is that the marketplace constitutes the "natural" environment for lesbian and gay movements:

> In the lesbian and gay movement, to a much greater degree than in any comparable movement, the institutions of culture-building have been market-mediated. ... Nonmarket forms of association . . . churches, kinship, traditional residence— have been less available for queers. This structural environment has meant that the institutions of queer culture have been dominated by those with capital: typically, middle-class white men. (xvii)

Queers have been consigned to the market, as they have been excised from the family. Warner ties this commodity-laden queer habitation to a particular class of citizen: "middle-class white men."

After the various celebrations of the indeterminate referents of the term "Queer Nation" cited above, Warner has brought the "unmarked" constituency out of the closet. While the umbrella notion of Queer Nation in its lack of denotation *might* signify a multicultural, multiclass, multigendered constituency, it in fact has been produced by class-specific, gender-specific agents. Warner's identification of these members resonates with Moraga's earlier assertion, but Warner's disclosure promotes an understanding of just how this constituency was formed. Queer Nation accommodates commodifying and nationalizing processes for a class of citizens who profit by them. The middle-class male citizen has the potential of being vested with substantial private property and discretionary income. His "unmarked" status allows consumer operations to be universalized and even extended into critical verities.

John D'Emilio would agree that there is a specific cooperation between capitalism and sexual politics. D'Emilio develops the historical rise of lesbian and gay self-identities and group organizations as within spaces that capitalism has provided. In other words, this particular category of political identity has been provided by the growth of capitalism and is dependent upon it. D'Emilio concludes his construction of "Capitalism and Gay Identity" by proposing the "building of an 'affectional community'" within the capitalist system for the successful struggle for "Civil Rights"

(475). If "community" exists within capitalism, then, it is not deployed against the division of property or the operations of class, but as an "affectional" bond that would extend the practice of Civil Rights to its citizens.

In fact, *Sexual Citizenship*, as David T. Evans entitles his book, hinges upon consumerist practices: "Sexual minorities have progressively become distinct, formal . . . participants within the citizenship of developed capitalism, whilst simultaneously becoming, not surprisingly for of course the two are closely connected, legitimate consumers of sexual and sexualised commodities marketed specifically for their use and enjoyment" (2). Evans historicizes this condition by first noting a change in capitalism's requirements for sexual behavior. If at first propagation, as Marx noted, and from which Foucault's argument proceeded, was a requirement for a massive work force, its subsequent need for "quality rather than quantity in first world economies has devalued procreative sexuality and progressively released the commodity potential of non-procreative forms" (37). It would seem that the increasing representation of leisure-time sexual pursuits in movies, on TV, in sex shops, etc., is in line with the rearrangement of the work force, whose numbers are being reduced by more efficient technologies, and with the required consumption of goods to keep the market strong. Moreover, Evans argues, the population is less likely to experience capitalism through the conditions of production than through consumption relations. This adjusted experience of the economy encourages the values of privatization and individualism (43).

Thus, the rise of a sexual politics that turns increasingly toward the representation of its sexual acts as politics is in confluence with the changing needs of capitalism. For consumers whose identity is based on a sex-radical agenda, the experience of pleasure moves through the field of commodities. If, in late capitalism in the first world, citizenship "involves essentially the question of access to scarce resources in society and participation in the distribution and enjoyment of such resources . . . sexual citizenship involves partial, private, and primary leisure and lifestyle membership" (64).

Queer strategies and the poststructuralist critique, in tandem, represent the new allure of the individual consumer, not only by elevating the status of the internal relationship to commodities, as in Benjamin's library, but through the celebration of a certain mobility—an internal morphing that moves the individual through a variety of positions. The same special-effects appeal of morphing in, say, *Terminator 2*, or in Michael Jackson's *Black or White* music video, now produces the spectacle of the new individualism offered up by poststructuralist politics. Fuss's notion of oscillation and multiple identifications is key to the process. The fragile, oscillating movement once located within the coalition-making process among communities has been transferred to a play within the individual, of multiple identifications. The links among different ethnic and sexual practices are, in fact, forged within individuals who may cross over their different divides as an internal process. Increasingly, this has become the model for the poststructuralist political critique. Chantal Mouffe's recent formulation of citizenship in her book *The Return of the Political* clearly illustrates how, in the time after the fall of the wall, the anti-essentialist position embeds differences within the individual. Within Mouffe's liberal democratic agenda, which, like Queer Nation, does not challenge the capitalist market or the state's "democratic" agenda, the citizen is constituted as no longer a "unified subject" but "a single individual can be the bearer of this multiplicity. . . . We can thus conceive the social agent as constituted by an ensemble of 'subject positions' that can never be totally fixed in a closed system of differences . . . but a constant movement of overdetermination and displacement" (77). As this citizen enacts within the processes of "subversion" and "overdetermination" among these positions, the agon of politics is subsumed by the individual. Queer Nation is likewise constituted as individuals who subsume coalition-building into their compound identities. Their own singular yet multiple identities serve as performative agents of the political agon. Such performativities are created through a shared class identification through consumerist practices and a privileged access to leisure pursuits.

What construction of nation, then, suits this citizen? How may she belong to any aggregation outside her own internal one? As we have noted, this nation represented no redistribution of property, took no account of dispossessed indigenous peoples. Within activist scenarios, it resided in a deployment of graffiti—a social writing across the face of dominant practices: stickers across billboards, signs in the subway, cards at a baseball game. It was an agitprop performance for the media, either for the video camera run by the demonstrators themselves, or for those of the networks. It was an intervention in the shopping mall, among consumer goods. This Nation originated in New York, bearing centrist, urban codes in its activism. Berlant and Freeman celebrate the field of Queer Nation as stretching out beyond "hegemonic spaces" into a "space of negativity" to occupy a "discursive field." Ultimately, they locate Queer Nation in the form of the fanzine (224–225). Certainly, the fanzine reveals a subcultural practice, in disjunction to the dominant, but within an addiction to commodification. Steven Seidman, who has aligned the poststructuralist critique with Queer Nation, comes to a conclusion similar to Berlant's and Freeman's, but is considerably less sanguine about it: "social practices are framed narrowly as discursive and signifying, and critical practice becomes deconstructive textual strategies. . . . There is an edge toward textual idealism" (132). Seidman's charge of "textual idealism" challenges these "fields" for their exclusion of material conditions such as geographical territories, wage practices, etc.

But perhaps the ground of the addicted text represents a necessary retreat from colonized territories. What if, for example, the sign "lesbian" has already been appropriated by the market? Not only, as Evans asserts above, has first-world capitalism encouraged leisure-time, nonprocreative sexual pursuits in order to sell more products, but, as lesbian critics Danae Clark, Kathy Griggers, and Sasha Torres have already articulated, "lesbian" has become a sign used to sell fashion apparel, prime-time television "pleasures," and other commodities. Danae Clark's "Commodity Lesbianism" claims that capitalism has even co-produced anti-essentialist strategies, confirming the commodified aspect of poststructuralist politics while charting the extent to which capital has colonized all possible alterities (195). Clark and others are working from the assumption that lesbian has become a fashion—a style—the market can employ to sell its goods. Along with a style, it has also become a form of entertainment. The homosexual is "put together from disarticulating bits and pieces of the historical discourse on homosexual desire, which becomes a narrative pastiche for middle-class 'entertainment'" (quotes John Les, 195).

With sexual citizenship circulating within market strategies, its Nation resides in the "aura of might" that surrounds its manipulation of commodities. Michael Taussig, in "Maleficium: State Fetishism," identifies this aura as the mark of the fetish of the dominant state (218). His argument takes a different turn from what I would accomplish here, but certain elements of it may be skewed into a description of the Queer Nation. One might perceive how that Nation borrows from the strategies of the dominant one to establish itself. In Taussig's discussion, it's possible to discover how the "unmarked" quality that haunts queer in its veiled constituency is revealed as the way the fetish produces its power: "Just the signifier . . . bereft of its erased signification gathered and dissipated through the mists of trade, religion, witchcraft, slavery, and what has come to be called science—and this is precisely the formal mechanism of fetishism (as we see it used by Marx and by Freud), whereby the signifier depends upon yet erases its signification" (225). The Nation of the queer, then, resides in the aura that its iteration of universalism and its erasure of referent produce. This is the "aura of might" that accompanies its circulation among commodities. It's as if Queer Nation took heed of Taussig's admonishment, based on Benjamin's reading of the surrealists, to "submit to . . . fetish powers and attempt to channel them in revolutionary directions" (229). This proposal is similar to Danae Clark's "subversive shopping" that calls lesbians to appropriate the market's use of lesbian to do their own shopping. It fuels the interaction with commodities—a cyborgean fusion without Haraway's utopic sense of it.

Queer Nation as an organization may already have come and gone. Its era was limited to only two or three years. However, its "aura," to purposefully borrow Benjamin's term, continues to surround the term "queer," which is circulating through broader and more complex discursive compounds than Queer Nation ever mobilized. Whatever the case, "queer" has come along with the marketing of what was once known as a community or subculture to its own constituents. Many of the booths erected at Pride marches and other "community" events now sell cups, jewelry, or T-shirts emblazoned with lesbian/gay insignia. The pages of the once-alternative *Lesbian News* are filled with ads for lesbian car dealers, real estate agents, dentists, lawyers, and the like. There are a multitude of opportunities to buy a membership in the Queer Nation. Perhaps this is a form of commodity separatism. It does, in one way, extend the traditional community practices of supporting one another—keeping the dollar in the ghetto. Nonetheless, it marks a different class than earlier handbills for women in the trades and the like, in its affiliations with middle-class accouterments, produced by dominant corporations such as Toyota or Coldwell Banker. And, while registering the positive factor that perhaps lesbians and gays are making more money, and that bisexuals and ethnic groups are willing to be associated with them within an umbrella term, the loss of a construction such as "coalition" connoting perhaps other classes and relations to the market means that the inward focus of the politics replicates the class and commodification of its citizens.

I would contend, however, that "queer" is the term for the fetish-effect, the aura of commodities used for "alternative" sexual pleasure that signify radicality by their appearance. The pierced nipple, the pierced nose, the leather chaps, the dildo, the retro-butch/femme look—all signify queerdom while suggesting its fetish effect.

Yet nothing seems more seductive and alluring in this practice than strapping on the dildo. Within the context of the queer and its national territories, the reconstruction of the "lesbian body" through the appendage of a penile commodity reveals the performative operations of market lesbianism.

COMMODITY DILDOISM

Strapping on the dildo has become the premier image of the new wave of lesbian sexual imagery and hermeneutics. Photos and ads of dildos for and with lesbians fill the pages of the underground chic 'zines as well as the slide screens of MLA panels on the lesbian. The dildo is "fleshed out" by the portrait of the lesbian with phallus-as-fetish. Similarly, the fashionable new focus on masquerade and performance makes the dildoed dyke appear alluring, plenitudinous, and postmodernly perverse and dispersed. What more or less could a girl want? In contrast, the earlier dowdy dyke, who had no market muscle, who inhabited the downwardly mobile community of lesbian feminists, and who eschewed the market for the "natural," lacked the allure of commodification. Attitudes toward her appearance were reminiscent of the oft-heard comments from Americans who traveled into East Berlin on a sightseeing day: boring, gray, and depressing without the visual excitement of billboards, display windows, brilliant commodities on the streets or on the people. The dowdy took too seriously, among other things, a utopian notion of equality in sex, and when she asked her date up to see her sketchings (up to her mommy's *jouissance* joint), they turned out to be old French feminist images of two lips and unseeable, ascopophilic holes. The appearance of the dowdy, a dutiful daughter of feminism with no sex toys or scenarios of power to play, and almost puritanical in her refusal of sexual images, has been obscured by graffiti such as ESSENTIALIST or FEMINIST by queer theory, and, in *Lesbian News* personal ads by the notice: No feminists need apply.

In contrast, the new dyke is born out of the rib of gay male subcultural images. She peaks in photo displays of her sex toys and clothes fashions, such as the photo essay in *Quim* entitled "Daddy Boy Dykes" in which the dykes are dressed as gay leather men, replete with mustaches. There, they pose as cock-suckers and ass-fuckers with dildos peeking out of their leather chaps. This new "lifestyle lesbianism" is configured as a reaction against that earlier dowdy's feminism as "a justifiable response to an over politicization of the personal" in which "this new attention to lifestyle [is] a freedom, a testament to the fact that their identity is now a personal choice rather than political compulsion" (A. Stein, 40, 41). It would seem that Danae Clark's "subversive shoppers" specifically correct earlier lesbian feminism.

This display of lesbian sexual identity as proximate to phallic display has deep roots within the tradition of lesbian appearance. Once and once again it is performed as butch/femme role playing. Likewise, it appears in lesbian s/m scenarios that often conflate penetration with phallic power and its vicissitudes of appearance. After all, as Teresa de Lauretis has already worked out in "Sexual (In)difference and Lesbian Representation," there are only certain ways in which lesbians can appear on the dominant heterosexual semiotic screen. However, the critical reception of the more traditional strategies of appearance, such as butch/femme role playing, has been figured through feminist theory, set against the backdrop of oppression. This tradition of configuring "lesbian" vis-à-vis "the gaze" addresses role playing as the only possible form of liberation in a system of representation locked tight by the erect phallus. Even Pat Califia, who would distinguish herself from orthodox lesbian feminist critiques, works off models of oppression for s/m practitioners and pornographers, pleading an almost civil libertarian case in her introduction to *Macho Sluts*. Thus, the running argument of the 1980s concludes that masquerading lesbians, oppressed, finally, by codes of invisibility, had little choice but to appropriate the phallus in order to appear. These politics of oppression allowed dykes and, for example, women of color to form coalitions and consonances among themselves, as well as with other political critiques such as socialism. Oppression is a gone concept in the new politics of commodification.

The newer theoretical argument that accompanies the dildoed dyke asserts that when the dyke straps on the dildo or gay male leather fashion wear, commodity fetishism overcomes dominant gender traps. Unlike the coalition politics of oppression, these are the politics of individual success. Cindy Patton in "Unmediated Lust?" works out how a dress code overcomes the older strategy of locating visibility vis-à-vis oppression:

> For the last few years the lesbian sex magazines have been quite openly playing with the (gay) boys. At first, there was a tinge of envy in these images, but once dressed for the occasion, we discovered that we had already been over this turf. ... We must now deconstruct any female desire that insists that it must be constructed against masculinity. We must create images for Monique Wittig's polemic assertion that lesbians are not women. (238)

Clothes make the man. The costumes of phallicized commodities provide the necessary deconstruction of earlier naturalized systems of genderfication and (hetero)sexualization. Some even "see" fashion wear as a form of activism: "My appearance tells people that I am a sexual outlaw and an urban gender terrorist" ("S/M Aesthetic," 42). Significantly, Patton's article appears in a book on lesbians and photography, for much of this new dyke posing and theorizing presupposes a camera somewhere or some version of *I Am a Camera*. Thus, the representational muscle of commodity fetishism is not merely in the buying of the dildo, in the posing, the sucking, or the watching, but also in the expectation of the photo of it and, ultimately, of the ad. The new dyke is constructed by her appearance in the marketplace of images—she is an ad man. Her politics are an ad campaign. Cameras are a dyke's best friend. Now this:

> In his account of the parallel rise of the photographic portrait and the middle classes, John Tagg characterises the medium as "a sign whose purpose is both the *description* of an individual and the *inscription* of a social identity." The latter function, Tagg argues, is performed both by the photograph's replacement of the earlier portrait media by which rising classes claimed their social place—the painted miniature, the silhouette and the engraving—and by its role as a commodity in itself, an object whose very purchase conferred a certain status on the purchaser. . . . Somewhere along this faultline, Krafft-Ebing's patient posed "in man's attire" with her woman lover, an image which . . . represented the social mobility traditionally afforded the "passing" woman. (Merck, 24)

The representational strategy of the new dyke, then, is a kind of photogynesis in which the dildo is a catalyst into the class of the visible. The status of commodity that the photo affords the new visible dyke is the motor for her upward mobility. The photo ad of dyke apparel, in assimilating the subculture, makes it literally class-y. Ironically, the link between apparel and political action for women has come full circle. While the women's movement began with burning bras, the lesbian one conquers by strapping on the dildo.

While these dykes are just stepping into their liberatory leathers, John Preston, a well-known gay-leather-scene pornhistoriographer, is already leaving his leather behind (so to speak). For Preston, the assimilation of gay subculture into the market-place has ruined its revolutionary potential: "Leather was gay sexuality stripped of being nice. It offended. It confronted. It took sex as its own ultimate value." But now "it's been codified, measured, and packaged. . . . As we all did it, we were also popularizing it, and romanticizing it" (10,11). Further, Preston argues, the marketing of the leather scene represses its politics, sexual identity, and sexual pleasure all at once. For him, the techno-market man fears sexual anarchy and strives for institutionalization: "Thus we have all the workshops, the endless patter of silly bottoms talking about 'the right way' to do things." Moreover, civil libertarian politics proceed from "the wimps who beg for acceptance from the larger society" (12). Preston's nostalgia signals what, for him, is the loss of an oppositional identity through leather and s/m practices that, once commodified, lose their sting.

What is at stake here is the construction of gay/lesbian appearance and sexual practice within the late-twentieth-century high-capitalist technomarket of commodity identities. As commodities create the appearance, the appearance also creates the commodification of the subculture. Images of gays and lesbians sell straight newspapers. For example, the *Los Angeles Times* ran an article in its "View" section on Northampton as a lesbian watering hole, titillating its readership with reviews of lesbian night at the local lingerie store (which found that lesbian night sold more lingerie than the former men's night did). Then, in a following week, the paper ran an insight article on how the new editor of the *Advocate* had increased its circulation by slicking up its look. In other words, the slick image of gay and lesbian subculture brings it closer to the *Times*. Traditional marketing structures govern the production of the new dyke image. The glossy *Out/Look* contrasts with the 'zines (sounds like "jeans"), which represent a similar market appearance of the rough and ready as alternative images to the glossy/dressy. What seems to be the new dyke look may be only the extension of fashion categories to the subculture. The ultimate accommodation to commodification is regarding it as an alternative political practice.

Straight critics of technoculture have already described how sexual identity and desire are produced through media marketing. Mark Poster, in *The Mode of Information*, constructs the notion of the "floating signifier" in television ads:

> The ad takes a signifier, a word that has no traditional relation to the object being promoted and attaches it to that object. . . . These floating signifiers derive their effects precisely from their recontextualization in the ad. Extracted from an actual relationship between lovers, romance or sexiness increases in linguistic power. In the ad, sexy floor wax is more romantic than a man or a woman in an actual relationship. . . . The commodity has been given a semiotic value that is distinct from, indeed out of phase with, its use value and its exchange value. (58)

This surplus sexual value deployed by the floating signifier cuts both ways in the representation of the new dyke. In strapping on the dildo and getting off on the pose of another woman going down on it, the dyke buys into the surplus sexual value of the recontextualized commodity. As the phallus, now a commodity, is recontextualized in lesbian sexual scenarios it takes, on the one hand, surplus sexual semiotic value. On the other hand (once an emblem of lesbian sexual desire), the appropriation of gay and lesbian images into straight culture semiotizes gay/lesbian as surplus sexual value in their recontextualization. Like the referent of the dildo in lesbian scenarios, gay/lesbian sexuality is without actual use or exchange value in the sexual economy of dominant heterosexual culture and is thus sexy as surplus. The effect, then, of the appearance of the new dyke is to capitalize her—her earlier dowdiness, just as the dowdiness of the erstwhile East Berlin (also newly capitalized) was in its distance from successful capitalist integration. For, as Engels noted, the "essential character" of capitalism is in the extraction of surplus value (700).

If Heiner Müller put image and text on separate tracks, the dildoed dyke leaves on track one. The image as commodity has come full-blown into its role as photo ad. "Lesbian" resides in the dildo's commercial allure, outside the dialectic and beyond the struggle. Performing lesbian, in this sense, is as a market function. The lesbian is only one of capitalism's operatives. There is no script—only the frozen image. The buck and the performance stop here as if finally sublated.

TELEDILDONICS

The same values that support the erection of the strap-on carry directly over into the coming production of teledildonics. "Dildonics" is a term from the 1970s, referring to a machine invented by a hacker named How Wachspress that converted sound into tactile sensations (Rheingold, 345). The term "teledildonics" refers to the possible link-up, through telecommunications systems, with other people through sensate materials. The mechanical, gendered dildo becomes dildo as "second skin."

Experiments with virtual "skins" are beginning to produce body suits laced with electronic circuits, emulating nerves that would stimulate the "meat." One future experience in cyberspace will be sexual scenarios that actually simulate, in the body, the "experience" of sex. Meeting in cyberspace, free to take on any cross-species, transgender appearance, the physical play will be signaled across the skin as sexual pleasure. Electronic personae, then, will be completely inhabitable, as another space for the sexual, bodily relationship.

In cyberskin, the photo that lingers in dildo performances will instead be screened across the body, as well as perceived by the eye. The sublime techno-sexual performance will be "in" the photograph, "as" the screen. Commodity fetishism, which heretofore relied on an imagined relationship to an object, will be reconfigured so that the commodity itself will produce the imaginary in the flesh. In one way, this seems the pinnacle of queer desire, composed of nothing but masquerade, cut free from identity and finally technologizing, commodifying the ontological trace of flesh. Teledildonics will not entertain a productive body, but will produce the body and the subject. Anything like the process of coalition would seem one-dimensional, production-oriented, and without immediate access to pleasure and satisfaction.

What's wrong with this picture? How can it be construed as problematic, without assuming the antiquated retro position of feminist or traditional materialism? After all, even the communist Müller could posit only a representational terrorism as a final strategy. The 1990s is the decade in which terrorism, at least in its 1970s version, finally plays its last act, in the rooting out of the final few (West) German terrorists from their hiding places in the erstwhile GDR and the "surrender" of Katherine Ann Power in the U.S.—the last of the "missing" Weather People. In this period between the final death throes of alternative practices that would challenge capitalism and state agendas and the techno-takeover by virtual systems, in the final episodes in which the uneven distribution of power remains visible, it would seem that there is only one scenario left to play: sadomasochism.

Lesbian sadomasochistic scenarios have "come" to the call. Explicitly imagining the power imbalances within sexual relations has, in many of the cultural icons, replaced the 1970s fantasies of equal sexual relations, now commonly referred to as "vanilla sex." Utopian fantasies that both players would play equal roles in lesbian seduction and foreplay are now considered to be "naive." Instead, performing power imbalances in s/m scenarios better suits the political climate of the late 1980s and 1990s. Lois Weaver and Peggy Shaw, who earlier performed those community pieces at WOW, have turned to scripting bitter, physically abusive power struggles in their new piece, *Lust and Comfort*. The queer dress style of leathers and piercings suggests traditional s/m fashions as the general sense of the new subculture. Yet, much of the U.S. tradition of scripting these scenarios, as in Pat Califia's writings, takes place in a space removed from the operations of class and national agendas. They presume "privacy" rather than private property and "consent" or a "safe word" as discursive operations powerful enough to enclose a separate place. If the costumes of power suggest class differences, or historical, national struggles, they are represented as if outside national agendas.

If the "live" body is on its way to the techno-sheath of sexual skin, in teledildonics it might be useful to examine an instance of how such performances of power could inscribe national agendas in their scenarios. On the one hand, teledildonics could be imagined as successful simulations of the "live" body, bringing complete transformations into sexual play. On the other, they might simply bring national and market agendas directly onto the skin of individuals—even in their most "private" acts. Given the potential in all electronic communication for others to "watch," or to "lurk" as it is termed online, all sexual play would be a performance for an audience. The camera presumed in strapping on the dildo would be embedded at multiple sites on the skin. *I Am a Camera* could be fully realized. S/m performances, then, as before an audience, gesturing state relations will be the future "performative." A review of a film that presumes all of these elements, implying its camera in the narrative, as well as other viewers, helps to illustrate just how this may work.

SEDUCTION: THE CRUEL WOMAN

The German film *Seduction: The Cruel Woman*, by Elfi Mikesch and Monika Treut resituates the lesbian s/m scenario within a play of market and national signs. In this film, lesbian s/m scenarios foreground the play of NATO relations, the "Big Sister" role of U.S. economic operations and U.S. feminism, the conflict of national competitions, the fascist legacy embedded in spectacle, the power relations in the camera's roving eye, and the cooperation between their performance and the commodification of it. Screening "live" performances already fetishizes the gaze within an uneven power dynamic.

The scenarios take place in a performance gallery, where they are performed for paying customers. The fee seems to be relatively high, since the dominatrix, Wanda, drives a late-model Mercedes Benz and dresses in various *haute couture* ensembles. While some forms of "personal" relations seem to prevail, they are always interwoven among professional responsibilities. The power relations of sadomasochist desire, fetishism, and role playing almost always occur at the site of business. No "private" or noncommercial site is established for the eroticization of power imbalances. "Dominatrix" symbolizes both Wanda's s/m role and her role as "boss" of the gallery. Along with her continual erotic persona, Wanda also exhibits some of the moods and manners associated with the workplace. She complains of fatigue in one instance from the hard night's work of dominating customers. Upon arriving at work, she hangs up her coat in the office, where one of her "slaves" sits before a computer terminal, presumably keeping accounts and appointments. She gives an interview to a newspaper reporter covering the opening of the new gallery, and she fires her long-term slave, Gregor. The business of the dominatrix is to run the show and the store.

The performance gallery is located on one of the piers of the Hamburg harbor. In its housing of s/m scenarios, it is not entirely unlike the warehouses and factories that surround it. The gallery opens out through its windows, warehouse doors in the performance spaces, and fantasies of its workers onto the harbor, where passing cargo ships, lading machinery, and dockworkers are revealed. The customers can see the harbor behind certain performances, and the performers can daydream about it. While the setting may seem like that of "poor theater" in its concrete walls and wharf location, it is in fact used to suggest a tough, unadorned backdrop for the entertainment of another class and toward lucrative ends. It sets the scene for "rough trade"—a subcultural term that associates rough sex with such trade. This backdrop is one familiar to gay subculture, represented for similar effect in other films such as Fassbinder's *Querelle*—locating seduction at the site of hard labor and trade. Here, "rough trade" may serve the pleasures of its practitioners, but is also employed as an exotic mise-en-scène for their affluent customers. Class difference is used to eroticize the setting. The muscular, sweating laborer, his/her "tools" and his/her rough environment are made the object of the leisured gaze.

Class codings are specific throughout the film to reference both the association of an upper class with such scenarios, and the erotics of class difference. Clients in evening dress are seen to arrive in expensive cars. There is an elegance to the scenes, provided by costumes and backdrops. Audience responses to the scenes are muted, subtle, and polite. Their behavior resembles that of high culture, such as at the opera or the symphony. Torture is not applied with too much vigor, pain is not registered with too much enthusiasm, and audience response is legislated by the conventions of politesse. The composition of the audience as wealthy brings an erotics of class into reception: the work of torture is performed for their somewhat distant and cool observation. The signs of fashion also work to construct an erotics of class. Wanda always dresses in high fashion, and when Justine arrives, in a flowered print dress, her middle-class attire is made to signify a kind of energetic, hard-working erotic, in contrast to Wanda's languorous, *faux* aristocratic demeanor. Ultimately, as an indirect quotation of European history, the energy of the middle class will "top" the aristocratic languor.

Fetishism is portrayed as a commodity in the s/m marketplace of performance. Commodity fetishism and the s/m fetish combine to reference the economic environment in which these erotic practices occur, rather than some internal, psychoanalytic process of subjecthood. The shoe fetishist works in a shoe store, arranging her desired objects in the display window. Her scenarios consist of fitting shoes on her customers. Likewise, the whip appears in a scene in which each lash is paid for by a customer. The fetish is also the site in which capitalist economic structures and national ones are conflated in the film. At one point in the whipping scenario, the whip is wiped clean by a dollar bill, which signifies the fetishism of the dollar, the enjoyment of the "strength" of the currency, and the s/m lashing of women's bottoms within one gesture. The dollar bill, while signifying the commodification of the erotics, also signifies a national currency in this German movie. The customer is figured as an American, while another American, Justine, the antagonist of the film, turns up her bottom for the lash. Gregor, the German "slave," simply manages the whip between the two.

Mikesch and Treut employ certain familiar elements of the American stereotype to represent affects of sex, power, and money. This confluence is nothing new, but operates in tandem with a traditional association in German thought between American high capitalism and sex. In the recent anthology *Nationalisms and Sexualities*, which addresses this intersection in a variety of ways, Sander Gilman's article entitled "Plague in Germany 1939/1989" cites earlier, seminal texts by Krafft-Ebing and August Forel, which conflate America and its high capitalism with the performance of illicit sexual power. Forel: "Americanism—By this term I designate an unhealthy feature of sexual life, common among the educated classes of the United States, and apparently originating in the greed for dollars, which is more prevalent in North America than anywhere else. I refer to the unnatural life which Americans lead, and more especially to its sexual aspect" (Gilman, 192).

While the American/German dialogue configures a certain national melodrama that organizes the narrative of the film, aspects of the use of fetishes suggest that it is not only America, as a nation, but structures of nationalism themselves that generally eroticize s/m scenarios. Within the German national history, spectacle is haunted by the ghost of Nazism. Hitler's power base was partially consolidated and promoted by spectacle. Moreover, it was an s/m spectacle in part, enacting the pleasure of allegiance to a führer and promising pain to some. The s/m scene has generally had a problematic relation to this particular spectacle, in the incorporation of Nazi symbols and gear into the scenarios. Most recently, the biography of Tom of Finland, one of the leading leather-porn illustrators of the gay male practice, revealed that his first lover was a Nazi. Thus, Finland's initial drawings of leathered-lust, which led to an entire style of gay s/m pornography, were literally based on erotic drawings of a Nazi. While the film *Seduction* does not engage directly with the Nazi lexicon of the spectacular, weapons of torture are enhanced by imagining their associations with national practices. The gallery sports a "trophy room" of fetishes, through which Gregor guides the newly arrived Justine. He plays his favorite device for her—an audio tape of a man screaming in pain. Gregor embellishes the screams with a narrative of the hangman, state torturers, and those in prison cells who have heard such screams. In other words, the setting for the screams revolves around state institutional sites of torture. Along with an opening scene of the film, which introduces the Lady Prime Minister of propaganda and protocol, and the lash of the dollar, these images of state torture create a leitmotiv of nationalism that weaves throughout the film. Ironically, Gregor produces this state setting for screams for the American who will ultimately take his job.

The narrative, however, is the primary device for the configuration of national competition. It begins with the arrival of an American, who is coming to visit Wanda. At first we hear only her broad American accent on Wanda's phone machine. We first see her when Wanda drives her onto the dock for unloading—as the American import. She is played by the American underground lesbian filmmaker Sheila McLaughlin, recognizable to many who would see this kind of lesbian film. McLaughlin is cast as Justine—a character name borrowed from Sacher-Masoch. Justine's arrival coincides with the gala opening of the new gallery space. Trailing images of U.S. lesbian cultural production behind her, McLaughlin/Justine enters the German performance of s/m power relations. Wanda inaugurates the gallery, in leopard-skin dress and pillbox hat, lounging on the upturned appendages of another woman, by introducing the "Lady Prime Minister in charge of propaganda and protocol." Wanda thus opens her gallery by offering the simulation of national protocol, to be witnessed by her new American apprentice.

Justine is soon discovered to be too earnest in her preference for one role over another, as she insists that she will not play a nurse. Wanda ties her up and abandons her in one of the rooms until her fantasies are catalyzed, and she "comes to power" by eagerly donning the nurse's costume to be whipped in the scene described above. Though Justine does turn up her bottom, she ultimately "tops" the tyrant Wanda, rising to eminence in the gallery as the manager of Wanda's slaves, or tamer of her "housepets" as she sometimes calls them. The signifiers of national characters in the film encourage a reading of this lesbian s/m narrative as mimicking the German/ American dialogue under NATO, in which the "friendly" Americans also emerge as butch tops. *Seduction: The Cruel Woman* situates lesbian seduction at a port of entry, the locus of import/export structures, conflating two national identities which have certainly played out s/m scenarios together for several decades with intimate fantasies of rough trade. Other films by Mikesch and Treut reverse the cultural exchange. Their next film, *The Virgin Machine,* opens in Hamburg but immigrates to San Francisco, where the German protagonist, through intercourse (so to speak) with the local lesbian s/m community, learns to abandon her European, Romantic notions of love for ungilded yet performative scenarios of power. She eventually throws her old eurocentric notions, in the form of her diary, into the San Francisco Bay. The two films together balance the trade between the ports of Hamburg and San Francisco.

The film not only reveals its participation in national and economic processes, it also foregrounds the operations of the camera in producing such scenarios. The galleries are under the surveillance of numerous video cameras that observe and record the scenarios. This surveillance system eroticizes the security practices in corporate and national work sites. Moreover, it suggests that the role simulation and the camera itself play in the production of the scenarios. In one scene, Wanda stands before the bank of screens that are playing back her scenario in the bathroom with the journalist who "came" to interview her, as she discourses on the nature of simulacra and desire. The film begins with a quotation by Baudrillard, and this scene promulgates some of the theory. Surveillance is another sex toy among the wares of the dominatrix. Her discourse on simulacra before the cameras extends her power over the scene: she owns the images, while the "bottom" was unaware of their production.

The camera of the film shoots scenes of its own vision beyond the dictates of the gallery to foreground its role in the scenarios. It returns again and again to pan the dark pilings beneath the pier, traveling along the water in the semi-dark to record the play of light and water along the rough cement. The opening shots of the film cut between a pan of the pilings and the journalist in white sandals and negligée crawling through vertical hanging leather straps. These cuts configure a parallel visual composition between vertical, hard pilings and soft straps. The pleasure of the man licking his way across a bathroom floor among the straps is set up to parallel the movement of the camera through the pilings. The camera also draws attention to its framing of individual scenes, by slowly traversing the visual space of the frame. Scenes are set up almost as tableaux, played at such a retarded tempo that the composition of their frame can be languorously explored by the camera. Such scenes provide a screen surface across which the camera can amble in a slow, plenitudinous fashion like the man licking his way across the bathroom floor. Images are thus packaged, owned, and fetishized. The camera, as in the play of the dildo, is a participant in creating the erotics of the scene. Although some scenes include dialogues, many are wordless. Gregor, harnessed to an antique yoke, makes his way across the floor on his knees, driven by the crack of the lash. The audience applauds, presumably for the effect of the image. Film, camera, and video are conveyors of the s/m scene and conversely, are produced by s/m relations. Thus, screening takes on specific attributes in relation to systems of sex, money, and power.

ANTI-COMMUNIST QUEERDOM

The fact that this section is framed by considerations of a West German film and Heiner Müller's East German performance practices suggests that the divided Germany, produced by the split in capitalist/communist ideologies and histories, is a site rich in the self-conscious performance of such operations. The United States seems to claim some remove in its history of political movements that configure, as many of the ethnic and homosexual movements have, only internal affairs. Yet, to beg once more the inscription of national and economic agendas in all cultural production is to insist that to write critical theory after World War II has been to write either, as Heiner Müller did, *for* communism or, in the case of U.S. production, *against* it. Having absorbed the Cold War discourse since early school days, and participated in the institutional backing of anti-communist funding projects, scholars in this country have been drawn into the propaganda wars.

Fittingly, this author discovered a history of the anti-communist agenda for cultural production in the U.S. in a GDR text entitled *Ost-West Kulturaustausch: Kooperation oder Konfrontation? (East-West Cultural Exchange: Cooperation or Confrontation?* [1987]). The book detailed the anti-communist agenda in the federal support for cultural and intellectual production. In 1953, the U.S. Information Agency (USIA) was created to act as the ideological arm of the state department—specifically for the production and dissemination of anti-communist propaganda. Under its aegis, cultural exchange programs such as the Fulbright are administered. "Public diplomacy" always included art and culture, but during the 1960s, the government began to fully realize and articulate the role of art and culture in the endeavor to "destabilize Socialism" (60–61). They were to function as "diversions" (63). In other words, they were not to be directly propagandistic in content, but used to lure developmental, third-world countries toward capitalism. As Armand Hammer, the art collector, put it in 1980, "the world is hungry for American culture," and that culture can create "subjects of freedom" (71).

The struggle intensified in the 1980s—at the same time as the proliferation of new cultural theories. In 1983, Charles Wick, president of the USIA, said in a speech before the Committee on Foreign Relations: "We are engaged, as never before, in the conflict of ideas. Our opponent is the Soviet Union . . . it is time for the USIA to become an important instrument of American foreign policy. The USIA has actually become the intersection in the fight for the minds of men." In 1986 he said, "The USIA is America's arsenal in the war of ideas" (65). By 1986, the USIA had a budget of $855 million, with new money earmarked for international TV satellite networks, as well as more fulsome cultural exchange programs. Screening capitalism was, therefore, a project of the state. Two of the TV networks are designed as Euronet and Afnet (Europe-Africa), leading up to the production of Worldnet. When Heiner Müller described the "despoiled shore" in "Eastman color," he was naming the new image-laden "voice of America"—more easily detectable from one of the alternative nations against which it was deployed. Such a powerful propagandistic campaign, waged in the U.S. for the last forty years and focusing in more and more tightly on cultural production, has intervened, at all levels, in the institutions of learning, scholarly travel abroad, museums, major theaters, concert halls, publication ventures, and touring companies. Some careers have been made by such patronage and others quietly destroyed by the denial of access to the network. To imagine critical writing in the U.S. during this time as apart from such influences would be naive at best.

Not surprisingly, there have been few revelations as to just how this national project affected the very structures of cultural, political, and intellectual work. In her book *Daring to Be Bad*, Alice Echols has traced how the fear of federal anti-communist infiltration helped to design the content and organization of early feminist groups. The paranoia produced by the knowledge that there were, somewhere, such infiltrators helped to bring about the demise of some groups. The invisible presence of such "observers" no doubt sculpted, to some degree, the topics to be discussed and the protocol—perhaps even influenced the nature of the political agenda. Only recently has the communist influence in the early years of the gay rights movement come to light in the history of the Mattachine society. Certainly, the McCarthy era, dedicated to rooting out communists and identifying lesbians and gays as unreliable witnesses of secret documents, along with the discovery of the British spies Donald McLean and Guy Burgess, revealed as homosexual, helped to organize the kind of closeting practiced during those years as well as the shape of the threat of discovery. The proximity of homosexual to communist, of closeted behavior to hidden spy, helped to form the community practices of two decades or more. There was once a relationship, for better and worse, between the homosexual identity and the communist one. In other words, the national agenda, which identified itself as capitalist against the enemy, has historically informed the signification of homosexual in the U.S.

One might ask, then, if some part of the market's interest in the sign "lesbian," for example, was as a "lure" to the freedom of capitalism within the international project. After all, it was outlawed in some "communist" countries, and the contrast might be found appealing. As long as a movement did not question capitalism, it could become useful to the propaganda mill. Therefore, movements that embraced private property, individualism, and commodification and that respected national territories could be made into a valuable cultural export—particularly if they are also "sexy." As oppositional movements, they also testified to the freedom of choice, while leaving national agendas intact. This might have been particularly useful in the interface with Cuba—the most proximate communist enemy. The oppressed condition of homosexuals in Cuba was generally known, and when Castro released several, as prisoners, into the U.S., a certain anti-communism grew up that was specific to the homosexual community. Feminist agendas have already been utilized in this fashion. The reports in China of the international women's meetings in Beijing in 1995 were broadcast over the Voice of America. The U.S., then, appeared as the nation where women could be "free," in contrast to their more controlled status in communist China.

The suppression of the influence of this particular state agenda within considerations of the political strategies of lesbians and gays, has been accompanied by an invisibility omission of class as a political category. A poignant record of the suppression of class difference within the feminist and lesbian movement has recently been published by Dorothy Allison. "White trash," a purely class identification without the ethnic one, presents a precise case in point. In "A Question of Class" Allison registers how she unknowingly devoted much energy to "passing" as middle-class in her political and personal life among lesbian feminist collectives. She notes that, in fact, her political identities as "feminist, radical lesbian organizer, and later as sex radical" were part of both belonging to a group and overriding her class background that would set her apart (16–17). Worse yet, the leftist movements, as well as "the myth of the poor in this country," identified a "good poor" to which she did not belong.

> I understood that we were the bad poor: men who drank and couldn't keep a job; women, invariably pregnant before marriage, who quickly became worn, fat, and old. . . . My cousins quit school, stole cars, used drugs, and took dead-end jobs pumping gas or waiting tables. We were not noble, not grateful, not even hopeful. . . . My family was ashamed of being poor, of feeling hopeless. (18)

Allison details ways in which this background as an oppressed political position was not recognizable to feminists, or lesbian feminists. She also records some of the subtle ways in which class informed lesbian desire and her own evaluation of other lesbian authors. Allison's "Bertha Harris, a Memoir" opens with a quotation from Harris's novel *Lover*: "The genuine class difference between women exists between those who had paradise and lost it, and those who never did but think they do" (201). She describes Harris's "lecture" on writing at a feminist institute in 1975 as challenging, frightening, rude, bold, and life-changing for Allison. Then she concludes:

> Bertha talked about class. . . . Class was a notion which in the early days of feminism got a lot more of lip service than examination. Bertha had her own approach. "In terms of class dynamics and psychology, they [great literary artists] are all lower class . . . direct, unequivocating, grabby, impolite, always ready

for a fight and with a nose that can smell bullshit a mile away. The ecumenical, appeasing, side-stepping, middle class mind never ever produces a great work of art, nor a great work of politics." . . . I gulped down Bertha's lauding of what trash might do like a thirsty woman sucks liquid. . . . DARE TO BE MON-STROUS, she told us. (206–207)

Many suggestive elements reside in this narration. Perhaps, as Allison learned, political behavior was marked with class manners and attitudes. Further, this same class training permeated the structures of thinking and writing. Finally, the now-familiar call of earlier lesbian feminists to be monsters and to identify with them had a class base to its meaning. Thus, the historical development of lesbian/gay politics during the era of the Cold War and anti-communist witch-hunts suppressed a critique of class operations within its political organization and abandoned a critique of the state and the economic system. Eventually, these omissions would produce a political movement such as Queer Nation—an organ of political resistance set within a greater cooperation with national and capitalist practices. The political strategies would be marked as middle-class, growing out of an environment that repressed "lower class," as Allison puts it, attributes.

BRINGING HOME THE MEAT

Recuperating the term "lesbian" from the pervasive notion of queer is to recover the strategy of specific denotation from a term that would lay claim to all semiotic territories. While exclusivity is certainly one property of denotation, it should not be confused with it. The charge of exclusivity is effective only when historically specific. In the time of the formation of immense "synergies" or monopolies, or global corporations, whichever term suits the public appearance of the enormous pools of capital, management of labor, and systems of defense which have been rapidly restructuring in the past few years, specific denotation, once proffered as "local" politics, organizes a site of resistance. Lesbian, operating as a specific sign, redesigns the strategies of the 1970s to fit the current state of global capitalism. As denotative, the term is imagined as one among "others"—not the hegemonic Other, but those who demonstrate that class differences, ethnic differences, historical and regional differences are still very much in operation. Admitting the specific limitations of a political position opens it up to the process of contradiction and coalition with those "others." This use of "lesbian" serves as a correction to "Queer," which may now be perceived, when in relation to economic and state structures, as emulating the corporate form of "collectivity" and the expansive gestures of global capitalism.

"Lesbian" not only readmits the politically positive sense of "others" through the organization of "exclusive" borders that provide the ground for contradiction, it redeploys visibility—not necessarily the visibility of "lesbians," as in the 1970s, but, by denoting differences, the visibility of those the new global economy would make invisible. As Grant Kester has put it, in "Out of Sight Is Out of Mind: The Imaginary Space of Postindustrial Culture," the capitalist assignation of its "other" to export-processing zones in the "third" world has served to make its "global assembly line" out of sight (72). This produces the illusion at "home," in the first world, that the class system declines as a "crisis-free technocracy" appropriates the realm of the visible (76). What remains in the visible is simply the "nonclass" of the unemployed "homeless," whose nomadic existence through the abandoned, desolate urban vacancies enacts the dark shadow of global capital's export-processing zones, capable of fleeing labor disputes and local, ecological legislations by nesting, temporarily, in underdeveloped countries, its technoexploitation.

As before, in the 1970s, "lesbian" intervenes as specific and visible within strategies of invisibility. Disclosing its configuration of national agendas and capitalist projects within its structuring, "lesbian" no longer connotes the condition of signifying an "outside" to the system, yet neither would it offer as its strategy an emulation of the dominant structure. "Lesbian" works only in coalition—as a site from which to enter into the struggles of coalition. It is in coalition with other movements concerning territorial rights, property rights, and class issues—in the international as well as within the national arena. "Lesbian" refers to the call to commitment to collectivization and dialogue from within a claimed space. Rather than claiming identity, it would claim space. "Lesbian" would redistribute the territories and challenge the formation of intellectual property through the dialectical movement of contradictions with "others." In other words, the materialist strategies of earlier movements may be brought forward onto new terrain. A specific strategy for the recapturing of territories is the lesbian version of "performing" within the new virtual spaces of technology. The body, the meat, the material, are retained as in resistance to any transcendental technological drive. The body is considered a productive site, tied to property rights and territorial divides. Performance, then, is the dialogue of contradiction and struggle with others who contest the homogenizing effects of Integrated World Capitalism and tele-presences that register commodification and transcendence.

Los Angeles: A Topography of Screenic Properties

What follows is a simple narrative of screens to illustrate their virtual, social, and material aggregations. Let it resonate with the study of stage and nation, community and subculture. The aim of the story is to situate screening within urban studies, postmodern geographies, and the politics of space, in order to more fully develop the topography of screens that produce cyberspace. While the coming space is, as yet, "unmarked," it will undoubtedly inherit the racial, gender, and sexual markers of these screenic practices. Each screen organizes its own virtual, social, and economic structure, but these discrete territories are becoming continuous with one another. Jody Berland, in "Angels Dancing: Cultural Technologies and the Production of Space," sums up the process: "Media produce not only texts and textual receptions, but also a continuous sensory and spatial reorganization of social life. Each technical innovation in the communication media has helped to produce new domestic, urban, industrial, regional, and national patterns of social and spatial relationships" (43). Each of these screens has already accrued a considerable critical space for its own. This narrative does not presume to fully represent those findings, but merely to illustrate how, through a proliferation of screens, a screenic consciousness and space has developed in contrast to that of print and text and how each serves a specific capitalist structuring.

Screens design social spacings not only through their narratives and structural, screenic functions, but also through their real estate. From their movie beginnings, the various screens associate with specific forms of real estate. Movie theaters were built to house the queen of screens, television grew up with suburban tract housing, and surveillance screens scan private, often corporate architecture. Moreover, screens have been related specifically to the urban geography of Los Angeles. Los Angeles has housed both the movie industry and network television. Its geography has developed along with screens, providing their images as well as their production. Whereas Los Angeles has been treated as the exemplum of postmodern geography by critics such as Fredric Jameson, Jean Baudrillard, and Edward Soja, I want to argue that its interaction with screens has developed an epistemological, perceptive sense of screening that functions in the way cyberspace seeks to emulate. The screenic consciousness configured through the interaction among Los Angeles and screens forms the habits and expectations of the space of the cyber of the late twentieth century.

Los Angeles, through its continual intercourse with screens, has accrued a universalizing effect that has encouraged many critics working in cultural studies and film studies to treat the city as if it is completely, virtually accessible—without a specific local, historical context. Visitors such as Baudrillard seem empowered to perceive its structural core in a glance. Likewise, some film critics are empowered to read its signification with no account of the historical relations between the production of the movie in Los Angeles and its images. The movie, then, and Los Angeles lose any local meanings and functions that might circulate between the product and the production. I want to locate Los Angeles alongside the movie and television industry, to illustrate how the movies sometimes work through local, historical problems of structuring the social space that produced them and how those solutions then take on a universalizing meaning. By treating specific movies, such as *Duel in the Sun* and *A Touch of Evil*, I hope to make some of those connections, returning Los Angeles to its specific, historical "place in the sun."

Queen of the Screens

Once upon a time, before the computer age, movies were the queen of the screen. Luminous and alone in their grand houses, they issued forth their narratives, camera angles, and cuts without intervention: sating by suturing. The opulence of their theaters, their stars, and Hollywood itself signaled their dominion. Melding gaze to narrative to star to industry, movies established the guidelines for the operations of screening in the cultural landscape. The architecture of the movie houses often emulated great gilded theaters, with portraits of unknown dignitaries, floral embellishments, cupids, and goddesses— all the accouterments of what seemed to be the European stages of culture. Early movie "theaters" even offered differently priced seats that organized different classes of theatergoers. The loges, with their larger, more comfortable seats that afforded better sightlines, were the new version of the first balcony in the traditions of live performance. But when the (sometimes) immense velvet curtains opened, they revealed not the stage but the screen, where the sweating meat of "live" performers had been absorbed by the technological gaze. The mortality of the stage, as Herbert Blau put it, based on " the fact that he who is performing can die there in front of your eyes; in fact, is doing so," was replaced by the fixed, ageless, repeatable, flat screening of the body (Blau, 83).

Stage space was collapsed into two dimensions. The screen absorbed both the stage space and the positioning of bodies upon it. The gesture, the blocking of movement in space, was replaced by an obsessive traversing of the planes of the body—particularly the face. The director Douglas Sirk once noted that, in fact, the face that offered up such planes to the camera was the "beauty" of the medium. As he said about his discovery of Zarah Leander: "the plane-ness (two dimensionality) of this face is filmically, exceptionally beautiful. This was also the face of Garbo and Ingrid Bergman" (Seiler, 40–41). These planes were what the spectatorial community gathered to view. In this sense, they came to the "theater" not so much to watch the movie, but to enjoy the pleasures of the screen—of screening. The illusion of three-dimensionality was more pleasurable than its actual representation by the stage.

Likewise, landscape and private property could be screened for the price of a ticket. The whole world could be captured within their grid. Movies rented out their "real estate" of the screen. At one end of the economic spectrum, the spectator could inhabit a luxurious surround—if only for an hour or two; at the other, one could get "in" off the streets—a service that movie theaters still serve for those without a domicile. The protagonist of *Stone Butch Blues* in New York, without a place to live: "It turned out to be true that 42nd Street was filled with all-night theaters. Admission was three dollars for kung fu movies endlessly slung together. I chose a theater and entered an all-male world." (228). Cheaper, more transient than a hotel, they offered a short-term occupancy that suited casual, sexual contacts. Samuel R. Delany: "I sat in the balcony of the Variety Photoplays Theater in New York, a tall, muscular white man in his mid-thirties . . . finished sucking off one black guy . . . only to climb over the back of the seats of the row between us and, steadying himself on my shoulder, grinned at me with the wet-lipped delight of the satisfied" (29).

Movie theaters served social functions that were, somehow, even better produced before the screen. Getting a little sleep was promoted by the repeated narratives, and sexual encounters by their images. Their real estate was marked by gender, class, and sexual practice. As the two passages above illustrate, meeting simple material needs at the movies was primarily the privilege of men. Those movie houses are located in the cheaper parts of the city and often rundown inside. *Stone Butch Blues* again:

> Many of the seats were broken. . . . I kept putting off going to the bathroom, but after a while I just had to. The stench hit me as I opened the men's room door. An older man was sitting on one toilet, a needle stuck in his arm, nodding. The tile was gummy with crud. There were no doors on the stalls. Most of the toilets were overflowing with shit and toilet paper. (228)

Here, the protagonist, a transgendered person, exhibits some anxiety in the gendered space of the cheap movie house inhabited by homeless men. Weekend nights in better parts of town suited the movie "house" to heterosexual dating practices, and their matinees allowed middle-class women and teenagers to "space out."

Movie theaters established themselves as a place, sometimes emulating places. The screen and its house could also capture the geographical, urban spaces that lay outside. The Arlington theater in Santa Barbara staged its screen within the *faux* space of a charming Spanish-style town (as Santa Barbara saw itself), with twinkling stars in the ceiling, little casitas around the sides, cozy amber lights illuminating their windows, and winding streets suggested between them. Grauman's Chinese Theater dressed its set in early Hollywood orientalist garb, as if housing the screen in some far-off, exotic land the viewer could enter.

Movies also screened out into the space of Los Angeles, producing it as the "home of the stars." Decades before amusement parks simulated cities, seas, and other environments, movies created a simulating effect throughout Los Angeles—mapping it as a topography of the screen industry. Stars' names were set into the sidewalk, turning Hollywood Boulevard into a hopscotch of movie personae. Tourist maps located the homes of stars. Restaurants, upscale shopping areas, and many of the public spaces of Beverly Hills provided the sites for "stargazing." Certain sites became monuments of star making and spotting, such as Schwab's drug store. Movie memorabilia spread out into retail stores, and stars' fanzines were delivered to the door. Immense billboards lined Sunset Boulevard, defining the parameters of the street with the faces of stars. The movie screen and its stars had the power to map Los Angeles in terms of its stars—one could almost imagine that the only map of Los Angeles is as an effect of the movies.

Early movies were filmed on the streets of Los Angeles, making it the inroads of screening and a familiar backdrop for narratives. Later movies, such as *Sunset Boulevard*, made its industry their subject, and narrativized its locations. The tourist might see a movie being shot—might become an "extra"—might appear on the screen, simply by traveling the streets of L.A. Openings spilled the event of the screen out into the streets, with searchlights charting the skies, and limousines lining the wide boulevards. On those nights, Grauman's Chinese Theater opened its glorious orientalist doors to industry dignitaries. The stars pressed their hands and feet into the cement to mark their "presence" in the city. These indentations then became a prime tourist spot, to view where, in Los Angeles, the hand or foot of a movie star had actually permeated the city pavement. Later, the studio lots themselves provided a nostalgic geography of familiar sets for tourists to visit. Movie Los Angeles was Hollywood and Beverly Hills.

The "rare" movie, alone, like Norma Desmond, in its opulence, grew up with L.A. in the 1920s and 1930s. Its singular, imperial quality simulated local monopolies. As movies monopolized the city through representation, the city monopolized Southern California by taking over the water supply, the harbor, and surrounding areas (Soja, 194). The movie industry, like the oil industry that drilled through L.A. County, and the citrus industry, soon in competition with housing tracts, all worked by accumulating site-specific pools of capital. However, as *Sunset Boulevard* (made in 1950, the era of the rise of TV) shot it, this style of economic, labor, and representational space was dated. Television was making the urban street, Sunset Boulevard, into the interstate *Route 66*. "It is already clear that both 'the city' and 'cinema' are in any case slipping into history. Spatial organization is increasingly determined by global information flows; the analytics and oneirics of cinema are becoming less powerful than the apparatus of visibility inscribed in and by television, video and multimedia" (Donald, 93). But the movie screen made one last stand during the rise of television—the invention of a screen that might be perceived as a transition into the all-encompassing screen of cyberspace.

In his book on virtual reality, Howard Rheingold relates the story of Morton Heilig, who wanted to produce something he called Sensorama—a complete realm of screenic senses. On the way to its development, Heilig became interested in the effect Cinerama had on the audience. Cinerama made its debut around the early 1950s, as television was beginning its flow out into the suburbs. Heilig describes his experience of watching Cinerama:

> When you watch TV or a movie in a theater, you are sitting in one reality, and at the same time you are looking at another reality through an imaginary transparent wall. However, when you enlarge that window enough, you get a sense of personal involvement. You *feel* the experience, you don't just *see* it. . . . I was convinced on the spot, sitting in that Cinerama theater of Broadway, that the future of cinema will mean the creation of films that create a total illusion of reality . . . with no frame between us. (Rheingold, 55)

The single "big screen" of the movies was on its way to the complete body-wrap that virtual reality systems work to provide. Empathetic structures of "pulling in" the viewer were replaced by the architecture and technology of the big screen. Although Cinerama did not last, the multi-million-dollar industry of special effects that now dominates the movie screen insists, similarly, on movie technology as the screen that can make the viewer "feel" the experience. While movies continue to insist upon the single screen as that which can "pull in" the viewer, the television industry has promoted the way in which the screen can move out to where the viewer lives.

The Flowing Locks of TV

I am using the letters TV to represent dominant network uses of television, much as movies stand for Hollywood productions and not cinema. As we will see, there is another use for television than TV would give us to understand.

TV leveled the first challenge to movies' dominion. Giant television studios edged up into West Los Angeles, challenging the real estate of the movie industry—their low-slung, 1950s-stucco look dating the studio's iron gates and guards. They replaced the projector and the can of film with the signal. Daily broadcasting fragmented stars, with their single screen and removed estates, into minor celebrities, available daily, or weekly, for one season. Oil was beginning to show signs of drying up, and citrus was being uprooted for housing tracts. The proliferation of TVs in homes reached out into the suburbs, beyond the urban movie houses. Los Angeles became less a city, in the eurocolonial sense of a center one could visit, and became instead the virtual capital of screens. Edward Soja describes this role in *Postmodern Geographies*:

> Los Angeles is everywhere. It is global in the fullest sense of the word. Nowhere is this more evident than in . . . its almost ubiquitous screening of itself as a rectangular dream machine for the world. Los Angeles broadcasts its self-imagery so widely that probably more people have seen this place . . . than any other on the planet. . . . even more so as the progressive globalization of its urban political economy flows along similar channels. (222–223)

The viewer did not need to go to the screen—the screen came into her home. If movies still staged the screen, early TV, reveals Lynn Spigel in "Installing the Television Set," set out to establish "the home as a theater" (1988, 12). With laugh tracks and stage set pieces, TV encouraged the isolated viewer, or family of viewers, to imagine themselves as part of a "live" audience. This internalization of the collective event makes a crucial turn from stage and performance to screening. Moreover, this move to private screening rested upon the ownership of private property. The at-home families "secured a

position of meaning in the *public* sphere through their new found social identities as *private* landowners" (Spigel 1988, 14). The ticket price for the "show"
rose substantially. If, as we have seen, the homeless might find a night's rest in
a movie theater (see "Queen of the Screens"), the TV screen demanded living quarters for its installation. The ownership of private property became part
of the admittance requirement. One result, before the invention of the suburban multiplex theaters, was the discounting of the urban movie house, which
became as derelict and dated in its appearance as the "inner city."

The crucial change TV brought to screening, in terms of the coming
cyberspace, was the increasing power of the individual to absorb the social.
On the way to the "performative," that internal, textual version of collective
performance, TV encouraged the small, isolated viewing unit to "imagine"
themselves as if within the wider collective. Laugh tracks encouraged the solitary viewer to laugh along with the rest of the "audience." The commonplace
address "you viewers at home," along with other forms of address that suggested that hundreds of people were tuned in, assured the solitary individual
or family that they were watching along with other "homes." Of course, this
simulated audience was a selective one. Presumably, the audience lived in
the white, middle-class suburbs and was composed of the hetero-normative
family unit. Watching "Ozzie and Harriet" implied that one resembled them.
While joining the new class of viewers and becoming part of a selective simulated audience, however, the middle-class housewife actually was even more
confined and isolated within the domestic space (21). And if, in the movie
theater, all spectators are more or less equally positioned in terms of the screen
(after the practice of differently priced loge and balcony seats), TV offered
the large screen only to those who could afford it, and put screen management into the hands of men. Spigel illustrates how, in ads for TV and its new
place in the home, the housewife was disciplined away from the operation of
the screen: "Specifically, there was something displeasurable about the sight
of a woman operating the technology of the receiver" (38). Cleaning up the
social space demanded a price beyond the down payment on a tract home.
It mandated a certain class of viewer and a gendering of the management
of social viewing space.

TV not only secured the suburban flight away from urban streets portrayed
as dangerous to women, whites, middle-class people, and children, but it proffered the home and the family as substitutes for other social and economic
affiliations. George Lipsitz, in his work on class and ethnicity in early network TV,
"reads" several shows representing the working class that portray outside affiliations, such as the lodge or the labor union, as unnecessary outings from the
domestic settings and family relations. Lipsitz ascertains that the change was
not merely fortuitous, but engineered by federal agencies, such as the FCC. In
order to diminish the strength of labor unions and collective practices that
developed during the war and to encourage consumerism and buying on
credit, through TV, the family domicile, removed from the workplace, was

elevated to a new identity-producing role that screened the allure of commodities. TV, then, became the prime tool for retooling "American" capitalism. Advanced through governmental agencies, it was more than a state stage—it was the state mode of economic and social production.

As TV exchanged the private sphere for the public one by emulating the collective audience of theater for the individual viewer, and sought to replace the working-class social spaces with its private, domestic one, it began to blur the lines between electrical and real space (see Spigel 1992). The promise TV offered and continues to offer is a "social sanitation," as Spigel puts it. Beyond the 1950s promise of moving to the suburbs, away from urban blight into controlled neighborhoods and safe streets, TV offered a surrogate social space that had been electronically cleansed **(see notions of cleansing away bodies and material conditions in chapter I, "Re-charging Essentialism," and section IIb, "Cyberspace")**. Spigel foresees how, in this way, TV set up the sanitized cyberspace that would follow on its heels:

> The utopian dreams of space-binding and social sanitation that characterized television's introduction in the fifties is still a dominant cultural ideal. Electronic communications offer an extension of those plans as private and public spaces become increasingly intertwined through such media as home computers, fax machines, message units, and car phones. Before considering these social changes as a necessary part of an impending "electronic revolution" or "information age," we need to remember the racist and sexist principles upon which these electrical utopias have often depended. (1992, 217)

Physical space and electronic space are conjoined through the project of TV and its role in the growth of the suburbs. The TV in domestic space and suburban space as well as the TV of social spacing thus controls and replaces any specific alliances among laborers that might prove disruptive, any sight of perversion or poverty in the social space, and any breach of private property and family normativity.

TV also altered the structures of the screen itself. Within the space of TV, the structural mode of the image began to change, and along with it, its structuration of economics. Early TV criticism noted the way in which the structure of TV's allure contradicted that of the movie. Networks with daily programming grew up alongside the single film openings. As John Ellis describes them, movies and their star system relied upon a "rarity value," whereas TV series and their stars operate by a "fairly constant presence on the medium, rather than on their rarity." Thus, the single, unique screening gives way to "repetition" (106–107). As TV criticism developed, this repetition of individual programs, accounting for the structuring of TV through units, gave way to the sense of "flow," as Raymond Williams identified it (Williams, 93). The viewer does not watch a TV show so much as TV itself, producing the sense that TV has two basic modes: on and off. As the networks increased their programming to extend throughout the day, they brought the possibility of constant screening into the home. Entertainment and edification were no longer whole, discrete experiences one somehow encountered or even focused upon, but effects of continual screening that accompanied quotidian tasks and pleasures. In the domestic context, the imperial regime of the gaze in the movies is reduced to the glance (Ellis, 137). Screening becomes a familiar, constant filter onto the world. TV introduced the habit of spending nights and even days before a screen, or in the presence of the screen, where work, entertainment, and social space all intermingled within its glow. Cyberspace was beginning to form more through the habits of living with the screen than through what was broadcast through it. The sense of being in the screened space at all times mounted as the distinction between inside and out of the screen diminished. Avital Ronell: "If TV has taught us anything—and I think it is helpful to locate it somewhere between Kansas and Oz, an internal spread of exteriority, an interruption precisely of the phantasmic difference between interiority and exteriority—the teaching principally concerns, I think, *the impossibility of staying home*" (1994, 310; italics hers). Ronell's use of home here is more the sense, in this argument, of the spread of screening until it seeks a final sublation into a cyberspace that can absorb all social and economic functions.

The economics of the TV screen brought an intensification of advertising and thus commodity fetishism into the domestic space. The classic capitalist project of creating a private, bourgeois space in contrast to the public one (see the discussion of Barker in section IVc, "Blanking Out") was being restructured by the screen. The marketplace entered the living room. Moreover, the marketplace entered every narrative and news broadcast. The effect of watching footage from Vietnam interspersed with ads for toothpaste or weight-loss programs intensified the role that commodity fetishism could play within multiple discourses and subjects. As TV time expanded throughout the day, the repetition of commercials pounded "home" the allure of commodities. Commodity fetishism flourished within "private" spaces, once designed as removes from the bustle of the marketplace. The screen became the prime site for flashing corporate images and logos. One could imagine how TV advertising could provide a kind of training ground for the way in which corporate logos become normalized in the operations of the computer screen. As they interpenetrate the functions of work or play, through screen blankers and logos situated within the software programs which run the functions, corporate emblems and ads on the computer function similarly to the way ads on TV interrupt news broadcasts, sports events, and dramatic narratives. Moreover, their flashing on the TV screen, in the "privacy" of the home, might have accustomed viewers of screens to the flashing of marketing images within spaces designated as private, such as the space of writing on the computer screen **(see "Blanking Out" for a fuller discussion of this phenomenon).**

Yet, if ads on TV are perceived as intervening in the home as "private," the property relations that secured such privacy in the housing tracts of the suburbs were, in fact, merely a simulation of ownership. In the suburbs, private property was somewhat of an illusion at base. Single-family dwellings, as they are termed, actually belonged to the corporations that both built the tracts and financed their mortgages. The corporations produced private ownership as an illusion to veterans, for example, who could secure a mortgage with no money down and thus no actual equity in the house. On the larger scale, this practice produced the illusion of a middle class that would collapse during the decade of the 1990s. The novelist Joan Didion provides a narrative of the Southern California "town" of Lakewood that traces the consequences of such an illusion. Didion, the daughter of several generations of California natives, recalls the "open farmland, several thousand acres of beans and sugar beets just inland from the Signal Hill oil field and across the road from the plant that the federal government completed in 1941 for Donald Douglas at the Long Beach airport" (46). She shares, along with Joan Irvine, the heiress of the Irvine ranch that became Irvine and part of the University of California at Irvine, a certain nostalgia for even this period of corporate farming, already caught between oil and airports. Didion offers a chilling portrait of the inauguration of the housing tract to be built on that farmland:

> The hundred-foot pylon, its rotating beacon visible for several miles, that advertised the opening, in April of 1950, of what was meant to be the world's biggest subdivision . . . seventeen thousand five hundred houses waiting to be built on the thirty-four hundred dead-level acres that three California developers had bought. . . . Each (house) would sell for between eight and ten thousand dollars, low F.H.A., Vets No Down. . . . Thirty thousand people showed up for the first day of selling. Twenty thousand showed up on weekends throughout the spring. . . . Deals were closed on six hundred and eleven houses the first week. (46)

Didion reveals that most of the buyers were aerospace workers, and, according to the 1990 census, 59,724 were white. Looking back from the sharp decline in employment in California, beginning in the late 1980s, and the concomitant decay of the real estate market, which has brought violence and drugs to this once-utopian tract, Didion asks: "What had it cost to create and maintain an artificial ownership class? Who paid? Who benefited? What happens when that class stops being useful? What does it mean to drop back below the line?" (48). Later, as TV is joined by other screens to create the topography of screens that will cyber California, Didion's questions will come back to interrogate the project. At this point, they offer a critical substrate for the founding of TV/tract space.

So, as TV simulated a collective audience for the solitary viewer in the suburban house, the housing tract simulated the house as private property and the mortgage as the certificate of middle-class standing. Corporations, then, began to screen the social space through their insistent ads on TV, their network programming, station breaks, and logos, as well as their design and ownership of the suburbs themselves. Visually, the tracts surrounding Los Angeles exchanged the unique single-family dwelling on a street for duplicate styles within the grid of a tract. Neighborhoods were determined by the parameters of these building projects. The corporate grid mapped the geographical terrain and its screen—its filter onto the world.

As corporate TV refined its economic grid, the time and repetition of commercials, the marketing moments atomized to the basic unit of the image. If images on the Müllerian stage represent commercial packaging, "the stream of visible images on television can be read as moments of economic circulation, decomposed into abstract markers of value in motion. . . . Any account of the 'political economy of television' hinges not only on the value of images but on the images of value" (Dienst, 38). In other words, as Richard Dienst summarizes in this passage from *Still Life in Real Time: Theory after Television,* TV has inverted the relation of image to value. From the perspective of the TV screen, Müller's stage still worries, through disjunction, the process of reification, whereas TV's acceleration of images has overcome the reified "thing" by its flow. Economic circulation produces value, rather than the things or units of labor that produce them. Thus, the image is merely a "decomposed marker" of that circulation rather than the representation of a "thing of value." The movie *The Thing,* made in 1951 to usher in the era of TV, already depicted the "thing" as frozen. When thawed into circulation, the "thing" was merely a dated horror, like Norma Desmond, haunting the new fast-talking military-industrial economy that was growing up on the outskirts of the suburbs. The 1982 remake of the movie revealed the interdependency between such "things" and the military-industrial compound. And flesh, as Romero's *Dead* trilogy would narrativize, was becoming the "meat" of cyberspace.

TV is the pioneer screen that represents circulation as economics and simulated space as the social. Discrete images only mark the motion of corporate circulation as value. Baudrillard describes this digital revolution in his book *Simulations,* regarding simulation as economic (re)production: "simulation characterizes, beyond the signifier and the signified, the pure form of the political economy of the sign—exactly as the floating of currency and its countable relations characterizes, beyond use and exchange value, beyond all substance of production, the pure form of value" (1983, 133). Yet Baudrillard was still "hung up" on the horns of the duopoly—the simulated binary as the operative form for circulation: "duopoly results from a *tactical doubling of monopoly.* In all domains duopoly is the final stage of monopoly. . . . You need two superpowers to keep the universe under control: a single empire would crumble of itself" (134–135). Baudrillard, the postmodern pessimist, is optimistic in this prediction about the future of socialist nations. He imagined that both superstructures were here to stay. As we will see, the now unimpeded growth of global capitalism will provide a "worlding" effect, where the contest of two different powers once played itself out. Before moving to this "new world order," however, we may review how the sense of a duopoly has carried over into other critical considerations of the relationship between TV and the viewer.

TV is positioned as the machine in the room, strapping the leash of ideology to the members of the household. In the attempt to establish some notion of resistance within the space of "mass culture," certain viewing practices have been established as sites for resistance. "Zapping" among channels has been offered up as one way to demonstrate a viewer's alternative use of the medium. Using the "mouse" of TV, the remote control, viewers zap between channels, cutting across programs. This practice may be perceived as subverting the programming, producing the viewer's own selection of narrative bytes and images. Although the composite of an evening's "zapping" may be unique to the viewer, the prefabricated nature of the images severely limits the effectiveness of the subversion. After all, asserting that zapping among corporate images is subversive is reminiscent of the argument for strategies such as "subversive shopping" put forward by the queer practitioners of performativity **(see sections Ia, "Queer Performativity," and "Commodity Dildoism")**. Hence, all the structures of the marketplace, advanced capitalism, and commodity fetishism remain securely in place. Rather than a subversion of TV by viewer, zapping may be interpreted as setting up another duopoly. "Subversive" viewing strategies and the machine itself produce the illusion of the two positions required for neomonopolistic practices. The viewer seems to mold the composition of images, yet is actually subject to them, performing within the corporate constitution of marketing. Caught between the corporate ownership of the house itself and the machine of corporate images, the viewer performs the scenario of anterior modes of ownership, privacy, and composition constructed by an earlier capitalist project.

Nevertheless, the remote control is the site where the viewer and the machine meet. As the mouse connects the body to the computer, the remote control ties the viewer to the TV (see section IVg, "Driving my Mouse," for the cyborgean context). Dienst describes the combination of tactile/digital relationships the manipulation of the remote control establishes with the airwaves: "zapping reveals how television channels are . . . grooves dredged out of airspace by the antenna and the knob. With zapping comes the union of two kinds of digitality—of the fingers and the signal" (28). Encountering the digital, the viewer thus emulates its microsegmentation of signal by zapping quickly across the airwaves. Tactility is reduced to the repetitious tapping of the limited keyboard of the remote control, but its effects seem more far-reaching and complex in their searching out of airwaves and the way they may bring home the channels. This is a complex relationship indeed between virtual complexity and tactile repetition. Before simply ascribing it to the remote control or the mouse, one might consider the piano keyboard as well in imagining the relationship. In fact, the early computer manuals encouraged the user to think of the keyboard more like that of the piano than that of the typewriter. As the operating site between two orders, TV's remote control negotiates the intermediate space into the cyberworld of signals and tactility. The signals the body would emit become increasingly limited as their virtual product increases in complexity. If the stage actor trained the breath, the limbs, the entire "instrument" as the body was regarded, in order to complete the gestures and diction of the stage, the virtual player focuses the energy of the body down into the confined space of the fingertips while the signal becomes more and more far-reaching, out into satellites.

Ghosting behind the flurry of fingertips tapping the controls is the image of the "coach potato"—the inert body behind the interface. How, then, to keep the body fit and within the system? The answer has been to commodify the interface between body and gesture—to aim the address of the body at another machine. In other words, if the reception of images from the machine of TV renders the body inert, simply reverse the direction—make the body produce the signal received by the machine—Nautilus. The em-bodied customer is the consumer, then, in both directions, paying to receive the images in an inert state and paying to send signals back to the Nautilus machines. Now we begin to perceive the full portrait of the new corporate citizen, dwelling in a corporately owned structure that is, in a sense, leased, positioned between TV and Nautilus machines. If in the early days of TV and suburbs the illusions of private property, private space, and individuality were retained to sell the new corporate structures of value, by the 1990s the circulation among machines and corporate ownership has overcome the illusion. If TV is perceived as altering spatial and social relations by its structuring of images—subsuming other, more traditional spatial relations through its own—then its "effect" becomes a new geography. Its early days, along with the suburbs, received federal assistance to establish the necessary credit to buy into the new order, but by now, transnational relations and global capitalism have replaced that national project.

TV's "worlding" image itself bears, as Richard Dienst puts it, "the unmistakable stamp of post–World War I Anglo-American optimism and liberal universalism" (5–6). Its collusion with national agendas has already been theorized by its leading critics. As noted in "Bringing Home the Meat," the USIA has had national agendas for global "net" transmissions for decades. But the exportation of "American" culture through entertainment has run away with the show. Commercial transmissions far outnumber the official state uses, and although they effectively aid in spreading U.S. cultural imperialism, they begin to create virtual nations that are different from the geographical one. A recent report in the *Los Angeles Times,* aptly entitled "The Global Village" (derived from Marshall McLuhan), charted the prime-time shows through the days of the week and across the globe, illustrating, for example, how "American" shows dominate the world:

> In fact, nearly every country on earth would count at least one American film, situation comedy, soap opera, game show, or action series among the top 10 broadcast within its borders on any given week. While on Monday France is watching Wheel of Fortune, Tuesday Greece is watching The Young and the Restless, Wednesday Kuwait is watching CNN World Report, Thursday Kenya is watching Sanford and Son, Friday Argentina is watching The Simpsons, Saturday Taiwan is watching MacGyver, and Sunday China is watching Tom and Jerry cartoons. (*LA Times,* October 20, 1992, H6–7)

One might begin to imagine that the networks themselves build virtual international communities that share something like "taste" or a particular relation to images and narratives. Varieties of representation, related to constructed appetites for particular commodities, may, in the future, define social aggregations more than municipalities or federations. William Gibson, in *Neuromancer,* creates a world in which the huge synergies "own" the very production of image—even one's own. In his novels, one's location among images and degree of recognition of their varying orders constitute one's sociality and economic condition at once.

However, as commercial satellites increase, along with the perfections of small-dish receivers that allow individuals to choose their channels outside cable companies, the possibility for the organization of other virtual nations or collectivities diversifies. Bruce Sterling's science fiction novel *Islands in the Net* imagines international communities of Poles, Rastas, Grenadians, installed on abandoned supertankers, collectively producing the technologies of life support systems, dedicated to "free" broadcasts, by "stealing" satellite time. Likewise, the film *Born in Flames* imagines a women's liberation army, composed of African American and lesbian women, who would finally be able to take over the major networks, spreading their revolution by broadcasting music, poetry, and a call to arms through "official channels." This sense of those outside the net stands in contrast, say, to TV's own series on itself, *Max Headroom,* which views the future of the industry as filming the world, screening it immediately, running the ratings by the minute to determine the next episode, and finally digitalizing its major reporter to live only on the screen, within the channels.

Yet video, the medium of TV, grew out beyond the channels to create its own screenic world of documentation, art production, and entertainment. Its inexpensive and relatively simple operating procedures brought the camera—the potential to screen—into the hands of individuals. Screens came into the service of personal entertainment formats, such as birthday parties and vacations. Subversive grassroots activist organizations began to produce alternative television, such as PTTV:

> Paper Tiger Television Collective (PTTV) was the brainstorm of a few media agitators who were interested in exercising the democratic mandates of public access cable TV in the early eighties. Since then, the Paper Tiger production philosophy has influenced the evolution of many New York City

video collectives and should rightfully be credited as a model for much quick-and-dirty media that evolved later in the decade. . . . PTTV demonstrates a methodology by which to reinterpret cultural misrepresentations using the very same tools of their production. (Saalfield, 24)

Such movements internal to the U.S. accompany what Tony Dowmunt has titled *Channels of Resistance,* an anthology dealing with global television and local empowerment—for instance, the struggle for the emerging new practices of television programming in South Africa, after the Broer Broederbond control and before the American global control. Likewise, the video workshop movement in the UK, which produces local shows in Northern Ireland, or by black video makers; Soufriere Community TV on the island of St. Lucia, video workshops among the Inuit in Canada, or the Maori in New Zealand.

Video, then, can produce the possibility of taking TV into local hands. The tradition of video imagines an individual, artistic use of the medium, a local or a "private" one. In contrast, movies and commercial TV seem to produce the public, commodifiable corporate face. The industry screen successfully pumps out mass entertainment and edification within transnational guidelines and for the exportation of national agendas. Yet local uses of TV and video produce an active interface with what was a one-way transmission. Video and local television have begun a practice of interactive screens that might contradict one another in the interface.

Transition: The Subject Position

Thus far in these sections on the screen, there has been no consideration of the subject. I have posed no such position in my paradigm, imagining that no such structure exists within this kind of corporate circulation. I assume that the notion of a subject position itself is extraneous to such circulation. However, Mark Poster, one of the major critics in this new field of technoculture, continues to interrogate the formation of the subject position vis-à-vis the new information technologies. In his new book, *The Second Media Age,* Poster situates the subject in the space between TV ads, on the one hand, and databases that form a new super-panopticon, on the other—somewhere between market forces and surveillance. Since this study is now at that same juncture between TV and surveillance screens, I want to attend to Poster's analysis as a way of getting at my own position.

Poster identifies TV ads as a "meaning structure" that, "keeping itself at the level of signifiers, meanings and images, powerfully invites the viewer to identify with the commodity." Lest the reader assume that the viewer is set up as modernist subject of intentionality and rationality, Poster cautions, "The ad stimulates not an object choice, a cognitive decision, a rational evaluation, but works at other linguistic levels to produce the effects of incorporation and attachment between the viewer and the product" (1995, 62). The structure of incorporation, without any sense of the possible pun in the word (corporation), is valorized by Poster as a poststructuralist correction to the modernist configuration of the subject. The subject does not exist prior to discursive operations, but is formed through them. TV ads aid in constructing the poststructuralist subject and to encourage a sense of it in their repetitious familiarity.

> Through these communications, the realist linguistic paradigm is shaken. The TV ad works with simulacra, with inventions and with imaginings. The modernist print-oriented communications associated with education, capitalism/socialism, bureaucracy and representative democracy . . . are displaced in favor of a postmodernist, electric-oriented communication in which identity is destabilized and fragmented. (62)

In other words, the way in which the circulation of TV ads works is to incorporate the subject through these images, making it fragmented and destabilized—a correction to the modernist formation. Here Poster and I, in one sense, do not disagree. His description of the subject forming within that circulation is similar to my own assertion that the body, or the viewer, is in the intersection between corporate ownership of land and of screen, addressing, through the body, the Nautilus. Poster celebrates this juncture, however, while I seem to decry it. Partially because he relegates considerations of ownership and means of production to the old modernist paradigm the new subject leaves behind. His focus is on the formation of the subject—the integer—while the space in which it forms remains unmarked, as if "free."

Poster's correction to "free" space comes in his discussion of the database as the new "super-panopticon." Following Foucault, he retains the negative charge on the term, but also, following Foucault, he employs the notion that the subject emerges within the operations of the super-panopticon, not separate from it (69). Databases, he argues, form a portrait of the individual. Although they operate by discrete fields of information, relational software functions permit combinations or "clusters" of information to link up to form "characteristics" of the "subject" of the database. To sum up his argument:

> Databases . . . constitute subjects in a manner that inscribes a new pattern of interpellation . . . far different from that of modernity with its discourses of print. . . . Once the form of representation embodied in the database is understood, it may be compared with other regions in the mode of information—television viewing, computer writing. . . . In each case the subject as coherent, stable rational center is refuted by heterogeneity, dispersion, instability, multiplicity. (90–91)

Poster notes that this interpellation is not necessarily positive, although it seems so when juxtaposed to his use of modernism. He emphasizes that such "multiple subject positions" require a new critical treatment rather than the deployment of a modernist critique such as the Marxist one, or one based on identity politics (76).

Poster's description of databases of individuals deployed for purposes of marketing or surveillance is helpful in reminding us that representations of identity are already constructed in cyberspace and already determine one's access to institutions and finances. These fields of data concerning one's employment status, buying habits, personal dwelling, and other sometimes unlike functions are already being conjoined in different nodes of identity, without the knowledge or effort of the individual involved. Some of these functions seem pleasurable—such as using a credit card to make a purchase. What Poster neglects to emphasize is that these "subject positions" are completely reified, completely commodified, in some databases and made to serve national agendas in others. They posit a portrait of the individual within corporate circulation. Those who do not appear there, those who accrue no weight or mass among data, are those who likewise can derive no benefit from the system, who have no access to it, such as the homeless and those who cannot qualify for credit cards.

Certainly, Poster is correct in assuming that the presuppositions about subject relations in liberal democracy, on the one hand, or within the fascist control of mass culture, on the other, do not really apply to the new "age," as he terms it. Yet his embrace of poststructuralism, in spite of his critical warnings, leads him into some unhappy conclusions. Similar to other critical writings on technology, Poster's poststructuralist "take" is not productive around the power differences embedded in gender systems, nor those in the operations of ethnicity. As it turns out, this "unmarked" fragmented, dispersed, and decentered subject of electronic circulation is also a correction of so-called "modernist" notions of ethnicity:

> Multiculturalists, postcolonialists and subaltern theorists sometimes further claim certain privileges for the subject position of the "minority" or "third world person" not simply as that of the oppressed but as affirming the ethnic characteristics of the group. In my view such cultural politics are not critical of the modernist position but simply shift the values or relative worth of two terms in the binary opposition. . . . To the extent that placing value on ethnicity promotes a recentering of the subject and supports the foundationalism or essentialism of the subject in question, then the subject position has little to do with postmodernity or the second media age. (41)

Poster's formulation is reminiscent of the same kind of correction that "queer performativity" brought to "lesbian community," treated in section Ia, "Queer Performativity," and in "Bringing Home the Meat." Without rehearsing those complete arguments here, perhaps it suffices to note the historical irony in reading this passage at this time, in the state of California, where anti–affirmative action forces have repealed university admission policies that took special account of minorities and women. The troubling split of so-called cultural theory, which aims at a political effect, and the current activist movement to (re)gain affirmative action, rests precisely on the notion of identity politics. While Poster's account of how the subject is formed in the new media age is compelling, this particular local situation (for me and Poster) heightens the sense that there is some privilege embedded in the practice of that multiplication of identity within the technologies and their critique. Does it assign to those expelled from the systems of education and employment the unfulfilled need for even a single identity that might secure their access to the system?

Even beyond this rather simple modernist historical observation on my part, it does seem that Poster's embrace, like that of many other critics in this field, of this unmarked, dispersed, morphing subject seems to agree with the sanitizing practices that the suburbs and cyberspace would deploy on the population, as argued in the section on TV and the suburbs. If difference only *seems* to occur, is only part of a playful masquerade, then actually homogeneity supports the emulation of heterogeneity. The continuing ownership of the cyberworld by white first-world men will be secured by this notion of the morphing subject.

It seems to me that the problem arises when the critical project attempts to attach a consideration of power differences around issues of class, "race," gender, and sexual practice to a formulation of the subject position. Repeating here the uses that feminist and ethnic activists made of the notions in the 1970s, in which "presence" means "showing up" and "stable identity" means a continuing dedication to struggling against oppressive measures aimed at women, ethnic majorities, and lesbians and gay men, in struggles such as those around affirmative action—rights actually gained through movements of identity politics—political uses of identity are confounded by a notion of the subject. They are required, for example, to produce an interiority peculiar to a bygone capitalist, modernist, or print age. In attempting to comply with such a structure of interiority, they take the "risk of essentialism" they were never designed to encounter **(see "Bringing Home the Meat" for the complete argument)**.

What's more, the screening described in this process has little to do with subjects. The screening process traced here screens out unwanted "properties" from the burgeoning new space of social and economic practices, and screens in corporate consumers. This process has little regard for "subjects." For this reason, the politics of space accomplish what the prior critical projects around subject formation confound. Within space, subjects operate as sites, unitary or not. They focus the critique on the nature of a location. Allucquere Rosanne Stone's notion of "warranting" citizenship through the reference to the envelope of flesh takes issue with the single location, the effect of establishing a unitary site, an integer, that location produces. She posits instead a multiple subject, multiple sites **(see section Vb, "The Transsexual Body")**. Poster argues for the dispersed, decentered postmodern subject. But multiplying or dispersing the subject is merely changing the nature of location. Poster's idea that databases produce a "multiple" subject that requires a "new arena of contestation" (93) actually begs the question of the "arena"—the nature of the space in which the subject is situated. Shifting the critical focus from the subject to space and how it is conceived does not, finally, return to a notion of agency, as debates over the subject position typically do. Rather, the politics of space attend to the function of the grid and *how* it locates subjects **(see section IIa, "Semio-Space," and the icon for this argument)**. To this end, let us return to the composition of screening to study its spatial politics.

Surveillance Screens

"Private" property turns the screen in the other direction—away from the individual and toward its accumulated capital. Surveillance screens proliferate in stores, apartment buildings, gated communities, cash machines, corporate offices, and universities. The experience of the screen as "watching" grew up with corporate organizations of capital and the resulting need for "security." Screening intervenes in the process of accessing one's own money, food, living quarters, workplace, and education. Individuals have become accustomed to the screening of themselves in parking garages and lobbies as a promise of their own security, as well as the security of other "owners." Movies have narrativized surveillance cameras, from the still shots of murders played in front of national emblems, as in Brian de Palma's *Blow Out,* which concluded its narrative in the Philadelphia Liberty Bell Parade before a giant American flag, to transnational intrigues around documentary doctoring processes, as in *The Rising Sun.* TV runs footage from surveillance cameras in grocery stores and banks in weekly programs such as *America's Most Wanted.* The needs of private property thus become the constraint on privacy. In 1991, Lotus produced a CD-ROM disk that screened the addresses, marital status, and estimated income of more than eighty million people, with no legal difficulty.

The cybersurveillance possibilities move beyond the camera to grids that can locate the exact location of a person or thing. The new BMWs already come with a screen in the dashboard that, when hooked into a satellite system, can map the driver's exact location. *The X Files,* the new TV program of futurist paranoia, developed a character who had been marked by a bar code so that he might be found by laser. Most critical considerations of these techniques associate "privacy," in this sense, the un-surveilled, with "freedom." Privacy Acts are designed to "protect" citizens from intrusive surveillance. What is really manifested here is the break between the old order of the private citizen, formed in the initial stages of capitalism, and the move into the global, corporate citizen who has no value of privacy or freedom, or at least of their necessary link.

Surveillance screens create an ambivalence about being screened. On the one hand, they encourage the screened to feel secure—protected by the net surrounding those who have the income to access their private spaces. In the same way that TV and the suburbs encouraged the viewer to imagine safety in terms of the screen, surveillance screens accompany one through open, social spaces that might invite danger. On the other hand, they create a log of one's actions—a visual database, such as the one Poster suggested as creating multiple subjects—that monitors and records one's movements for the use of the security forces attached to them and the owners of the forces. The screened citizen must trust these forces to act in her own interest. Further, they encourage, by their camera eyes, the feeling that danger might lurk in these spaces. Their very sign of protection also instigates fear and caution. They provide the sense that only the thin surface of a screen lies between the "private" or, more properly, the "corporate" citizen of property and danger.

Octavia Butler, in her novel *Parable of the Sower,* imagines a Southern California in which the retreat into Planned Unit Developments (PUDs), walled-in communities with their own security guards, and within the protection of surveillance screens is no longer effective. The dispossessed break the screens, climb over the walls, outnumber the security forces, and walk the freeways. Only a company town with "foreign" security forces offers complete, secure surveillance in exchange for indenture, but slavery, for the African American protagonists of Butler's novel, is not inviting. Accordingly, surveillance promises security while suggesting danger, protects income and access while threatening the indenture of the "company town."

On neither side of surveillance, danger or protection, does the category of the "private" produce an effective strategy of protection. The notion that "privacy" protects the individual and that surveillance systems invade that privacy, as we have seen, is a notion born of a particular interest that the passing phase of capitalism had in creating that "private" citizen. Emulations of privacy, effective as they may be for inducing nostalgia, or for encouraging cooperation with systems of surveillance, are simply that—performances of a prior civil and marketing structure. They have been effectively employed by the corporate owners of housing tracts, as well as the corporate designers of ads, to bring the consumer/viewer/screened into the circulation of corporate value. The "private" property the surveillance screens seem to protect is more often the property of institutions and corporations, in which the screened citizen is encouraged to believe that she has some equity.

The ambivalence that surveillance screens produce in the screened citizen they track marks, perhaps, the transitional moment in which the corporate or global capitalist circulation of value has not quite fully accomplished the destruction of the bourgeoisie, the private, middle-class citizenry of its prior project. As the "middle" dissipates, the wall of screens offers the secure but dangerous divide between the dispossessed and the corporate and perhaps indentured "citizen."

Videopathy

Video countersurveillance is understood to be a way to turn the surveillance strategies back on to the dominant. ACT UP! protects its activists' "live" demonstrations by recording them (Saalfield, 29). Offered as proof against what the networks may offer, groups such as this one seek to circulate their video through the legitimating channels. In this function, when television runs these videos it provides what Avital Ronell, in "TraumaTV," calls a simulation of "a call to conscience" (312). The video footage gains credibility as it circulates. When it appears on network news and in documentaries and is even quoted in a mini-series or film, it functions as a conscience-calling cry for the truth. Yet, in gaining its moral strength through circulation, video, in itself, signifies less cultural value than its circulation among screens. As we have seen, screenic practices consist more and more of the quotation of other screens— digitation of images that reproduce in different visual landscapes. This circulation among screens is "native" to the computer screen. All its images are borrowed from elsewhere, digitally reproduced, and transmitted. Cyberspace may be an intense form of screenic circulation—an eddy or cyclone of screens.

The Rodney King uprising offers a social example of screenic circulation. Initiated by video countersurveillance footage, the footage of the police beating circulated across news programs and documentaries. Public access to these images brought a legal and social charge of racism to the police proceedings. Once the inequitable decision of the jury was known, the news screened the looting of electronics stores, where people were stealing TVs and VCRs. TVs and video cameras were being taken hostage by the ghetto: a "racial" retribution on screens, prompted by the judicial interpretation of video as evidence. However, counter- and state surveillance entwined in complex operations, as the looting was recorded by television news cameras and tried, in court, on that evidence. The beating of Reginald Denny, pulled from his truck onto the street, registered, through numerous broadcast interviews with onlookers, urban experts, and Denny himself, a complex urban paranoia, as the intersection at which he was beaten was tested for its ethnic "dangers." Repeated runs of the Denny beatings, surveys of the fires in L.A., along with the lootings created a new mapping of the city on figuratively "colored" grids.

The Rodney King uprising, located at the intersection of screen technology and fictions of race, performed the new urban geography of screening. Los Angeles, first the "home of the stars," then the virtual capital of the TV screen, acquired its geography, particularly its racialized geography, through the circulation of screens. The Rodney King uprising seems, now, to have been the first in a new TV series on race relations in L.A. The O.J. Simpson case absorbed the television screen. Aerial TV cameras followed Simpson's car along the freeway grid, while the networks split the screen between maps of L.A. and shots of the white Bronco. Surveillance, TV programming, the freeway, the city, shots of Simpson's Hertz commercials, footage of his football "runs" all screened, through a complex circulation, the sociopolitical space of Los Angeles.

Screens have also been "taken" by lesbians and gays—not only as countersurveillance technology around the AIDS crisis, but as entertainment. Some lesbian and gay bars in West Hollywood "homosexualize" the screen by making what might be termed "house" movies. Like house music, house movies cut, in this case, film bites, to sync them with contemporary dance music. One such lesbian house movie, for example, cut from shots of Garbo in *Queen Christina* to clips of muscle-women workouts, to soft porn, set to music by k. d. lang. The acquaintance with movies is presumed to be so acute that the stars and movies in the seconds-long cuts may be immediately recognized in order to create a camp cutting across associations. Movies are screened by the bars, and the bars by the consequent videos running alongside the dance floor, where "live" flirtations are playing nightly. Some bars have become known for this, such as the Revolver in West Hollywood, which at one time had its own production company for producing and distributing such tapes. In these locales, a certain semiotically interactive screening takes place, in which the recognition of clips draws in the viewer, who, through camp associations, makes them into a mise-en-scène for the lesbian bar.

More than semiotically interactive, video games have invited the spectator into a limited co-production of the screening . Arcades of animated, interactive screens draw primarily young men into their dim rooms in shopping areas and on campuses. One can turn to screens from the process of studying or shopping to compete with their software. Nintendo, Atari, and Sega have brought these screens into homes. The computer joins the other interactive screens with word processing and data management functions, locating people in front of screens throughout the workday. Now, one can work all day in front of a screen, play with one in the store on the way home, watch one at home at night, or go out to see the movie screen in her new complex. Thus, screens have now become central and dispersed in the production of social and physical space. The screen is enshrined in the movie house, available in the electronics store, commonplace on vacations and in social celebrations, a tool in the workplace, "on" as the TV broadcast, and on watch as the security agent among the architecture of living spaces. Screening creates "subversive" uses, transmits the American imperialist cultural agenda, substitutes for the most personal of diaries, links worker to product, player to game, person to person, nation to nation, and all to its own virtual "globe." The mode, uses, and association of each screen merge to create a topography of screens, across which labor, entertainment, sexual lives (porn videos), travel, family meetings, video conferences of workplaces, whole virtual nations are distributed. Controlled by the interests of business and national agendas; in part, loose, out into the streets in the hands of individuals and subversive, political groups. The screenic discourse of today.

Screenic Discourse as Grid

The huge lines of spectators jostling each other Saturday and Sunday before the windows of the temples of film are disappearing because they reform from now on, and as punctually, at the freeway entrances. It's simply the case that what had pushed the masses toward the cinema armchairs now forces them into the seats of their automobiles.

From this perspective, the evolution of movie houses may be revealed as useful for analysis of the cities.... After the age of architecture-sculpture we are now in the time of cinematographic factitiousness; literally as well as figuratively, from now on architecture is only a movie. (Virilio1991, 63–64)

The urbanscape of Los Angeles, home of movies and television networks, has developed in an eerie consonance with screening. As Virilio suggests in the above quotation, the complex sprawl of the Los Angeles basin and its simulated-style architecture could be perceived as structural resonances of the movie theaters themselves. But the deeper consonance between the screen and the city is the way in which both constitute their representation through a grid. Virilio relates the seats before the movie screen to positions on the highway. What do movies and L.A. have in common? Both screening and the grid organize points in space. L.A. as grid has become a commonplace of critical treatments of the city. Since L.A. is not organized around a central "downtown" district, but spreads out along its freeways, it is perceived through a grid of travel—as a vector of vehicles. Here is how Mike Davis describes it in *City of Quartz*: "Los Angeles's polymorphous landscapes and architectures were given a 'comprehensible unity' by the freeway grid in a metropolis that spoke the 'language of movement not monument'" (73). Here is how it appears in David Brodsly's *L.A. Freeway: An Appreciative Essay* : "An urban environment of distinct points on the highway grid . . . a set of freeway-defined vector relationships.... whose magnitudes are measured in minutes and whose directions are disembodied place names" (25).

L.A. then, appears only as a grid—its basic organization is homologous to the process of screening. L.A. is the city of screens—a city which produces the screen, is populated by the screen industry and screen addicts—and a city constituted by screening. But if the city exists as grid, what is the import of that representation? The art critic Rosalind Krauss identifies the grid as the primary structuring of the aesthetic sensibility of the twentieth century. For Krauss, the grid has been used to produce the condition of abstraction: "In the flatness that results from its coordinates, the grid is the means of crowding out the dimensions of the real and replacing them with the lateral spread of a single surface. . . . pure relationship" (9). Krauss contends that the grid functions as the "antinatural, antimimetic, antireal," evacuating the analogic, the sequential, and the narrative, for spatial structure. Krauss situates this phenomenon within modernism, but if one extends the notion beyond painting (Krauss's focus) to the conditions of cyberspace as screen, or L.A. as grid, the same abstracting effects may be perceived. In the case of a city, this abstract nature of its constitution goes against its traditional representation. A city traditionally signifies a centralizing embodiment of cultural production. New York, for example, functions as an embodiment of U.S. cultural production. In fact, the traditional comparison between New York and Los Angeles makes this exact point. Some argue that Manhattan, in its compressed island form, provides the appropriate center for cultural production. One can "see" the arts, "walk" among them, and pass the producers on the street. New York fleshes out, on its streets, the abstract. If, as postmodern geographers argue, L.A. appears only as its freeway grid—its intersecting vectors where channels change—it produces itself as an abstraction rather than an embodiment.

The dynamic interplay of grids between screens and L.A. is more complex than simply freeway to framing device. Star sightings, freeway crossings, studio lots, the impressions in cement, the dispersion and interventionist assimilation of screens—the circulation of screening through all of these elements constitutes Los Angeles. This screenic circulation displaces the "somewhere" that tourists such as Frederic Jameson cannot seem to find: "the latest evolutionary mutation of late capitalism toward 'something else' which is no longer family or neighborhood, city or state, or even nation, but as abstract and nonsituated as the placeness of a room in an international chain of motels or the anonymous space of airport terminals" (116). Jameson is desperately seeking the city in its traditional centering, embodied state. "Abstract" and "anonymous" are conflated to produce a negative sense of this screenic entity. The passage is marked by a eurocentric melancholy for centers. The West Coast still functions as the distant endpoint of the eurocolonial process, not quite "in touch" with centrist, corporeal urban models that have, in the past, represented an "unalienated" state. Ironically, Jameson is nostalgic for an earlier, eurocolonial stage of property relations. The codes of visibility he would elect belong to another form of private property.

The grid also serves to represent perception itself. Krauss contends that, historically, the visual arts developed the grid from the science of optics:

> An interesting feature of treatises written on physiological optics is that they were illustrated with grids. Because it was a matter of demonstrating the interaction of specific particles throughout a continuous field, that field was analyzed into the modular and repetitive structure of the grid. . . . By its very abstraction, the grid conveyed one of the basic laws of knowledge—the separation of the perceptual screen from that of the "real" world. (15)

The grid is the field theory of optics—a perceptual field established by moving particles. Compare this insight with Benedikt's report on how the screen of cyberspace produces movement and location:

> There are a finite number of finite-sized pixels on any video monitor screen, and it is not unreasonable to define the real (2-D) size/area of an object as the absolute number of pixels that comprise it. An object that is moving itself or is being "dragged" across the screen will retain its size and shape because the distribution of pixels over the screen is uniform. . . . Any traveling, one-pixel "particle" that, on a uniformly pixellated screen, would travel at a constant pixel/sec . . . velocity, would, to us, decelerate and accelerate as it traveled through areas of varying pixel density. (155)

If L.A. appears only as grid, the conditions of its visibility are congruent with those of perception itself. Thus, as one perceives L.A., one perceives perception itself. Moreover, the conditions of its visibility as grid are homologous with the structural devices of the computer screen. The computer's simulation of space and location is homologous with the way L.A. is constituted—through movement across or within a grid. In the case of L.A., these particles or pixels may be cars, which determine the grid of the freeway as the perceptual representation of its location.

As the grid invokes the condition of perception, it also functions as an icon. A historical example might provide a way into that complex iconic structure. Krauss finds that before grids appeared in their abstract form, they appeared as windows or mirrors in Symbolist paintings. As such, they functioned as geometric panes that both admit light into the room and reflect images (16). Recalling once more the icon on the computer screen—a window in and out of software functions—we can see how the grid of the screen that simulates location works with the icon/window effect that moves between different orders of functions. In the city, the grid also functions in an iconic fashion, suggesting both the topography of the city and the structure of perception. Grids abstract representation as they bridge two orders of things.

Within the cyberpunk imagination, this gridding, screenic effect unites cyberspace with "real" space. Screening space provides the link between online social structures and traditional ones. With precisely this conflation, Pat Cadigan begins her short story "Death in the Promised Land":

> The kid has his choice of places to go—other countries, other worlds, even other universes . . . but the kid's idea of a hell of a good universe next door had been a glitzed-out, gritted up, blasted and blistered Apocalyptic Noo Yawk Sitty . . . topping the hitline for the thirteenth week in a row, with post-Apocalyptic Ellay and post-Apocalyptic Hong Kong. . . . Perhaps the kid could have explained to her . . . (how) he had come out of post-Apocalyptic Noo Yawk Sitty with his throat cut. (258)

"Ellay" is a purely cyber Sitty, where the protagonist spends his money and his social time. Cadigan's "murder in virtual reality" is a reminder that such grids are not without menace and danger, even though they are primarily, in the cyberfuture, a space for entertainment. She plays the now-familiar trope in cyberpunk that what happens to the body, or the chosen icon of the player, in cyber-reality actually affects the "real" body. The order of influence reverses. The homological relations between the "real" city and the cyber Sitty produce a continuous plane upon which the body is situated. Homology produces what simulation cannot: the direct exchange of conditions from one order of things to the other. Thus, the entire relationship between the two worlds is an iconic one.

Even more prescient is Cadigan's notion that considerations of material wealth also invert in the online world:

Yeah. Stuff in AR. In the Sitty. Everybody who goes in regular's got stuff in AR. So I got this nothing job. . . . I live in a hive on Sepulveda. But I got stuff in AR. I got a good place for myself, I'm in the game with the name and the fame. I even got myself a few passwords. I put in plenty of time to get all that. . . . I spent some big sums doin' it. If I give it away, then I got *nothing*. (280)

As in most cyberpunk, Cadigan has caught a future that already exists. The sums that people are spending on (the appropriately named) America Online, in the chat rooms, or in the games are an investment in that online existence— one that pays off in the space of that exchange. In the sense that they have "earned" a certain status and a certain access to programs, the players "got stuff." Contrasting this condition with a low-paying job and probable social iso- lation makes the point that the investment inverts from the "real," where the players have little or nothing to ante up, to the online, where they may fantasize what they will. In spite of the difference between the two conditions, however, the correspondence between them is completely operable.

As technology and global capitalism form what many predict will be a two-class society of the "haves and have nots," their investment in cyber-real- ity may be the only terrain where they may meet. The owners who are invest- ing and reaping "real" rewards from the business (as Bill Gates of Microsoft is doing) are withdrawing into secure spaces from those who will exchange what little they have for "stuff" in cyberspace. Their only intercourse will be online, for it seems that even the suburbs do not offer enough protection anymore from what used to be "urban blight," or dense areas of poverty. In California, those with "stuff" in the "real" world are moving into Planned Unit Develop- ments (PUDs)—gated communities with their own security forces. Cyberspace may eventually provide the only safe space for the exchange of valuables. The exchange of material goods is already taking place online. More and more businesses are opening web sites, paying computer designers to con- struct ever more alluring icons for their store fronts. The user can "enter" a commercial space and, with the online exchange of money through credit card transactions, buy goods. The new synergies signal the structuring of the emerging space of commercial transactions. The attempt of Viacom and QVC, the shopping channel, to buy Paramount would permit exactly what Cadigan foresees in her short story. **(See section IVg, "Driving My Mouse.")**

The conflation of entertainment with business has already confused where "value" resides, as Cadigan's character illustrates. Considerations of the ludic, as we have seen in the section on the body and elsewhere, confuse traditional notions of business and learning. This observation is central to the argument here, which would establish just how screening, throughout the twentieth century, has operated to set up a circulation among screens wherein all social properties actually garner value. In other words, no single screen will establish social value. The circulation among screens and screening will situate value as an effect of that circulation.

The correspondence between cities and Sitty, for example, will provide the exchange mechanism for citizenship and value.

The actual structures of value screening institutes have been developing through a long progression and combination of screens. The project of this chapter is to trace those different types of screenings and to suggest a common space in which they all interact. The movie screen began a process of screening that subsumed screenic effects to narrativity. Thus, the pleasures of the narrative screen and the movie "house" disciplined the surround—in particular Los Angeles and its environs—within a specific screenic form. As we will see in the following discussion of two Hollywood movies, a particular structuring of social relations was instituted through an iconic interaction between the movie and its city. Additionally, video screens, through their circulation of functions, from camcorders to surveillance screens, inured people to the conflation of screening as a record of private pleasure and screening as securing private property. Security, surveillance, and pleasure circulated among one another through the proliferation of video screens. Finally, property and social relations are caught up in the circulation among screens, in which the various screenic functions actually determine their "real" value.

The experience of this screenic circulation is what Margaret Morse terms "distraction." In her article "An Ontology of Everyday Distraction: The Freeway, the Mall, and Television," Morse theorizes how what has here been represented as "screening" is an experience that moves through social and geographic space to find, in their intercourse, a new kind of sensibility:

> The late twentieth century has witnessed the growing dominance of a differently constituted kind of space, a *nonspace* of both experience and representation, an elsewhere which inhabits the everyday ... a distracted state—such as driving, shopping, or television watching. . . . *Nonspace* is ground within which communication as a flow of values among and between two and three dimensions and between virtuality and actuality ... can "take place." (196)

Morse takes the notion of *I Am a Camera* out into new realms. This spatial organization of knowledge predominates across orders of things, reconfiguring them as if on or in a screen and thus creating a sense of space that replaces old structures of subjectivity. Stretching across city, perception, and cognition, this sense of space allows simultaneous cohabitation: the space of implosion, where resonances link with one another in a dense, semiotic simultaneity.

However, as Cadigan indicated, the zone of screenic effects is not neutral. For example, the freeway does not cut through just any part of cities but divides poor communities—ethnic neighborhoods. "Better" neighborhoods are removed from the freeway, enforcing stabilized sound spaces that promise access without disruption. As Foucault and others have worked out in detail, there is a disciplinary aspect of the screen, which, as surveillance, keeps its various points "in order." In the next section, I want to explore the disciplinary aspects of the icon and the grid as they have been narrated in movies and on the stage. The disciplinary uses of the iconic in the movies could be enforced through the focus on images whose presence in the field determines the narrative and representational value of the field, or frame. I hope to demonstrate just how these functional elements have accrued a tradition of narrative and affect that they bring back into the screenic process itself, so that any participation in gridding, in "distraction," bears their weight—to illustrate how movies train the viewer in how to interpret the grid.

The Icon: Duel in the Sun

In classical Hollywood movies, "empty" space is established in a variety of ways. In some movies, empty space is outer space—the dark place evacuated by light and land. Opening camera shots explore outer space as something silent and dark. Other movies open onto a landscape which serves as an empty space of "open" possibilities, but which, during the narrative process, becomes a socially contested one. However, for landscape to function as empty, it opens out without vertical grandeurs, such as mountains, trees, or any active borders. The desert has traditionally worked this way, as recently as in *The Sheltering Sky,* in which the eminently photographable desert signifies the empty, existential ground upon which sexual actions falter.

Contradictorily, space's emptiness is dependent upon the sense that something exists within it. Harking back to Euclid, space extends from the "point" of view. With no blockages of that view, splayed open as desert or the dark regions of "outer" space, freedom is ascribed to the "point" of view. Once again, Michael Benedikt conjectures the simulation of space through its phenomenological history, which is the experience of space as movement:

> Space presents itself to us in the *freedom to move.* . . . We come to reflect upon how the very possibility of movement depends on the preexistence of different and discrete locations for the same thing (including our bodies), locations between which continuous movement—that is, movement through all intervening locations—must occur over time. (127)

In film, this movement is the movement of the camera. Wide, sweeping shots over the desert both scan its expanse and offer some notion of freedom—unimpeded movement. Yet, as the camera moves, an expectation mounts, a sense of some other point or "presence" suggests itself to the viewer. In other words, with movement comes the mark of agency and presence as well as temporality. Something or someone is looking—is there in the camera. And some other one is "out" there. This premonition is mined as an eerie sense in movies of outer space. The "thing" is already there, lurking beyond the camera's view. The eerie sense signals that what is there is contaminated.

If one accepts the phenomenological base for the conception of space, that space as abstraction devolved from the experience of movement, then space is not empty, but only not yet filled by that body. No "real" or empty space exists beyond its function as a register of movement. In the shots of outer space, one might then trace the sense of eerie contamination back to the body. The concept of absolute or empty space, created through unimpeded movement, though displaced onto movement, can be traced back, through movement, to the body. The body is there and was already there. The contamination is that physical presence. Unlike the clean, empty "point" in geometry, its surrogate, the body, has come, in science fiction and new virtual theories, to be referred to as "meat." Meat and blood contaminate the emptiness. "Presence" contaminates the empty. Socially, the "already there," lurking somehow beyond or behind the gaze, the already-there-body casts the indigenous as contaminated.

Now, the body, the point, introduces another space—the "inner" space of its own site. In that way, it serves as an icon, a window between spaces. Henri Lefebvre, in his materialist history of the production of the notion of space, accounts for it this way:

> Absolute space was made up of fragments of nature located at sites which were chosen for their intrinsic qualities (cave, mountaintop, spring, river). . . . Typically, architecture picked a site in nature and transferred it to the political realm by means of a symbolic mediation . . . statues of local gods or goddesses. . . . A sanctified inwardness set up in opposition to the outwardness in nature, yet at the same time it echoed and restored that outwardness. (48)

Thus, the point in space animates it, engenders an inner space that is inhabiting it, whether it be, as Carson McCullers once put it, "A Tree, a Rock, or a Cloud," and, we might add, a camera, a person, or any "point" of view.

The narrative of the movie *Duel in the Sun* brings together many of these seemingly disparate points in its treatment of space. The opening shots freely pan the "empty" desert to discover a rock, where the camera stops and deliberates. The rock is the icon, the "point" from which the narrative unfolds. A voice-over by Joseph Cotton describes the rock as a monument to the indigenous people, "the Comanches," who named it "Squaw's Head Rock." With the point comes the contamination of the meat, of blood, as Cotton continues, "those of Indian blood still speak of Pearl Chavez, a half-breed girl from down along the border" who was "a wild flower" and whose death both monumentalized and contaminated the space of the desert. Like clicking onto the icon, and opening the window, the film cuts from Squaw's Head Rock to a flashback of the "squaw," mother, dancing wildly in a Mexican border town. This is a movie about space, then, and the body in space. The narrative of *Duel in the Sun* tells the history of the space of the desert, its literal border, and its privatization. It is about "free-ranging" cattle, enclosure, the coming of trains, the suppression of the native peoples, and the coming of the law to the "Wild West." Space, then, opened out through the monument, becomes relativized and historical. The screen presents a particular history of empty, free space, signified by the West. The narrative of the movie assigns these affects of the properties of space. The icon disciplines space by sacrificing its indigenous contamination to the new, white law.

How do these explicit points of the narrative discipline, through the movie screen, the space of Los Angeles in 1946, when King Vidor made the film? California and Los Angeles were identified as the West in both civic ad campaigns and popular lore. In 1946, L.A. was only about fifty years old. The "creature of real-estate capitalism," it was still luring its population and economic resources out to the West through deliberate real estate advertising (Davis, 25). Kevin Starr describes it as "a melange of mission myth (originating in Helen Hunt Jackson's *Ramona*), obsession with climate, political conservatism . . . and a thinly veiled racialism, all put to the service of boosterism and oligarchy" (in Davis, 26). L.A. made movies that mythologized—screened—race relations within its drive to populate its space. The movies presented a history of semi-arid lands in "the history of race relations as a pastoral ritual of obedience and paternalism" (Davis, 26). Few documents managed to disrupt the pastoral story. In 1946, Carey McWilliams published *Southern California Country: Island on the Land*, which deconstructed the mission myths, telling the story of genocide and native resistance as the land was wrested from them during the 1850s and 1860s, but its persuasive affects were slim compared to the power of the movies. A bloody L.A. was emerging through detective novels, such as those by Raymond Chandler, and the *noirs* shot the dark side of the city. Aldous Huxley's *Ape and Essence* (1948) satirized the city, and the novel by Chester Himes of embittered racism in L.A., *If He Hollers Let Him Go*, was published in 1945. Meanwhile, the water barons and subdividers of the San Fernando Valley were quickly enclosing the wide-open spaces into corporate ownership, and the population began to move out east to the desert, where they rested or retired in Palm Springs, surrounded by real estate booms, water rights, and the border. In order to adjust the darkening picture of Southern California as a site of violent discrimination and property struggles, Hollywood adopted the Good Neighbor Policy. Films about Mexico in the time of the "Zoot Suit Riots" in 1943 marked the beginning of L.A.'s filmic displacement of racial uprisings that would continue through Rodney King.

Duel in the Sun, relying upon traditional values of space, screens the unruly space of L.A. in the 1940s by offering the story of how "Western" space was historically properly enclosed, divided, and controlled. In so doing, the movie conflates the proper assignment of location to real estate with the proper performance of gender roles and sexuality to "race." Thus, the "duel" in the film's title is not really, as it would seem to suggest, one violence against another, but the violent dual*ism* that notions of race, gender, class, and female sexuality deployed to maintain colonial control. The film converges several histories into one in order to control this particular compound. The old, slave-owning, fertile, green South is set up as a model of control against the lawless, dry (empty) desert. Herbert Marshall, an actor associated with urbane love

Fig. 4 Jennifer Jones in shoe polish as Pearl Chavez with Lillian Gish.

stories, plays Pearl's father, marked with the elegance of the plantation South in wasted decline. His true love, Lillian Gish, also from earlier cinema, plays the role-model mother/wife on the Texas hacienda, with the values of the "old" South in conflict with the ways of the new frontier. Gish is married to someone else, with whom she no longer shares a bed or any intimate space. She is accompanied by her black maid, played by Butterfly McQueen as stupid and lazy, yet with a certain nostalgia assigned to her character through the repetitive singing of the song "Sometimes I Feel Like a Motherless Child." So the old slave-owning South is present as high culture, refinement, but sterile and sexually incapacitated; while the frontier is cast as the lawless, sexualized, feminized border which requires the coming "law" to "tame" the space. Pearl, the hot halfblood, does not fit into the colonial hacienda. (See fig. 4.) Coming from "below" the border, she takes up with the wild son, who is dedicated to the "wrong side of the law." The story concludes with Pearl and her lover slowly shooting each other to death, as they continue to crawl toward each other at Squaw's Head Rock.

The lovers' blood monumentalizes the icon, the point which organizes the desert space in the same way L.A. architecture monumentalizes the culture it dislocates. With mission towns, where indigenous peoples worked for the colonial Spanish priests, romanticized as quaint tourist spots, and the prevalence of *faux* "Spanish" architecture in housing developments, the historical displacement of both the Indians and the Mexicans is made alluring—made to signify the desirability of California. Pearl, the bygone genderized and racialized outlaw, becomes the eroticization of real estate. Her exclusion from it lends it allure. The big screen, the multi-million-dollar production, the big stars, what constitutes Hollywood's epic style produces a cultural appetite big enough to consume the space as monumental.

Hollywood adds another practice that successfully displaces any possibility of ethnic Other, while representing it: what I call "Spanish in shoe polish." The casting of Jennifer Jones, a recognizably famous white actress, in shoe polish as Pearl marks another kind of colonial practice. Whatever appears to be indigenous, or Mexican, is always already white. Spanish in shoe polish works like *faux* Spanish architecture to create the allure of the historical and con-temporary inhabitancy of the space of the West by the ethnic Other through its displacement. The screenic practice and the social practices in Los Ange-les reinforced one another in the ways in which they circulated these myths of space and icons to bring narrative pleasure to the movies and to the pur-chase of real estate. This has long been a revered practice, from *Othello* per-formed in blackface to white men playing Indians in *Dances with Wolves*. At-tacks on such casting practices also have a long tradition. The first film pro-duced by the "Good Neighbor Policy" was *Juarez*, in which the "first Mexican hero of the American screen" was played by Paul Muni (Woll, 61). Likewise, Elia Kazan's *Viva Zapata!* (1951) cast Marlon Brando in shoe polish as the Mexi-can revolutionary hero. Political disagreements about Kazan's casting with Gabriel Figueroa, head of the Mexican film technicians' union, resulted in Figueroa's question: "Suppose a Mexican company came up to Illinois to make a picture about Abraham Lincoln's life with a Mexican playing the lead . . . ?" (quoted in Woll, 94). Kazan interpreted these political attacks as "commu-nist"—an effective way, at that time, to erase the issues of race and cultural difference by conflating them with the federal anti-communist agenda. The epithet "communist" substituting for "Mexican" further displaced the actual struggle for civic and legal space that ethnic peoples were leading in L.A. through legal channels and the "Zoot Suit Riots" to the international frame-work of the Cold War. Border patrols were reaching international heights. The screening of colonial space and dislocation would give way in the 1950s to fantasies of invasion.

An underground film, *Lust in the Dust*, set out to invert some of the dominant structures that *Duel* would enforce. The film opens with the transvestite Di-vine, in revealing blouse (in imitation of Jennifer Jones's costume), astride a mule, crossing the western "badlands." Unlike the establishment of Squaw's Head Rock, the bloodied icon that polices space, as the source, the point from which the narrativization of space unfolds, this film sets the farcical trans-vestite portrayal of racialized and genderized lust as over "coming" the desert on an ass. *Lust's* plot turns when the wonderfully huge Divine, with obvious falsies, in ruined Spanish drag, is discovered to have half a map to buried gold tattooed on her buttocks. Mapping, the grid of value, displayed here as the map to gold on transvestite buttocks, is farcically inverted. The affect that *Duel* would narrativize onto the icon and the social mapping of space is sexualized, transgendered, and "sent up." Notably, all of the various elements are repeated in the compound: the grid, genderizing, racializing, private property, the body, and so on. The epic scope of *Duel* is exchanged for the epic size of Divine. *Lust* also brings on a familiar actor from earlier movies, Tab Hunter. But this blonde one-time pin-up of innocence ironizes his lust for Divine. Cross-dressing and other inversions thus manage to wiggle through the web. With the grid "behind," this send-up makes the colonial controls of space and lust asinine. Immense Divine leaves nothing out of her inversion.

The Grid: A Touch of Evil

Unfortunately, not all underground films serve to invert the grid. One of the most pernicious examples of screening the space of Los Angeles with racist, homophobic effect, is a film by Orson Welles entitled *A Touch of Evil*. This film is explicitly about the border. It is set in a fictional border town called Los Robles, described on a billboard at the edge of town as "Paris of the Border." As good Mexicans are played by familiar white actors in shoe polish, such as Charlton Heston, the border is recognizably Venice, California—the pun from Paris to Venice part of the typically ironic, layered references in avant-garde treatments. The repeated shots of the Venice arcade, along with its canals, the town's trademarks, have multiple functions. For a moment, I would like to defer the complex narrative functions the border takes on through the film, in order to focus on the way this "shooting on location" reads through the film's narrative.

The anxiety about borders and the threatening ambivalence they raise along the divisions of sex, race, and gender are conveyed through the narrative and its relation to the sequence of shots. But these same anxieties are allayed by the shots of Venice as the sign for Mexico. Venice, built as a kind of Southern California simulacrum of "the Italian," suggesting the playful, sexual, decadent stereotype of "the Italian" inherited from Northern European cultural attitudes, here becomes a double sign for North/South cultural difference. The role of the double simulacrum (Mexican border town/Venice, California; Venice, California/Italy) is to reassure, through avant-garde irony and the intellectual pleasure in unraveling complex references, that what may look like any referential (political) reality is already swallowed up by the representational process. The irony serves to diminish the enforcing of borders that the film is shooting along with the displacement it encourages of those "Southern" manners by avant-garde troping.

This strategy of location is conjoined with the positive hero, Vargas, played in shoe polish. There is one important sequence that illustrates the way the conjunction between the two strategies works. Hank Quinlan, the bad but

Falstaffian white cop, played by Orson Welles, first meets Miguel "Mike" Vargas (Heston), the good Mexican cop, through the following sequence: Quinlan, in conversation with his cohorts at the scene of the crime, says, "I hear you even invited some kind of a Mexican"; cut to Heston, entering in front of a billboard that says WELCOME STRANGER TO PICTURESQUE LOS ROBLES PARIS OF THE WEST. Notice how the white actor as Mexican enters on a racist line delivered by the bad guy with the play on the location in Venice in the background. The compound of elements reassures us that racism, national agendas, and the "real estate" of properties are here only devices employed by avant-garde cultural producers to shock us with the seeming radicality of taboos, but save us through the aestheticizing of them. In other words, the Mexican border becomes either an inside joke or simply the syncretized shreds of a culture assimilated in Southern California through a simulation (assimilation) of its past. Any lingering reminders of exclusionary practices become titillating as they play into the complexity of the signification. Screening emphasizes its entertainment value in order to make palatable its structuration of social space.

Gender and sexuality are screened along with race and place by other characters in shoe polish. The first is the madame of a bordello in Mexico, played by Marlene Dietrich. She wears a black wig, black eyelashes, ethnically marked clothes, excessive jewelry, and dangling earrings, cooks chili, and smokes a cigarillo. Actually, she is more reminiscent of Divine than of Jennifer Jones. Nevertheless, Dietrich ends the film in Spanish, looking fondly at the dead sheriff with the epitaph "He was some kind of a man" and exiting with the word "adios." Dietrich signals the bygone era of World War II, with her German accent and her tough, smoking ways reminiscent of her traditional persona. If Italian is playful, exotic, and like the Mexican, German is by now a nostalgic sense of masculinized, tough women who nevertheless remain accessible to men. As Dietrich concludes the film, crossing back to Mexico, she closes the narrative as the unredeemed Mexican in shoe polish, the touch of evil where the erotics, the scopic economy of the film, is situated. The ambivalence over the "foreign" is solved by lawful Heston/Vargas and the unredeemed foreign woman, whose exoticism is hauntingly nostalgic and always available.

Counter to Dietrich is the other woman in shoe polish—Mercedes McCambridge as a butch lesbian in a Mexican gang. McCambridge is set up as the woman who would threaten Janet Leigh, the white woman without shoe polish. The image of the Mexican butch gang member is used to animate racism and homophobia together. Although her role is a minor one, her representation in the film is the most central to the Los Angeles that Venice borders, for Mexican gangs were prominent in the city, in the courts, and in the press. They were becoming the dangerous border where ethnic claims were made from within the city. Like Venice, they were already part of L.A., but unlike Venice, they defended their ethnic territory with violence. Situating the butch lesbian within the gang opened up the space of taboo within issues

Fig. 5 McCambridge entering Leigh's motel room.
Courtesy of the Academy of Motion Picture Arts and Sciences.

of colonial management. Here is how she is portrayed. Janet Leigh, who is lawfully married to Heston, is caught alone in a motel room by the gang. We first meet Mercedes as only a whisper to Janet through the motel walls: "Honey, you in the next room?" delivered with sexual innuendo. We haven't seen her yet—we probably assume the whisperer to be a man. She tells Janet that the men are going to come into her room—that they have marijuana—menacingly, she offers her some. So now drugs have been introduced into the scene. Sex and drugs, lawless stimulants of pleasure, belong to this voice, this gang. Cut to the first shot of Mercedes. She and another woman are seen in the mirror: Mercedes in leather jacket with the gang-style haircut of two-fenders-and-a-waterfall; the other woman a total femme, in tight clothes, hanging on her. She says, "The fun is only beginning." (See fig. 5.) The second shot of Mercedes is from inside Janet's motel room, as she enters with the gang. Cut to Dietrich on the phone in her brothel (sex is everywhere Mexicans are). Cut to Mercedes entering Janet's bedroom with the blonde close behind her. The male leader of the gang speaks to her in Spanish (some of the only Spanish spoken in the film) and Mercedes answers in English, marked with a heavy accent, pleading, "Let me stay. I wanta watch." The gang leader orders the men to control Janet: "Hold her legs"; shot of men lifting her; "Close the door"; the viewer is closed out the other side of it, but imagines an ensuing rape.

What was at that time called "Mexican," what we would now call "Chicano," gangs were developing the Pachuco style in the 1940s. McCambridge's haircut signifies the post–zoot suit look. Prior to the Zoot Suit Riots on June 3–13, 1943, the "Sleepy Lagoon Case" in 1942 had already filled the papers. Hollywood got involved. The racist conviction of the Mexican youth inspired the formation of a Defense Committee that included the Screen Artists' Guild—including Orson Welles. In fact, in 1944 Welles wrote the foreword to a collectively written committee pamphlet against the trials (Mazón, 25). Mario Mazón in his study of the riots makes a point that elucidates the ascription of illicit sexuality to the gangs, upon which Welles was playing:

> Zoot-suiters had girls, and this became one of the sorest conflicts between them and servicemen. "The *pachuquitas* were very appealing to American servicemen, and jealously guarded by the Mexican-American boys. They scandalized the adults of the Anglo and Mexican communities alike, with their short, tight skirts, sheer blouses, and built-up hairdos." Indeed, one interpretation of the riots was that they emasculated the zoot-suiters. (64)

A Touch of Evil brings on that *pachuquita,* but on the arm of a butch lesbian. They are not across the border, but coming into the bedroom of the most modest, innocent, and lawful citizens.

The displacement of peoples is still working through its *faux* strategy, as Venice signals, but the plaster of "Paris" is cracking. The ambivalence about borders is merely the residue of the attempt to imagine borders when they have already given way. The underground use of the screen reveals the fault lines of its own fracture. Venice in this film is already beginning to register, through a play on borders, the "inner city," where white women without shoe polish may be raped by Mexicans and butches. Perverts and ethnics gather there. The shifting sense of borders is how the inner city appears, full of "aliens" of all sorts. The movie screen can no longer discipline L.A. Thus, the movie screen, the single screen that, in movies such as *Duel,* screened the entire West, will soon give way to a panoply of satellite screens, safely ensconced in suburbia. The heroic movie screen was beginning to have seen better days. It was leaving town, in the white flight, to be viewed in suburban living rooms. Yet the glimpse of that butch lesbian was more prescient than Welles could ever have imagined. Her heroic times were still ahead, when, leathered and pierced, her "queer dyke" appearance would attend the coming of cyberspace.

In the meantime, the movie screen still had space to narrativize. The anti-communist mythology of the 1950s turned the screen from narratives of colonial management to staving off invasions from "outer" space. The military-industrial compound could be portrayed as securing the "natural" borders. Shots of the desert, "empty" space, would find a different kind of contamination lurking in their scenic "points"—radiated or alien monsters threatened to take over the free space. The narrative and iconic referent of space changed, but the structures of screening remained in place. What was landing was the first contact of the virtual—murderous *Heavenly Creatures.*

In Black and White: Adrienne Kennedy

The playwright Adrienne Kennedy staged the iconic screening of the movies in her play *A Movie Star Has to Star in Black and White.* Rather than the screen's organization of screened space, Kennedy takes one of the movie industry's own icons, the "Columbia Pictures Lady," to open her play. At first, the opening image of the "Columbia Pictures Lady" may seem to operate like the single point that configures the traditional space of meaning. In other words, the "lady" seems to be a monument that fixes space, claims it, and ensures its regularized ownership. This "lady," however, actually works to the contrary. She enables a stage space that reveals how the mandate of "*Black and White*" works in the movies, while also "fleshing out" a narrative of an African American woman's life.

The "Leading Roles," as Kennedy designates them, are played by actors who "look exactly like" Bette Davis, Paul Henreid, Jean Peters, Marlon Brando, Montgomery Clift, and Shelley Winters. The movie stars appear in tableaux from their films *Now, Voyager, A Place in the Sun,* and *Viva Zapata!* Within the tableaux, the men remain silent, while the women speak the dialogue of the play's "protagonist," Clara, an African American woman in her thirties. The "Supporting Roles" are assigned to Clara's family: her mother, father, brother, and husband. Thus, the icon of the movie Lady yields, through stars, a plethora of interrelated movies, that play out the melodrama of an African American family. The signs of ethnicity, movies, and gender signify through this circulation between screen and stage.

To review more specifically how this structure works, the opening stage directions for Scene II follow:

> There is no real separation from the hospital room (of her family drama) and Viva Zapata and the ship lights in Now Voyager. Wedding night scene in Viva Zapata. Yet it is still the stateroom within the ship. Movie Music. MARLON BRANDO and JEAN PETERS are sitting on the bed. They are both dressed as in Viva Zapata. (90–91)

The tableau from *Zapata* is taken from the scene of the wedding night, on which Zapata (Marlon Brando) asks his new wife (Jean Peters) to teach him how to read. In the play, this wedding night is set against Clara's prior disclosure that she is pregnant and must remain in bed because she is hemorrhaging and wishes to avoid a miscarriage. In the tableau, Jean Peters is bleeding black blood onto the sheets, while Brando pulls them off—sheet after sheet drenched in black (92). Further complicating the playing space for the scene, Kennedy notes in the stage directions, that the Zapata scene is also set within the ship scene with Bette Davis and Paul Henreid from *Now, Voyager*. (This is the oft-cited scene in which Henreid lights the two cigarettes.) Three narrative spaces combine, so that the space of the single woman, Bette Davis, who sacrificed her personal life for her married lover is inhabited by Jean Peters, who is now married but, in a scene that marks their class difference, is asked to teach her revolutionary Mexican husband how to read, while she hemorrhages as Clara and speaks her lines: "I saw my father today. He's come from Georgia to see my brother. . . . When I was young he seemed energetic, speaking before civic groups and rallying people to give money to the Negro Settlement" (91). Certain elements of the casting should be noted. Remember, Marlon Brando and Jean Peters are playing Mexicans in shoe polish. Yet, as a Mexican revolutionary, the white Peters speaks lines about a black civil rights worker. This exchange between "color" and the invisible white, which stabilizes the role of Zapata in one Hollywood movie is reversed in Kennedy's play as the Anglo actor, as Mexican, speaks the lines of the black Clara, who stands near them onstage—lines that specifically refer to the civil rights movement.

Onstage, Brando and Peters are set within a scene in the hospital, played by black actors. Their bed is drenched with blood, which is actually Clara's hemorrhaging, but is black blood. Brando's only action in the scene is to pull sheet after sheet from the bed. As Deborah R. Geis notes in her article "A Spectator Watching My Life: Adrienne Kennedy's *A Movie Star Has to Star in Black and White*," there is "a conflation of menstruation, defloration, pregnancy" and ink (177). The black blood signifies Clara, but also ink, in that Clara is a playwright, who is writing lines from Kennedy's first play, *The Owl Answers*. Further, female sexuality, represented by the conjugal bed, inscribed with the blood of miscarriage and creative production, is also set on the ship upon which Bette Davis gains self-respect and a certain independence, though she is still masochistically tied to the love of a man. The movie actors maintain the "stills" from their movies, while the actors who portray the members of the African American family are blocked in the conventions of stage realism. The complex circulation of character, plot, and signification entangles racial, gendered, and sexual markers within a structure of representations which ultimately renders them indecipherable.

The catalyst for this flow is the movie screen. The Columbia Lady issues forth these women stars who represent both patriarchal victims and independent producers of civic, and in Clara's case creative, work. Collapsed into these simultaneous narratives and scenic sites are the contradictions in the female gender engendering public narratives. "Color" slips through characters and actors marking civil oppression as well as revolutionary projects. "Color" is a dynamic, in the field of representation, between the black woman playwright and the screen of Anglo actors which invites her participation, allows her narrative, and closes her out. Screening through stars allows the stage simultaneity and porosity. They open the movie space, like windows out into the play that is happening on their borders. Kennedy constructs the movie screen as the space of simultaneous cohabitation.

In *People Who Led to My Plays,* in the category titled "Zombies, mummies, the Cat Woman, ghouls, ghosts, vampires, monsters, werewolves," Kennedy explains that this sense of cohabitation actually came from the movies themselves: "The Wolf Man held a power over me. Metamorphosis and that change of identity would, twenty years later, become a theme that would dominate my writing. The characters in my plays and stories would also change personae at an alarming rate" (17). Kennedy is the wolfman and Bette Davis at once. There is no fast boundary between identity or her creative process and the films she has seen. Movies make animation possible. Their exclusionary screenings serve rather to invite the African American narrative to cohabit their spaces with them. Ironically, the stage they supplanted in their movie "theaters" deploys their frozen, timeless images to animate the "live" performance of the African American woman protagonist. The icon of their screening process, the white "Columbia Pictures Lady," is frozen in place, the disciplinary screening bounded by the African American play. Movie stars are contained and frozen. The "live" is animated through its containment of the screened.

Performing City: Chicano Chariots of Fire and Drive-By Art

Chicanos found a way to colorize the grid of L.A. If L.A. is located by its grid of freeways, the low riders, Chicanos who customize their cars, pixillate the presence of Chicano road culture through their auto bodies. Low riders, as their name suggests, drive down close to the street. Manipulating the proximity of car to road through hydraulics, they critique the high-riding Anglo bourgeoisie. Low, cherried-out, dark cars menace the so-called freeways of power. The car of choice is the Chevy from the forties: the auto body of the Pachuco— a road-warrior quotation of the Zoot Suit uprisings. The memory of the Pachuco pride and menace to Anglo superiority is embodied in the Chicano assimilation of the Chevrolet into the Chevy. The car, then, screens the road it drives on, projecting the image of Chicano pride onto the gridlock called L.A.

Moreover, the cars themselves become screens of airbrushed Chicano images. Flames on the hood extending back from the grill image the danger of the car's movement, its burning thrust onto the freeway grid. Like the flames of entry into the earth's atmosphere, these cars flame their way into the visible city. Chicano Magic Realism rides on the hoods, the door panels, and the trunks. Images of the imaginary Aztlán adorn the bodies: Aztlán, the imagined political state of the Chicanos, comprising, through ancient Mexican myths, the land taken from these people by the Anglos. Images of Aztec warriors, skeletons from Day of the Dead, Catholic icons, urban dreams, and utopian cities screen the car's territory back to Chicano culture. The moving picture, here, is projected onto the streets. The vast state and corporate constructions of roads, cities, and cars are resisted by personal custom production in garages, by the drivers themselves.

Unfortunately, the low riders' culture is macho. Like the superhighway, it's boys' territory. So the hoods are also adorned with sexualized, objectified images of women, who appear to be splayed out across the powerful engine of the driver. For this reason, the *machismo* embedded in the custom car culture is critiqued by Chicana feminists, though Chicano cultural nationalists insist that it is a "political expression of ethnic identity that transcends gender ... 'a symbolic principle of the Chicano revolt'" (Mirandé and Enriquez, 242). Nevertheless, the principle of custom car culture as political is important in a region where more than a quarter of a million people have been displaced by freeways (Brodsly, 32). These moving pictures take back freeways which have cut through primarily ethnic neighborhoods, indissolubly dividing up those communities. For the commuters who whiz through these communities, blind to the conditions around them, the freeway becomes a screen: a monolinear, accelerated space for internal images to play, or for the windshield to serve as a screening of the social realities beyond, equalizing them, bringing them, like a moving picture, to the driver. For the middle-class commuter, the freeway from the protected suburbs to the civic center is protected from the sight of the bordering ethnic communities. The low riders bring the images back onto the roads into the geography of the visible.

If the Chicanos take back the streets and freeways with their cars, the Chicanas take back the city with their murals. They provide a kind of drive-by art in the time of drive-by shootings. One example is Judith Baca's mural project that extends one-half mile. It illustrates a mural of history of L.A., painted by 450 teenagers from various ethnic backgrounds. Similarly, Las Comrades, a women's performance collective, produces a kind of drive-by performance practice on the border itself. Returning that site to the indigenous people and their imaginary through performance. Chicano low riders, *muralistas,* and border performers color the grid of Los Angeles and its territories. Assimilating the space of a discrete unit, namely, middle-class Anglos in this case, they cohabit the already existing borders with the icons of their existence, making the City of the Angels into an *altare,* or altar of cultural icons. Yet, while the grid is colored and cohabited, it still remains decidedly heterosexual, maintaining dominant divisions of sexual difference and the assignment of sexual preference along the axis of gender.

Performing City: Lesbian Neon Lust

The neon artist Lili Lakich has assimilated windshield as screen and its vision into the urban night as sculptures of lesbian lust. Her neon art performs city and car. In her book *Neon Lovers Glow in the Dark*, Lakich records the memories of traveling at night, charged by the neon signs that made the cities come to life:

> Urban centers have become dark, dismal and fearful because the neon which brought brightness, color, liveliness and light into the streets has been removed. Concrete and glass structures just don't have the kind of life that store fronts with neon illuminations have. You can go to Las Vegas at 4 a.m., for example, and feel energized, alive, lively—as if life is unending. (8)

For Lakich, neon makes the cities livable. Their potentially dangerous nights are illuminated by its playful colors. In contrast, the seemingly safer suburbs turn a dark, less playful eye onto the night—uninviting compared to the city's colorful glow. Lakich's art embeds that city night in its neon forms and colors. Lakich quotes Mayakovsky: "After electricity, I lost interest in nature" (10). As Lakich quotes the city lights with her neon, she quotes the car with her incorporation of brushed aluminum. The aluminum backings to the pieces reflect the neon—are the surfaces for its play. They relate the neon glow to the effects on a polished auto body.

Lakich's auto bodies and glowing tubes illuminate a lesbian L.A. For example, *The Red Hot Mama* is made of aluminum, lacquered with candy-apple red paint (a favorite with car customizers), and cut into the shape of a female torso. She lies on her side, with a red neon tube for the pubis, one leg raised: open and ready. The lust is candy-apple neon polish, which, as Lakich puts it, with its glow "rages against the dying of the light" (22). With her electric pubis, *The Red Hot Mama* draws down desire with burning agency. She is not woman-as-car and man-as-driver, but the palpating auto made erotic, penetrating the night with her light. Car, woman, neon sign are city come to life as a lesbian love of women's bodies hits the road.

From long nights driving on the road, wearily scanning through the windshield, Lakich created *Vacancy/No Vacancy* (fig. 6). With motel sign for heart, the cool torso signifies what Lakich describes as "a contemporary madonna who put forth her availability or lack of it in no uncertain terms. A flick of the switch will change her from a willing seeker of intimacy to a woman who needs nothing from anyone" (18). The blinking motel sign becomes a sign of woman's active desire, read out onto her own brushed, aluminum body. She is both car and motel, switching off when she feels like it: tough lesbian lover of one-night stands. The viewer sees her as a last hope for rest, or a direction to remain on the road.

Neon is also reminiscent of the signs outside the dark lesbian bars. In her piece *Oasis: Portrait of Djuna Barnes*, Lakich seats Barnes in just such a bar, sporting a rakish man's hat, with cigarette in hand on the bar, a drink before her, and a neon palm tree behind. Barnes is the butch smoker, drinker, bar girl—the urban dyke who defies respectable notions of femininity and love. In the bar, she wallows in the hurt of a breakup, or the impossible desire of a

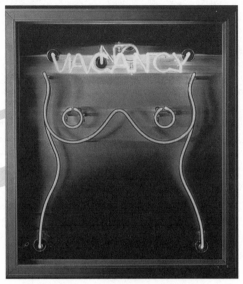

Fig. 6 *Vacancy/No Vacancy*,
neon sculpture by Lili Lakich.
Copyright 1972. Collection: Marion Rothman, Carlsbad, Calif.

crush. Her urban oasis is a drink before the already "potted" palm. In this piece, Lakich plays on the association of neon with an outsider status, and with emotion:

> I chose the medium of neon because no one had considered it a medium worthy of fine art. It was a medium for advertising, not art. (And advertising sleazy bars, shoe repair shops and cheap motels at that.) I felt there was some connection between the stigma of neon and the equal contempt with which emotions are regarded in our culture.... I believe in emotion. I believe in wallowing in it. (18)

One might add that lesbian also occupies that outsider status. The urban nighttime lesbian haunts the public oases of bars.

Not only are the images tough, but the materials with which Lakich sculpts are industrial, technological artifacts. She designs the electronics of these signaling tubes that flash and darken in sequences. A photo of her with drill and industrial goggles standing before a wall-size work reveals the artist as worker, as technician. Like the low riders, she takes on the materials of advanced capitalism, of corporate construction, to make them serve her own personal, subcultural images.

Lakich's sculptures, through the light of neon, screen the city. The aluminum backings screen the light, as well as the wall behind them onto which it spills. The image exists only in that glow in the dark. Perhaps Lakich is working something like a reversal of Walter Benjamin's theory of the "aura." While Benjamin argued that technology extracts the aura, the unique presence in time and space of the representation, divesting it of its material form (*Illuminations*, 220–221), Lakich gives only the glow. The aura, produced by technology and urban quotation, is all there is.

Ironically, some of Lakich's neon is now housed in the city's own simulation of itself. City Walk, a four-block commercial and retail development in Universal City, billed as a distillation of the essence of Los Angeles, includes a store for part of Lakich's neon collection. City Walk is a theme park of Los Angeles itself, erecting neon signs and old store fronts inside, in a mall-like atmosphere, designed for safe shopping. It is a "distillation" of Los Angeles under controlled circumstances: the kind of control that *Duel in the Sun* narrativized, *A Touch of Evil* portrayed as faltering, and drive-by, low-riding art would subvert. Los Angeles, the city that has defined the virtual, now houses its own sanitized simulation. The screening it hoped for is in place through private security guards and interior, guarded streets. The cars are parked outside. The neon illuminates mall reconstructions of the streets. Not yet online as "Ellay," Cadigan's projection of it, L.A. as City Walk verges on its screenic sublation in cyberspace. Yet, in spite of its secure premises, it is lit, at least partially, by the glow of lesbian desire.

The Bottom

Unjustifiably, I felt the need for something like a conclusion. This desire is the mark of ambivalence that prevails throughout this book between the fragmenting dislocating qualities of the virtual and the ordering principles of print. Conclusions have no place in the matrix, but bottoms might. The Domain-Matrix could, in the pun on Dominatrix (the top), happily be followed by a bottom. The bottom would be the recipient of her marvelous power in order to play out the s/m scenario. Likewise, the position of bottom performs a completing role in the tradition of print. The bottom of the page arranges its ending in space. In spatial organization, the bottom represents the weight that organizes the other directions. In class positioning, the "lower" reveals the oppressive, destructive results of privilege and profit, and is often deemed the possible site for revolt. In the several orders surveyed in this work, then, the bottom holds the place that might reveal, conclude, or perform. Thus, I want to place a bottom at the end of this work.

Situating cyberspace has a tradition of ambivalence as well. Critics swing between articulating the wish for ecstatic transcendence and crying doom. Katherine Hayles legislates between the two positions in "The Seductions of Cyberspace," concluding:

> The positive seduction of cyberspace leads us to an appreciation of the larger ecosystems of which we are a part, connected through feedback loops that entangle our destinies with their fates. . . . Hailing us on multiple levels, connecting physicality with cirtuality, it opens new vistas for exploration even as it invites us to remember what cannot be replaced. (188)

Hayles's sense of ecosystems is a positive one—the linking aspect of the medium that might incur accountability for the conditions it shares and produces. The last sentence is particularly haunting. Vivian Sobchack at the 1994 MLA performed the power of what cannot be replaced, as she spoke about her new prosthetic limb. Remarking that it would probably outlast her into the future, and that it was stronger than the rest of her body, requiring endless exercise to accommodate it, she introduced the notion of pain and loss to "stand" against the ecstatic embrace of the cyborg body. If Hayles and Sobchack are cautionary, others, such as Arthur Kroker, are prophets of doom. Ironically, today, those close to the Marxist critique adopt a pose of hopeless warning. As visitors to L.A., Jameson and Baudrillard have remarked, in celebrated places, the apocalyptic nature of its cityhood. Arthur Kroker's books attribute spasms, vomits, decay, and a nasty image of "recombitant capitalism" that is, in fact, fascism to the new virtual organization of the screen. In contrast, Allucquere Rosanne Stone celebrates the new space for identification or identity, creative social organization, and safe, virtual sex that the new screen might bring. I find all of these perspectives to have merit.

In the section on L.A. and the screen, I have attempted to balance between the disciplinary effects of screening and certain interventions. If, as I have argued, L.A. is already a kind of cyberspace, organized through a circulation of screens that inherit the disciplinary strategies of the various screenic traditions, I have also suggested how those dominant points in space may still be animated as Chicano low riders move through the matrix, bearing their own flaming images, as well as how lesbian neon images might illuminate the city night. Moreover, the section on transcendent corporate screening is balanced against the section on "bringing home the meat" of "live" performance, materialist concerns, and embodied communities.

It seems that a new radical role may be possible for "live" performance. As the century wears on, it seems "live" performance has been cast in the role of dinosaur—an extinct form of performance supplanted by screens and by the incorporation of performativity. The corporate nature of screens and of globalism is in a position of ascendancy, with cyberspace as its final sublation. Virtual identities and virtual space represent all the allure of global forms of commodity feitshism. They transcend, along with screens, the limiting failures of the "meat." However, within this "new world order" reanimating the fleshly body, reassigning agency to it might become a strategy for intervening in the seamless screenic world. The limiting and the failing qualities of the body pose a contradiction to the screenic spectacle of power. The slow, uncertain labor of coalition creates a counterposition to inclusive strategies that emulate global corporate unities. Dialogue signifies a discourse of several voices contradicting one another rather than emulating agreements that have never really been made. The bounded nature of performance plays against the unbounded reach of cyber-corporate space.

THE BOTTOM

MENU

HELP

FIND

PRINT

OPEN

PREV

NEXT

235
PAGE

The difference is that the body is within the screenic order. The two separate tracks of print and image, body and spectacle have merged, recontextualizing body and performance within the screen. How can that body overcome its Euclidean piercing—the discipline by point? How can a field be imagined, a space, that is organized differently? As an academic, I think first of "field of study" as the object of such an interrogation. But any space as field or field as space raises similar concerns. In one sense, the field is, as I indicated at the "beginning" of this work, something like Wittgenstein's "the world is all that is the case." The field is proposed at the outset, and the critical work is in creating its subdivisions. The "Domain-Matrix" proposes a similar ground for critical work, with thought-bites scattered across its topography. The very notion of trying to organize some complete critique or notion may be precisely beside the "point." Yet the technological and corporate space is speeding into existence while we pause to ponder. Consequences are already taking their toll in unemployment, habits of fervent social isolation, worldwide communications, liberatory connections among people, sexist and homophobic images online and in the games, the privileging of violence, etc. Field cannot simply function as the status quo, in its grid effect. Nevertheless, proposing the field alters the methodology and the ideas in its traversal. I had a firmer notion of how the body and performance related to the screen and performativity when I began to write than when I finished. As I distributed issues around gender, sexuality, and ethnicity within the field, my critical control of their signification seemed to weaken. The field overcame its subdivisions, and I began to feel as if some form of globalism were overcoming my critique of it.

As L.A. became a more persistent element in the process of writing, the new conditions in California came more to the fore. While insisting that the history of Hollywood and Southern California is marked in their screenic discourse, I began to see a certain subtext in this writing that had evaded me. In part, this book feels as if it is driven by some *sehnsucht*—some longing for the vitality, familiarity, and elegance of eurocentric notions that are failing to fit the new design. California and the matrix seem to mark the end station of their applicability. As Los Angeles turns east, to become part of the Pacific Rim, and away from the perception that it is the westernmost part of the United States—the last frontier of eurocentric culture—its context for critical considerations is radically altered. As the population becomes increasingly Asian American, increased by massive immigrations from Vietnam, Taiwan, Japan, Korea, and the Pacific Islands, and as California and the West Coast develop as cybercenters, in places such as "Silicon Valley" and Microsoft headquarters near Seattle, it seems that new syncretisms will inevitably emerge that will bring together "Eastern" models with cyberspace. Cyberpunk has already imagined this merger, in films such as *Blade Runner* and Gibson's novel *Mona Lisa Overdrive*. In those science "fictions," L.A. is a place where

DOMAIN-MATRIX

236
PAGE

 PREV

 NEXT

 OPEN

 PRINT

 FIND

 HELP

 MENU

Asian and Asian American images and influences meld with a punked-out urban sprawl designed to market cybersystems. I would need to begin to retool my entire intellectual training to work with these developments. Watching the international women's conference in Beijing made me aware that the location for that forum was almost more definitive than the forum itself. While I have tried to responsibly represent the Chicano and Mexican history and influence in California, I realize that I might do so insofar as that culture maintains elements of its eurocolonial past, in religious institutions and cultures.

How can this new ethnographic position be structured into the matrix? Should we begin to throw the *Y Ching,* or theorize out from its presumptions, as John Cage did decades ago? Reconsider the strong influence that Zen practices had on the Beats in the 1950s, and the Hippies in the late 1960s and 1970s? Imagine now, in spite of the 1980s yuppie turn from such models, that their influence is somehow retained in the intellectual structures of the 1990s? What about the consideration of the game Go in Deleuze and Guattari as the illustration of new constructions of exteriority? Possibly. As the section here on voudou exemplifies, there is a movement to model critical thinking on designs outside of the eurocentric context. Yet the same drive is clearly both liberating and assimilating all in one.

Facing the consequences of all the above developments, I have lost the sure footing that feminist theory, lesbian critical practice, and a materialist methodology once offered me. So instead of trying to reconstitute a style that no longer actually holds in my own intellectual experience, I have sought to replicate the way in which my own set of certitudes, doubts, obsessive returns, and bold assertions spread themselves across the intellectual space of my endeavors. Certainly, this approach emulates the traditional practice of the "bottom"— particular to this author—the "butch bottom." Hanging onto my critical amulets, I enter the scenario with the "Domain-Matrix." I am disciplined by her, but I maintain my role; I am ignorant of her plan, but capable of improvising within it; I beg her to recognize my body, to bind me, to seduce me, while performing in the anxious space of her far-reaching domain and power, whose boundaries are, by definition, beyond my purview and my control. I am seduced and pleasured by her spectacle, but wary of its consequences. I fully expect some final satisfaction, but assume it will never be dispensed. I realize that it works only within strict parameters, but want it never to end. Recollecting once again the title of the book about insurgencies, *Weapons of the Weak,* I might imagine a different configuration of political intervention that relies on weakness as a weapon. The point is not to succeed. The hope that "we shall overcome" only emulates the Domain-Matrix. Instead, playing the bottom, while denigrating even that role as efficacious or conclusive, might be the only "point" that succeeds precisely where it fails.

Playing the bottom does not mean doing nothing in these tough times for the homeless, who are tossed like garbage out of the transcending net, the unemployed, who gather below its gleaming ascendancy, or the gender, the pervert who is excluded from those mass meetings of "Christian" men in sports stadiums, creating the new citizen as a "promise keeper." Emphasizing failure, incapacity, vulnerability, boundary, contradiction, and the exigencies of the flesh is a way of working against the key element in all these systems: transcendence. As the net, the World Wide Web, global capitalism, and the critical strategies that emulate them work by transcendence (employing a male-specific Christianity as an emotional engine), strategies that emphasize failures and fallibilities may serve to retain those spoiling aspects of the flesh. Sporting different genders and sexual practices in cyberspace may serve as a laboratory for social change—maybe playing within the new virtual communities, or even nations. Expertise in these matters and the spread of these playful identities may be one way of redesigning the new cyberspace. There is little profit in hanging onto the structures of print culture in the time of cyberspace. Learning new models of organization that do not emulate focus, or looking for those values is exciting, creative, and full of promise. At the same time, I am reminded of one of the common examples of cyberspace. It goes like this: If you want to understand cyberspace, think of it this way—your money is already in cyberspace. Money, or value, is already virtual on those credit card transfers—represented by a code on a card. Perhaps, as Mark Poster suggests, this is a new kind of subject position, constructed as if the wish list of poststructuralist strategies. Then I remember Margaret Atwood's chilling novel *The Handmaid's Tale,* in which the fascist, patriarchal order takeover happened in one day, when the women went to the bank machine and found that their accounts had been closed. The ambivalence between celebrating cyberspace and fearing it, learning new operations within it and opposing its anti-bodies, which renders me unable to conclude, may be the best I can do.

I imagine these futures as a woman. Identifying as a woman removes me from any major identificatory relationship with queer and aligns me with the traditional sense of lesbian. Throughout, the term "lesbian" has signified concerns of gender as a woman, in coalition with other women whose oppression may be differently or similarly configured by operations of class and ethnicity. In fact, the emphasis on coalition springs from that feminist or woman-identified lesbian position. While there are complex and compelling arguments for sexual practice as disengaging gender, I remain unconvinced that the category of women will not continue to operate to my disadvantage in the future. I have sought to reassert lesbian, lesbian feminist coalition building, and lesbian socialist feminist strategies against global capitalism in this time of the coming cyberspace. And those queer performativitists are correct in aligning such identifications with performance. Thus, the "butch bottom" position that the text organizes remains in coalition with other women.

SOURCES

Allison, Dorothy. "A Question of Class." In *Skin: Talking about Sex, Class, and Literature*. Ithaca: Firebrand Books, 1994. 13–36.

———. "Bertha Harris, a Memoir." In *Skin*. 201–207.

Aristotle. *Metaphysics*. In *The Basic Works of Aristotle*. Ed. Richard McKeon. New York: Random House, 1941.

Artaud, Antonin. *The Theater and Its Double*. New York: Grove Press, 1958.

Atkinson, Ti-Grace. "Lesbianism and Feminism." In *Amazon Expedition*. Albion, Calif.: Times Change Press, 1973. 11–14.

Augustine. *The City of God*. Trans. Marcus Dods. New York: The Modern Library, Random House, 1950.

Bachelard, Gaston. *The Poetics of Space*. Trans. Maria Jolas. Boston: Beacon Press, 1994.

Barglow, Raymond. *The Crisis of the Self in the Age of Information*. London: Routledge, 1994.

Barker, Francis. *The Tremulous Private Body: Essays on Subjection*. London: Methuen, 1984.

Baudrillard, Jean. *Kool Killer oder der Aufstand der Zeichen*. Berlin: Merve Verlag, 1978.

———. *Simulations*. Trans. Paul Foss, Paul Patton, and Philip Beitchman. New York: Semiotext(e), 1983.

Belsey, Catherine. *The Subject of Tragedy*. London and New York: Methuen, 1985.

Benedikt, Michael. *Cyberspace: First Steps*. Cambridge: MIT Press, 1992.

———. "Cyberspace: Some Proposals." In *Cyberspace: First Steps*. 119–224.

Benjamin, Walter. "The Paris of the Second Empire in Baudelaire." In *Charles Baudelaire: A Lyric Poet in the Era of High Capitalism*. Trans. Harry Zohn. London: NLB, 1973. 9–67.

———. "Unpacking My Library." In *Illuminations*. Ed. Hannah Arendt. New York: Schocken Books, 1977. 59–67.

Bergson, Henri. *Time and Free Will*. New York: Harper Torchbooks, 1960.

Berland, Jody. "Angels Dancing: Cultural Technologies and the Production of Space." In *Cultural Studies*. Ed. Lawrence Grossberg, Cary Nelson, and Paula Treichler. New York and London: Routledge, 1992. 38–55.

SOURCES

240
PAGE

 PREV

NEXT

 OPEN

 PRINT

 FIND

 HELP

 MENU

Berlant, Lauren, and Elizabeth Freeman. "Queer Nationality." In *Fear of a Queer Planet*. Ed. Michael Warner. Minneapolis: University of Minnesota Press, 1993. 193–229.

Bey, Hakim. *T.A.Z.: The Temporary Autonomous Zone*. Brooklyn: Autonomedia, 1992.

Beyond Cyberpunk. Hypercard stack by Mark Frauenfelder, Gareth Branwyn, and Peter Sugarman. Louisa, Va.: The Computer Lab, 1993.

Blau, Herbert. *Take Up the Bodies*. Urbana: University of Illinois Press, 1982.

Bolter, Jay David. *Writing Space: The Computer, Hypertext, and the History of Writing*. Hillsdale, N.J.: Lawrence Erlbaum Associates, 1991.

Bornstein, Kate. *Gender Outlaw*. New York and London: Routledge, 1994.

———. *Hidden: A Gender*. In *Gender Outlaw*.

Braidotti, Rosi. *Nomadic Subjects: Embodiment and Sexual Difference in Contemporary Feminist Theory*. New York: Columbia University Press, 1994.

Brodsly, David. *L.A. Freeway: An Appreciative Essay*. Berkeley: University of California Press, 1981.

Brook, Peter. *The Empty Space*. New York: Atheneum, 1968.

Brossard, Nicole. *Mauve Desert*. Trans. Susanne de Lotbiniere-Harwood. Toronto: Coach House Press, 1990.

———. *Picture Theory*. Trans. Barbara Godard. New York: Roof Books, 1990.

Bryson, Norman. *Vision and Painting: The Logic of the Gaze*. New Haven: Yale University Press, 1983.

Bukatman, Scott. *Terminal Identity*. Durham: Duke University Press, 1993.

Butler, Judith. "Imitation and Gender Insubordination." In *inside/out: Lesbian Theories, Gay Theories*. Ed. Diana Fuss. New York and London: Routledge, 1991. 13–31.

———."The Body You Want." (interview) *Artforum* (November 1992).

———."Critically Queer." *glq: A Journal of Lesbian and Gay Studies* 1:1 (1993): 17–32.

Butler, Octavia. *Dawn*. New York: Popular Library, 1987.

———. *Parable of the Sower*. New York: Warner Books, 1993.

Cadigan, Pat. "Death in the Promised Land." *Asimov's Science Fiction* 19:12&3 (1995): 258–308.

Califia, Pat. *Macho Sluts*. Boston: Alyson, 1988.

———."Daddy Boy Dykes." *Quim* (Winter 1991): 32–35.

Cartwright, Lisa. *Screening the Body: Tracing Medicine's Visual Culture*. Minneapolis: University of Minnesota Press, 1995.

Case, Sue-Ellen. "Tracking the Vampire." *differences* 3:2 (1991):1–20.

Castle, Terry. *The Apparitional Lesbian*. New York: Columbia University Press, 1993.

Chee, Alexander S. "A Queer Nationalism." *Out/Look* (Winter 1991): 15–20.

Cixous, Hélène. "The Laugh of the Medusa." Trans. Keith Cohen and Paula Cohen. In *New French Feminisms*. Ed. Elaine Marks and Isabelle de Coutivron. Amherst: University of Massachusetts Press, 1980. 245–264.

———. "Castration or Decapitation." Trans. Annette Kuhn. *Signs* 7:1 (1981): 36–55.

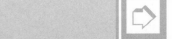

Clark, Danae. "Commodity Lesbianism." In *The Lesbian and Gay Studies Reader*. Ed. Henry Abelove, Michele Barale, and David Halperin. New York: Routledge, 1993. 186–201.

Combahee River Collective. "A Black Feminist Statement." In *All Women Are White, All Blacks Are Men, but Some of Us Are Brave*. Ed. Barbara Smith, Gloria Hull, and Patricia Scott. Old Westbury, N.Y.: Feminist Press, 1982. 13–22.

Conley, Verena Andermatt. "Communal Crisis." In *Community at Loose Ends*. Ed. Miami Theory Collective. Minneapolis: University of Minnesota Press, 1991. 49–69.

———. "Eco-Subjects." In *Rethinking Technologies*. Ed. Verena Andermatt Conley on behalf of the Miami Theory Collective. Minneapolis: University of Minnesota Press, 1993. 77–91.

Crimp, Douglas. *AIDS DemoGraphics*. Seattle: Bay Press, 1990.

Davis, Mike. *City of Quartz*. New York: Random House, 1992.

Davy, Kate. "Fe/Male Impersonation: The Discourse of Camp." In *Critical Theory and Performance*. Ed. Joseph Roach and Janelle Reinelt. Ann Arbor: University of Michigan Press, 1992. 231–247.

Delany, Samuel R. "Street Talk/Straight Talk." *differences* 3:3 (1991): 21–38.

de Lauretis, Teresa. "The Technology of Gender." In *Technologies of Gender*. Bloomington: Indiana University Press, 1987. 1–30.

———. "Sexual (In)difference and Lesbian Representation." *Theatre Journal* 40 (1988): 155–177.

———. "The Essence of the Triangle, or Taking the Risk of Essentialism Seriously: Feminist Theory in Italy, the U.S., and Britain." *differences* 1:2 (1989): 3–37.

Deleuze, Gilles, and Felix Guattari. "The Treatise on Nomadology—The War Machine." In *A Thousand Plateaus*. Minneapolis: University of Minnesota Press, 1987. 351-423.

D'Emilio, John. "Capitalism and Gay Identity." In *The Lesbian and Gay Studies Reader*. Ed. Henry Abelove, Michele Aina Barale, and David M. Halperin. New York: Routledge. 1993. 467–476.

Deren, Maya. *Divine Horsemen: The Living Gods of Haiti*. London: Thames and Hudson, 1953.

Derrida, Jacques. "The Double Session." In *Dissemination*. Trans. Barbara Johnson. Chicago: University of Chicago Press, 1981. 173–285.

Dery, Mark. "Black to the Future: Interviews with Samuel R. Delany, Greg Tate, and Tricia Rose." *Flame Wars: The Discourse of Cyberculture, South Atlantic Quarterly* 92:4 (Fall 1993): 735–778.

Dhairyam, Sagri. "Racing the Lesbian, Dodging White Critics." In *The Lesbian Postmodern*. New York: Columbia University Press, 1994. 25–46.

Didion, Joan. "Letter from California: Trouble in Lakewood." *The New Yorker*, July 26, 1993, 46–65.

Dienst, Richard. *Still Life in Real Time: Theory after Television*. Durham: Duke University Press. 1994.

Doane, Mary Ann. "Film and the Masquerade: Theorising the Female Spectator." *Screen* 23 (1982): 74–88.

SOURCES

242
PAGE

 PREV

 NEXT

 OPEN

 PRINT

 FIND

 HELP

 MENU

Dolan, Jill. *The Feminist Spectator as Critic.* Ann Arbor: UMI Press, 1988.

Dollimore, Jonathan. *Sexual Dissidence: Augustine to Wilde, Freud to Foucault.* Oxford: Clarendon Press, 1991.

Donald, James. "The City, the Cinema: Modern Spaces." In *Visual Culture.* Ed. Chris Jenks. London and New York: Routledge, 1995. 77–95.

Doty, Alexander. *Making Things Perfectly Queer: Interpreting Mass Culture.* Minneapolis: University of Minnesota Press, 1993.

Dowmunt, Tony. *Channels of Resistance.* London: British Film Institute and Channel Four Television, 1993.

Duel in the Sun. Dir. King Vidor. 1946.

Duggan, Lisa. "Making It Perfectly Queer." *Socialist Review* 22:1 (Jan.–Mar. 1992): 11-31.

Eco, Umberto. *A Theory of Semiotics.* Bloomington: Indiana University Press, 1979.

Ehrenreich, Barbara; Elizabeth Hess; and Gloria Jacobs. "Beatlemania: Girls Just Want to Have Fun." In *The Adoring Audience.* Ed. Lisa A. Lewis. London: Routledge, 1992. 84–106.

Ellis, John. *Visible Fictions: Cinema Television Video.* London: Routledge, 1982.

Engels, Friedrich. "Socialism: Utopian and Scientific." In *The Marx-Engels Reader.* Ed. Robert C. Tucker. New York: Norton, 1978. 683–717.

Evans, David T. *Sexual Citizenship: The Material Construction of Sexualities.* London: Routledge, 1993.

Fehervary, Helen. "Enlightenment or Entanglement: History and Aesthetics in Bertolt Brecht and Heiner Müller." *New German Critique* (Spring 1976): 80–109.

Feinberg, Leslie. *Stone Butch Blues.* Ithaca: Firebrand Books, 1993.

Fernández, Charles. "Undocumented Aliens in the Queer Nation." *Out/Look* (Spring 1991): 20–23.

Feuer, Jane. "The Concept of Live Television: Ontology as Ideology." In *Regarding Television.* Ed. E. Ann Kaplan. Frederick, Md.: University Publications of America, 1983.

Fiske, John. "The Cultural Economy of Fandom." In *The Adoring Audience.* Ed. Lisa A. Lewis. London: Routledge, 1992. 30–49.

Flanagan, Bob. *Bob Flanagan: Supermasochist. REsearch* I:1 (1993).

Fuss, Diana. "Inside/Out." In *inside/out.* New York and London: Routledge, 1991. 1–10.

Garber, Marjorie. *Vested Interests.* New York: Harper Collins, 1992.

Garner, Rochelle. "The Mother of Multimedia." *Wired* 2:4 (April 1994): 52–56.

Geis, Deborah. "'A Spectator Watching My Life': Adrienne Kennedy's *A Movie Star Has to Star in Black and White.*" In *Intersecting Boundaries: The Theatre of Adrienne Kennedy.* Ed. Paul K. Bryant-Jackson and Lois More Overbeck. Minneapolis: University of Minnesota Press, 1992. 170–178.

Gibson, William. *Count Zero.* New York: Ace Books, 1986.

———. *Neuromancer.* New York: Ace Books, 1986.

———. *Mona Lisa Overdrive.* New York: Bantam Books, 1988.

Gilman, Sander. "Plague in Germany 1939/1989: Cultural Images of Race, Space, and Disease." In *Nationalisms and Sexualities.* Ed. Andrew Parker, Mary Russo, et al. New York and London: Routledge, 1992. 175–200.

Glamuzina, Julie, and Alison J. Laurie. *Parker and Hulme: A Lesbian View*. Auckland: New Women's Press, 1991.

Goldberg, Jonathan. "Recalling Totalities: The Mirrored Stages of Arnold Schwarzenegger." In *The Cyborg Handbook*. Ed. Chris Hables Gray. New York: Routledge, 1995. 233–254.

Grahn, Judy. *The Highest Apple*. San Francisco: Spinster's Ink, 1985.

Grosz, Elizabeth. *Volatile Bodies: Toward a Corporeal Feminism*. Bloomington: Indiana University Press, 1994.

Hall, Stuart. "Cultural Studies and Its Theoretical Legacies." In *Cultural Studies*. Ed. Lawrence Grossberg, Cary Nelson, and Paula Treichler. New York and London: Routledge, 1992. 277–294.

Haraway, Donna. "A Cyborg Manifesto: Science, Technology and Socialist Feminism in the 1980s." In *Simians, Cyborgs, and Women*. New York: Routledge, 1989. 149–181.

———. Interview with Constance Penley and Andrew Ross. In *Technoculture*. Ed. Constance Penley and Andrew Ross. Minneapolis: University of Minnesota Press, 1991. 1–20.

Harper, Phillip E.; Frances White; and Margaret Cerullo. "Multi/Queer/Culture." *Radical America* 24:4 (Sept.–Dec. 1990): 27–37.

Hart, Lynda. "Identity and Seduction: Lesbians in the Mainstream." In *Acting Out: Feminist Performances*. Ed. Lynda Hart and Peggy Phelan. Ann Arbor: University of Michigan Press, 1993. 119–137.

———. *Fatal Women*. Princeton: Princeton University Press, 1994.

Hausman, Bernice L. *Changing Sex: Transsexualism, Technology, and the Idea of Gender*. Durham: Duke University Press, 1995.

Hayles, N. Katherine. "The Seductions of Cyberspace." In *Rethinking Technologies*. Ed. Verena Andermatt Conley. Minneapolis: University of Minnesota Press, 1993. 173–189.

———. "Virtual Bodies and Flickering Signifiers." *October* 66 (Fall 1993): 69–91.

Heavenly Creatures. Dir. Peter Jackson. 1994.

Hebdige, Dick. *Subculture: The Meaning of Style*. London and New York: Methuen, 1979.

Hennessy, Rosemary. *Materialist Feminism and the Politics of Discourse*. New York and London: Routledge, 1993.

Huettich, H. G. *Theater in a Planned Society*. Chapel Hill: University of North Carolina Press, 1978.

Hughes, Holly. "Polymorphous Perversity and the Lesbian Scientist: An Interview by Rebecca Schneider." *The Drama Review* 33:1 (1989): 171–183.

Irigaray, Luce. "The Power of Discourse." In *This Sex Which Is Not One*. Trans. Catherine Porter. Ithaca: Cornell University Press, 1985. 68–85.

———. "Questions." In *This Sex Which Is Not One*. 119–169.

Jameson, Fredric. *Postmodernism, or The Cultural Logic of Late Capitalism*. Durham: Duke University Press, 1992.

Jenson, Joli. "Fandom as Pathology: The Consequences of Characterization." In *The Adoring Audience*. Ed. Lisa A. Lewis. London: Routledge, 1992. 9–29.

SOURCES

 244 PAGE

 PREV

 NEXT

 OPEN

 PRINT

 FIND

HELP

 MENU

Jones, Lawrence. "Versions of the Dream: Literature and the Search for Identity." In *Culture and Identity in New Zealand*. Ed. David Novitz and Nill Willmott. Christchurch: GP Books, 1989. 187–211.

The Joy of Cybersex. Ed. Phillip Robinson, Nancy Tamosaitis, et al. New York: Brady, 1993.

Kennedy, Adrienne. *People Who Led to My Plays*. New York: Alfred A. Knopf, 1987.

———. *A Movie Star Has to Star in Black and White: Adrienne Kennedy in One Act*. Minneapolis: University of Minnesota Press, 1988. 79–100.

Kern, Stephen. *The Culture of Time and Space, 1880–1918*. Cambridge: Harvard University Press, 1983.

Kester, Grant H. "Out of Sight Is Out of Mind: The Imaginary Space of Postindustrial Culture." *Social Text* 11:2 (Summer 1993): 72–92.

Krauss, Rosalind E. *The Originality of the Avant-Garde and Other Modernist Myths*. Cambridge: MIT Press, 1987.

Kroker, Arthur. *Spasm: Virtual Reality, Android Music and Electric Flesh*. New York: St. Martin's Press, 1993.

Kroker, Arthur, and Michael A. Weinstein. *Data Trash: The Theory of the Virtual Class*. New York: St. Martin's Press, 1994.

Kushner, Tony. *Angels in America: A Gay Fantasia on National Themes. Part Two: Perestroika*. New York: Theatre Communications Group, 1994.

Lakich, Lili. *Neon Lovers Glow in the Dark*. Los Angeles: Peregrine Smith Books, 1986.

Landow, George. *Hyper/Text/Theory*. Baltimore: Johns Hopkins University Press, 1994.

Lanham, Richard. A. *The Electronic Word: Democracy, Technology, and the Arts*. Chicago: University of Chicago Press, 1993.

Laurel, Brenda. *Computers as Theatre*. Reading, Mass.: Addison-Wesley, 1991.

Lefebvre, Henri. *The Production of Space*. Trans. Donald Nicholson-Smith. Oxford: Basil Blackwell, 1991.

Lévi-Strauss, Claude. "Caduveo: A Native Community and Its Life Style." In *Tristes Tropiques*. Trans. John and Doreen Weightman. New York: Penguin Books, 1992. 178–197.

Lewis, Lisa. "'Something More Than Love': Fan Stories on Film." In *The Adoring Audience*. Ed. Lisa A. Lewis. London: Routledge, 1992. 135–159.

Lipsitz, George. "The Meaning of Memory: Family, Class, and Ethnicity in Early Network Television Programs." *Camera Obscura* 16 (1988): 79–116.

Lyon, David. *The Electronic Eye: The Rise of Surveillance Society*. Minneapolis: University of Minnesota Press, 1994.

Mâle, Emile. *The Gothic Image*, Trans. Dora Nussey. New York and London: Harper and Row, 1958.

Mazón, Mauricio. *The Zoot Suit Riots*. Austin: University of Texas Press, 1984.

McCaffrey, Anne. *The Ship Who Sang*. New York: Ballantine Books, 1969.

McDonough, Thomas F. "Situationist Space." *October* 67: 59–77.

Merck, Mandy. "'Transforming the Suit': A Century of Lesbian Self Portraits." In *Stolen Glances: Lesbians Take Photographs*. Ed. Tessa Boffin and Jean Fraser. London: Pandora, 1991. 22–29.

Merrell, Floyd. *Sign, Textuality, World*. Bloomington: Indiana University Press, 1992.

Miller, D. A. "Anal *Rope*." In *inside/out*. Ed. Diana Fuss. New York: Routledge, 1991. 119–141.

———. *Bringing Out Roland Barthes*. Berkeley: University of California Press, 1992.

Millot, Catherine. *Horsexe: Essay on Transsexuality*. Trans. Kenneth Hylton. Brooklyn: Autonomedia, 1990.

Mirandé, Alfredo, and Evangelina Enriquéz. *La Chicana: The Mexican-American Woman*. Chicago: University of Chicago Press, 1979.

Mondo 2000: A User's Guide to the New Edge. Ed. Rudy Rucker, R.U. Sirius, and Queen Mu. New York: Harper Perennial, 1992.

Moraga, Cherríe. *The Last Generation*. Boston: South End Press, 1993.

———. *Heroes and Saints: Heroes and Saints and Other Plays*. Albuquerque: West End Press, 1994.

Morse, Margaret. "An Ontology of Everyday Distraction: The Freeway, the Mall, and Television." In *The Logics of Television*. Ed. Patricia Mellencamp. Bloomington: Indiana University Press, 1990. 193–221.

Mouffe, Chantal. "Democratic Citizenship and the Political Community." In *Community at Loose Ends*. Minneapolis: University of Minnesota Press, 1991. 70–82.

———. *The Return of the Political*. London: Verso, 1993.

Moulthrop, Stuart. *Victory Garden*. Hypertext Novel. Watertown, Mass.: Eastgate Systems, 1993.

Müller, Heiner. *Die Bauern*. In *Die Umsiedlerin oder das Leben auf dem Lande*. Berlin: Rotbuch Verlag, 1975. 19–118.

———. *Cement*. Trans. Sue-Ellen Case, Helen Fehervary, and Marc Silberman. Milwaukee: New German Critique, 1979.

———. "The Walls of History." *semiotext(e)* 4:2 (1982): 36–107.

———. DESPOILED SHORE MEDEAMATERIAL LANDSCAPE WITH ARGONAUTS. In *Hamletmachine and Other Texts for the Stage*. Ed. and trans. Carl Weber. New York: Performing Arts Journal, 1984. 123–135.

———. *GUNDLING'S LIFE FREDERICK OF PRUSSIA LESSING'S SLEEP DREAM SCREAM*. In *Hamletmachine and Other Texts for the Stage*. 59–79.

———. *Hamletmachine*. In *Hamletmachine and Other Texts for the Stage*. 49–58.

———. "Brecht vs. Brecht: I shit on the order of the world I am lost." In *Germania*. Ed. Sylvere Lotringer. Trans. Bernard and Caroline Schutze. New York: Semiotext(e), 1990. 124–133.

———. *Zur Lage der Nation*. Berlin: Rotbuch Verlag, 1990.

Mulvey, Laura. "Afterthoughts on 'Visual Pleasure and Narrative Cinema.'" In *Visual and Other Pleasures*. Bloomington: Indiana University Press, 1989. 29–38.

———. "Visual Pleasure and Narrative Cinema." In *Visual and Other Pleasures*. 14–26.

Novack, Cynthia. *Sharing the Dance: Contact Improvisation and American Culture*. Madison: University of Wisconsin Press, 1990.

Novak, Marcos. "Liquid Architectures in Cyberspace." In *Cyberspace: First Steps*. Ed. Michael Benedikt. Cambridge: MIT Press, 1992. 225–254.

Ost-West-Kulturaustausch: Kooperation oder Konfrontation? By Falko Raaz. Berlin: Dietz Verlag, 1987.

SOURCES

246
PAGE

 PREV

 NEXT

 OPEN

 PRINT

 FIND

 HELP

 MENU

Patton, Cindy. "Unmediated Lust? The Improbable Space of Lesbian Desires." In *Stolen Glances: Lesbians Take Photographs*. Ed. Tessa Boffin and Jean Fraser. London: Pandora, 1991. 233–240.

Penley, Constance, and Andrew Ross. "Introduction." In *Technoculture*. Ed. Penley and Ross. Minneapolis: University of Minnesota Press, 1991.

Perry, Anne. *Silence in Hanover Close*. New York: Fawcett Crest, 1988.

Phelan, Peggy. *Unmarked: The Politics of Performance*. London and New York: Routledge, 1993.

Pickover, Clifford A. *Mazes for the Mind: Computers and the Unexpected*. New York: St. Martin's Press, 1992.

Piercy, Marge. *He, She and It*. New York: A Fawcett Crest Book, 1991.

Pietz, William. "The 'Post-Colonialism' of Cold War Discourse." *Social Text* 7:1–2 (1988): 55–75.

Poster, Mark. *The Mode of Information: Poststructuralism and Social Context*. Chicago: University of Chicago Press, 1990.

———. *The Second Media Age*. Cambridge: Polity Press, 1995.

Poundstone, William. *Labyrinths of Reason: Paradox, Puzzles, and the Frailty of Knowledge*. New York: Doubleday/Anchor, 1990.

Preston, John. "What Happened? An S/M Pioneer Reflects on the Leather World Past and Present." *Out/Look* 4:3 (1992): 8–15.

Pryse, Marjorie. "Zora Neale Hurston, Alice Walker, and the 'Ancient Power' of Black Women." In *Conjuring: Black Women, Fiction, and Literary Tradition*. Ed. Marjorie Pryse and Hortense J. Spillers. Bloomington: Indiana University Press, 1985. 1–24.

Reagon, Bernice Johnson. "Coalition Politics: Turning the Century." In *Home Girls: A Black Feminist Anthology*. Ed. Barbara Smith. New York: Kitchen Table: Women of Color Press, 1983. 356–368.

Reinelt, Janelle. "Staging the Invisible: The Crisis of Visibility in Theatrical Representation." *Text and Performance Quarterly* 14 (1994): 1–11.

Rheingold, Howard. *Virtual Reality*. New York: Summit Books, 1991.

Roach, Joseph. "The Artificial Eye: Augustan Theatre and the Empire of the Visible." In *The Performance of Power: Theatrical Discourse and Politics*. Ed. Sue-Ellen Case and Janelle Reinelt. Iowa City: University of Iowa Press, 1991. 131–145.

Robinson, Phillip, and Nancy Tamosaitis. *The Joy of Cybersex*. New York: Brady, 1993.

Ronell, Avital. *The Telephone Book*. Lincoln: University of Nebraska Press, 1989.

———. "TraumaTV: Twelve Steps beyond the Pleasure Principle." In *Finitude's Score: Essays for the End of the Millennium*. Lincoln: University of Nebraska Press, 1994. 305–327.

Roof, Judith. *A Lure of Knowledge: Lesbian Sexuality and Theory*. New York: Columbia University Press, 1991.

Rouse, John. "Heiner Müller and the Politics of Memory." *Theatre Journal* 45:1 (1993): 65–74.

Saalfield, Catherine. "On the Make: Activist Video Collectives." In *Queer Looks*. Ed. Martha Gever, John Greyson, et al. New York and London: Routledge, 1993. 21-37.

Savran, David. "Queer Masculinities." Unpublished manuscript.

Schulman, Sarah. *My American History.* New York: Routledge, 1994.

Scott, James. *Weapons of the Weak: Everyday Forms of Peasant Resistance.* New Haven: Yale University Press, 1985.

Scott, Melissa. *Trouble and Her Friends.* New York: Tom Doherty Associates, 1994.

Sedgwick, Eve Kosofsky. "Queer Performativity: Henry James's *The Art of the Novel." glq: A Journal of Lesbian and Gay Studies* 1:1 (1993): 1–16.

Seduction: The Cruel Woman (Verführung: die grausame Frau). Dir. Elfi Mikesch and Monika Treut. 1985.

Seidman, Steven. "Identity and Politics in a 'Postmodern' Gay Culture: Some Historical and Conceptual Notes." In *Fear of a Queer Planet.* Ed. Michael Warner. Minneapolis: University of Minnesota Press, 1993. 105–142.

Seiler, Paul. *Zarah Leander.* Hamburg: Rowolt Taschenbuch Verlag, 1985.

Shapiro, Judith. "Transsexualism: Reflections on the Persistence of Gender and the Mutability of Sex." In *Body Guards.* Ed. Julia Epstein and Kristina Straub. New York and London: Routledge, 1991. 248–279.

Singer, Linda. "Recalling Community at Loose Ends." In *Community at Loose Ends.* Ed. Miami Theory Collective. Minneapolis: University of Minnesota Press, 1991. 121–130.

"S/M Aesthetic." *Out/Look* 1:4 (1989): 42–43.

Smith, Paul. "Laclau and Mouffe's Secret Agent." In *Community at Loose Ends.* Ed. Miami Therory Collective. Minneapolis: University of Minnesota Press, 1991. 99–110.

Smyth, Bernard. *The Role of Culture and Leisure Time in New Zealand.* Paris: UNESCO, 1973.

Smyth, Cherry. *Lesbians Talk Queer Notions.* London: Scarlet Press, 1992.

Soja, Edward W. *Postmodern Geographies.* New York: Verso, 1989.

Spigel, Lynn. "Installing the Television Set: Popular Discourses on Television and Domestic Space, 1948–1955." *camera obscura* 16 (January 1988): 11–46.

———. "The Suburban Home Companion: Television and the Neighborhood Ideal in Postwar America." In *Sexuality and Space.* Ed. Beatriz Colomina. Princeton: Princeton Papers on Architecture, 1992. 185–217.

Stein, Arlene. "Style Wars and the New Lesbian." *Out/Look* 1:4 (1989): 34–42.

Stein, Gertrude. "Pink Melon Joy." In *Geography and Plays.* New York: Something Else Press, 1968. 347–376.

———. "Arthur A Grammar." In *How to Write.* Craftsbury Common: Sherry Urie, 1977. 37–101.

———. "Finally George: A Vocabulary of Thinking." In *How To Write.* 273–382.

Sterling, Bruce. *Islands in the Net.* New York: Ace Books, 1989.

Stone, Allucquere Rosanne. "Will the Real Body Please Stand Up?: Boundary Stories about Virtual Cultures." In *Cyberspace: First Steps.* Ed. Michael Benedikt. Cambridge: MIT Press, 1992. 81–118.

———. *The War of Desire and Technology at the Close of the Mechanical Age.* Cambridge: MIT Press, 1995.

Stone, Sandy. "The *Empire* Strikes Back: A Posttranssexual Manifesto." In *Body Guards.* Ed. Julia Epstein and Kristina Straub. New York: Routledge, 1991. 280–304.

——. "Split Subjects, Not Atoms; or, How I Fell in Love with My Prosthesis." In *The Cyborg Handbook*. Ed. Chris Hables Gray. New York: Routledge, 1995. 393–406.

Taussig, Michael. "Maleficium: State Fetishism." In *Fetishism as Cultural Discourse*. Ed. Emily Apter and William Pietz. Ithaca: Cornell University Press, 1993. 217–247.

——. *Mimesis and Alterity*. New York: Routledge, 1993.

Tomas, David. "Old Rituals for New Space: *Rites de Passage* and William Gibson's Cultural Model of Cyberspace." In *Cyberspace: First Steps*. Ed. Michael Benedikt. Cambridge: MIT Press, 1991.

Torres, Sasha. "Television/Feminism: *HeartBeat* and Prime Time Lesbianism." In *The Lesbian and Gay Studies Reader*. Ed. Henry Abelove, Michele Barale, and David Halperin. New York: Routledge, 1993. 176–185.

Touch of Evil. Dir. Orson Welles. 1958.

Virilio, Paul. *The Aesthetics of Disappearance*.Trans. Philip Beitchman. New York: Semiotext(e), 1991.

——. "The Third Interval: A Critical Transition," In *Rethinking Technologies*. Ed. Verena Andermatt Conley. Minneapolis: University of Minnesota Press, 1993. 3–12.

Warner, Michael. "Introduction." In *Fear of a Queer Planet: Queer Politics and Social Theory*. Minneapolis/London: University of Minnesota Press, 1993. vii–xxxi.

Wiegman, Robyn. "Introduction: Mapping the Lesbian Postmodern." In *The Lesbian Postmodern*. New York: Columbia University Press, 1994. 1–20.

Williams, Raymond. *Television: Technology and Cultural Form*. New York: Schocken Books, 1975.

Witt, Charlotte. "Aristotelian Essentialism Revisited." *Journal of the History of Philosophy* 27:2 (April 1989): 285–298.

Wittig, Monique. *The Lesbian Body*. Trans. David LeVay. Boston: Beacon Press, 1986.

Woll, Allen L. *The Latin Image in American Film*. Los Angeles: UCLA Latin American Studies, 1977.

Young, Iris Marion. "The Ideal of Community and the Politics of Difference." In *Feminism/Postmodernism*. Ed. Linda J. Nicholson. New York and London: Routledge, 1990. 300–323.

INDEX

INDEX

254 PAGE

PREV

NEXT

OPEN

PRINT

FIND

HELP

MENU

INDEX

256
PAGE

 PREV
 NEXT
 OPEN
 PRINT
 FIND
 HELP
 MENU

SUE-ELLEN CASE

is Professor of English at University of California at Riverside. Her book *Feminism and Theatre* was the pioneering text in that field. Subsequently, her article "Towards a Butch-Femme Aesthetic" opened the debates around lesbian role playing. She has served as the editor of *Theatre Journal* and has edited several anthologies of plays and feminist critical work on the theater.